HAPPY
BIRTHDAY MATT,
WELCOME TO THE
CLUB RADOONAS
MANHOOD. MAY YOU DO
OUR FATHER'S WILL AND
MAKE HIM PROUD. Jesse

365
MEDITATIONS
for MEN
by MEN

365 MEDITATIONS for MEN by MEN

S. D. Sharpe, Editor
Christian Coon, Tim Gossett,
James A. Harnish, Joseph L. Harris,
J. Ellsworth Kalas, Andy Langford,
Russell T. Montfort, James W. Moore,
Ramon Presson, Stacy L. Spencer,
Shane Stanford, John Underwood

Abingdon Press
Nashville

365 MEDITATIONS FOR MEN BY MEN

Copyright © 2008 by Abingdon Press

All rights reserved.

This book is printed on recycled, acid-free paper.

Library of Congress Cataloging-in-Publication Data

365 meditations for men by men / S.D. Sharpe, editor.
   p. cm.
   ISBN 978-0-687-65198-6 (binding: pbk., adhesive-perfect)
   1. Christian men—Prayers and devotions.   2. Devotional calendars.   I. Sharpe, Sally D., 1964-
II. Title: Three hundred and sixty-five meditations for men by men.

   BV4843.S55 2008
   242'.642—dc22

2008016604

08 09 10 11 12 13 14 15 16 17—10 9 8 7 6 5 4 3 2 1
MANUFACTURED IN THE UNITED STATES OF AMERICA

Contents

Introduction

Man's search for meaning is the primary motivation in his life.
—*Viktor Frankl,* Man's Search for Meaning

There is a longing deep within every man's heart to discover meaning and purpose in life; to lead a life of significance as opposed to a life of "success"; to live a life of adventure, conquest, and victory; to make a difference and leave a positive, enduring mark on the world. Yet, as Henry David Thoreau observed, "The mass of men lead lives of quiet desperation." Although Thoreau penned these words more than a century ago, they still ring true today. So many men—including devoted Christian men—wake up one day and realize they are leading lives of quiet desperation, silently "losing themselves" as they strive to meet unrealistic expectations, overcome mounting work and family pressures, and battle unrelenting temptations. These challenges can easily sidetrack men, causing them to lose their spiritual focus.

Whether consciously or unconsciously, many men subsequently spend their time and energy and resources searching for significance in pursuits and people and things that can never fully satisfy. Some simply give up on ever finding lasting meaning and purpose in this world. Others find themselves somewhere in between. In any case, the result is often the same: a pervading sense of exhaustion, futility, or hopelessness.

Yet there is a remedy to this cultural epidemic, and it is found in reclaiming and living out every man's true purpose, which is found in God alone. As Saint Augustine wrote, "Thou hast made us for Thyself, O Lord, and our hearts are restless until they rest in Thee." The apostle Paul expressed it this way: "Everything, absolutely everything, above and below, visible and invisible . . . *everything* got started in [Christ] and finds its purpose in him" (Colossians 1:16 *The Message*).

365 Meditations for Men by Men is intended to help men focus on their relationship with God and, consequently, find real meaning and purpose in life. Twelve different Christian men share their reflections on what it means to be a man who seeks to follow Christ each and every day. Drawing upon the lives of men in the Bible as well as their own personal experiences, the writers present timeless truths and valuable life lessons that will speak to men of every age and experience. In addition to offering inspiration and encouragement, they provide counsel on practical matters such as how to

- know God;
- get your priorities in order;
- become spiritually fit;
- be holy and righteous;
- make a difference;
- be equipped;
- step up;
- take risks;
- stand firm;
- serve God wholeheartedly.

As you make your way through the year (whether you start in January or June), you will be undergirded by a sense of brotherhood—an assurance that you are not alone on this journey. With this confidence, may you boldly and courageously pursue a full and abundant life in Christ!

S. D. Sharpe, Editor

About the Writers

Christian Coon (SEPTEMBER) has been pastor of Christ United Methodist Church in Deerfield, Illinois, since 2001. He and his wife, Anne, have two children, Caroline and Ethan. Christian is a native Iowan and is an avid runner, blogger (www.genxrev.com), and movie watcher.

Tim Gossett (APRIL) is the Educational Consultant for Iowa Religious Media Services in Urbandale, Iowa, the nation's largest ecumenical resource center. He is the author of six youth ministry books, including *A Walk with God for Graduates*, and he has worked for the past twenty years in campus ministry, youth ministry, Christian education, and as a freelance writer/editor. Tim lives in Ames, Iowa, with his wife, Kathryn, and (hopefully, by the time you're reading this) an adopted daughter.

James A. Harnish (OCTOBER) is a husband, father, grandfather, and University of Florida Gator football fan. He also is senior pastor of Hyde Park United Methodist Church in Tampa, Florida, and the author of several books including *Passion, Power, and Praise: A Model for Men's Spirituality from the Life of David* and *Journey to the Center of the Faith: An Explorer's Guide to Christian Living*.

Joseph L. Harris (AUGUST) is assistant to the bishop and communications director for the Oklahoma Conference of The United Methodist Church. In addition to serving as a youth director, pastor, and district superintendent, he has been publisher of the *United Methodist Men* magazine, the first general secretary of the Commission on United Methodist Men, and the first president of the World Fellowship of Methodist and Uniting Church Men affiliated through the World Methodist Council. Joseph has been married to Nancy for thirty-two years. They have two adult children, Sarah and Joseph Jr.

J. Ellsworth Kalas (FEBRUARY) is an administrator and professor of preaching at Asbury Theological Seminary in Wilmore, Kentucky. Before going to Asbury in 1993, he served for five years as the associate in evangelism with the World Methodist Council, and as a United Methodist pastor in Wisconsin and Cleveland for thirty-eight years. He has been a presenter on DISCIPLE videos, is the author of the *Christian Believer* series, and has written more than thirty books, including the popular Back Side series; *Longing to Pray: How the Psalms Teach Us to Talk with God; Strong Was Her Faith: Women of the New Testament; What I Learned When I Was Ten;* and *A Hop, Skip, and a Jump Through the Bible.*

Andy Langford (JUNE) is a United Methodist pastor in North Carolina. He received degrees from Davidson College, Duke University Divinity School, and Emory University. Andy has written almost twenty books on worship, weddings, church reformation, evangelism, and spirituality. Most important, he is the son of Tom and Ann Marie; brother to Jay, Tim, and Hugh; uncle to many nieces and nephews; husband of Sally; father of Ann Green and Sarah; and now father-in-law to Nathan.

Russell T. Montfort (MAY) retired after forty-three years as a United Methodist pastor in western North Carolina; Bonn, Germany; and West End United Methodist Church, Nashville, Tennessee. He holds degrees from Kentucky Wesleyan and Duke University. He has been married for fifty-four years to Ruth Nance Montfort. They are the parents of two adult children, Leslie Montfort Marsicano and Joel Montfort, and the grandparents of three grandchildren: Chris, James, and David. Russ currently works as a custody advocate for The Center for Children's Rights in Charlotte, North Carolina. He and Ruth also teach adults with developmental disabilities in their church. He is the author of two books: *Who's in Charge Here?* and *Buck and the Band of Angels.*

James W. Moore (JANUARY) is the author of more than forty books, including *Yes, Lord, I Have Sinned but I Have Several Excellent Excuses; You Can Get Bitter or Better; Some Things Are Too Good Not to Be True;* and *Faith Is the Answer, But What Are the*

Questions? In 2006 he retired from twenty-two years as senior pastor of Saint Luke's United Methodist Church in Houston, Texas. Prior to that he served for twelve years as co-pastor with D. L. Dykes of First United Methodist Church in Shreveport, Louisiana, in addition to pastoring several churches in Tennessee and Ohio. Currently he is minister in residence at Highland Park United Methodist Church, where he spends his time preaching on occasion, teaching, and writing. He and his wife, June, make their home at Heritage Ranch in Fairview, Texas. They are the proud parents of two children and grandparents of five grandchildren.

Ramon Presson (MARCH), an ordained minister, is a clinically certified marriage and family therapist and the founder of LifeChange Counseling and The Marriage Center of Franklin (Tennessee). An award-winning poet, avid journaler, and local newspaper columnist, he has written numerous feature articles for major Christian magazines and is the author of seven books, including the Love Talks series with Gary Chapman. Married to Dorrie for twenty-one years, he and his wife have two sons, Trevor and Cameron. Ramon's blog, "SightLines: Seeing God in All of Life," may be found at www.RamonDPresson.typepad.com.

Stacy L. Spencer (JULY) serves as senior pastor of New Direction Christian Church in Memphis, Tennessee. Under his leadership, the ministry, which began in 2001 with sixty members, has amassed a membership of more than ten thousand with two worship facilities. He holds degrees from Drew University, Southern Theological Seminary, and Western Kentucky University. The Kentucky native is married to Rhonda, and they happily parent four sons: Calvin, Omari, Jordan, and Jaden.

Shane Stanford (DECEMBER) serves as the staff leader/teacher for *The United Methodist Hour*, a television and radio program broadcast to more than five million homes a week. He is the author of two books, *The Seven Next Words of Christ* and *The Eight Blessings*. He also has written for a variety of religious periodicals. Shane is married to Dr. Pokey Stanford. They are the parents of three daughters: Sarai Grace (10), Juli Anna (7), and Emma Leigh (2).

John Underwood (NOVEMBER) is a native Oklahoman and a full-blood member of the Seminole Tribe of Oklahoma. For the past fourteen years, he has made his home in Nashville, Tennessee. John has a degree in education and works in retail management. He and his wife are co-contributors to *365 Meditations for Couples* and the proud parents of two beautiful daughters.

JANUARY

New Beginnings

JAMES W. MOORE

JANUARY 1   GOD CAN BRING HEALING
                                     WHERE IT HURTS

So if anyone is in Christ, there is a new creation: everything old has passed away; see, everything has become new!
(2 Corinthians 5:17)

Years ago I heard a story in a sermon about Edgar Dewitt Jones, renowned pastor and author of the early twentieth century. As the story goes, Dr. Jones was preaching a revival, and when he gave the invitation, a huge, burly man came storming down the aisle. The man was obviously moved, penitent, and remorseful. Big tears were streaming down his cheeks. He marched right to the front, extended his hand to Dr. Jones, and said, "Preacher, you said tonight that God could save anybody, no matter who they are or what they've done. I want to believe that. I want God to save me. But I want you to know I've done everything. I've done it all. So many times I've broken the Ten Commandments—all of them. I'm a Swedish blacksmith by trade, and I have been a terrible sinner. I don't know whether God can help me or not."

Dr. Jones took the man's massive hand, looked deep into that eager face, and said to him, "Sir, you are in luck. God is specializing in Swedish blacksmiths tonight!"

Whatever your problems may be, God is specializing in *you* today. God is the Great Physician, and God can bring healing where it hurts. That's a good thing to wrap our arms around as we move into the new year—a time for new beginnings. Join me this

13

month as we consider how we can experience some new beginnings in our lives!

O God, you are the Lord of new beginnings and new life. You are the Great Physician. Bring me the healing I need, and be with me in the new year. I pray in Jesus' name. Amen.

JANUARY 2 NEW LIFE

We are more than conquerors through him who loved us. For I am convinced that neither death, nor life, ... nor anything else in all creation, will be able to separate us from the love of God in Christ Jesus our Lord. (Romans 8:37-39)

The words of Louise Fletcher Tarkington are especially pertinent for the start of a new year: "I wish that there were some wonderful place called the Land of Beginning Again."

Well, there is such a place! This is the good news of the Christian faith. It's the great promise of the Bible. We can be forgiven. We can make new beginnings. We can start over. We can have a new chance. We can become a new creation. By the miracle of God's redeeming grace, we can have new life!

The start of a new year is a great time to make resolutions. It is also a great time to ask God to come into our lives and give us new life.

At the start of this new year, O God, make me a new creation. Give me new life, new beginnings, new birth; and enable me to be your servant. Help me live each day in the Spirit of Jesus Christ, my Lord and Savior. Amen.

JANUARY 3 THE GOOD NEWS OF THE CROSS

For the message about the cross is foolishness to those who are perishing, but to us who are being saved it is the power of God. (1 Corinthians 1:18)

A popular story from the Second World War tells about some Marines who were shipwrecked. After days of floating in a raft, they saw land. Their fears began to be dispelled, and they made their way to shore where they said prayers of gratitude to God for saving them.

Soon they saw signs of life on the island and realized they weren't alone. Immediately they began to wonder: *Are we safe here? Will the people welcome us or kill us?* And their fears returned.

Then one of the young Marines climbed a tree to see if he could get some indication of what they might expect. Suddenly he called down to the others: "We're saved! I see a steeple with a cross on it!"

Isn't that great? The cross meant that the spirit of Christ was there and they didn't need to be afraid.

Neither do we, because nothing—not even death—can separate us from God's love. That's the good news of the cross! And that's good news we need to take with us throughout this day, this week, this month, and this year!

Teach me, Lord, to trust you and the way of the cross. In Jesus' name. Amen.

JANUARY 4   GOD REDEEMS!

"Where, O death, is your victory? Where, O death, is your sting?"
(1 Corinthians 15:55)

On September 14, 1986, Bob Brenley of the San Francisco Giants tied a major league record by committing four errors in one inning at third base against the Atlanta Braves. The errors led to four unearned runs in the fourth inning.

At Bob's last time at bat in the bottom of the ninth inning, the count was three and two. Bob hit a home run and won the game 7-6. As he circled the bases with his game-winning home run, a radio announcer reportedly said, "Well, folks, Bob Brenley just redeemed himself." The jeers turned to cheers. A nightmare became the dream of a lifetime.

An athlete may be able to redeem himself by his own ability, but when it comes to our spiritual lives, only God can redeem. Only God can turn defeat into victory, death into life. This is the message of our Christian faith.

"For God so loved the world that he gave his only Son, so that everyone who believes in him may not perish but may have eternal life" (John 3:16). Christ died and rose again! And because he lives, we, too, can live through faith in him. We, too, can be resurrected. We, too, can move from defeat to victory.

In what ways do you need to experience God's resurrection power?

O God, resurrect me and give me a new start, a new beginning, a new vision, a new life. Amen.

JANUARY 5   PRACTICE WHAT YOU PREACH

"You must faithfully keep all my commands by obeying them, for I am the Lord."   *(Leviticus 22:31 NLT)*

Several years ago I asked some children to write down the one thing that would make our world a better place. I was impressed with their responses. If we will listen, we can learn much from them:

- "Each person should try to be a light in the world and an influence for good."
- "More love and less violence."
- "All people should act like brothers and sisters because, after all, we are God's family."
- "Go out and do what you know is right—and stand up for what you know is right."
- "Learn the Christian faith and stick to it."

Do you see what the children are saying to us? They are saying: Live your faith; practice what you preach; see yourself as God's co-worker in this world. These are good things to think about as we move into the new year.

O God, watch over me, walk with me, and help me "practice what I preach" in the spirit of Jesus Christ. In his name I pray. Amen.

JANUARY 6   SEND ME

Then I heard the voice of the Lord saying, "Whom shall I send, and who will go for us?" And I said, "Here am I; send me!"
(Isaiah 6:8)

Imagine you are at a football game and fifty players are huddled with their three coaches. The referee blows his whistle to start the game, and a crazy thing happens. The fifty players stand on the sideline, and the three coaches run out onto the field to play the game. Some of the players shout, "Go get 'em, Coach! You can do it!" But none of the players goes onto the playing field. They expect the coaches to do it all.

If you saw that at a football game, you would think, *This is the craziest thing I've ever seen!* Yet that's the way some people relate to the church. They think the ministers and staff are supposed to do it all while the other church members stand by and watch.

That idea is certainly not biblical. Jesus didn't call a single priest or rabbi to be one of his disciples; he called lay people. *He is calling you right now.* Can you hear his call? And can you say with Isaiah, "Here am I; send me"?

Here am I, Lord; send me; use me. Let me be your servant this day and every day, in the name of Jesus. Amen.

JANUARY 7   CELEBRATE EACH DAY

This is the day that the LORD has made; let us rejoice and be glad in it.   (Psalm 118:24)

A first-grade teacher walked into her classroom one morning and found six-year-old Johnny standing in front of the room, sticking his stomach out. "Johnny," she asked, "why are you standing there with your stomach sticking out?"

"Well," said Johnny, "I had a stomachache this morning, and I went to see the nurse. She said if I could just stick it out 'til noon, maybe it would be OK."

Unfortunately, many men go through life like that: no sense of purpose; no great cause; no celebration of life. They just "stick it out 'til noon." They give in to boredom and apathy, to premature old age, or to fear and anxiety. They do nothing exciting and take no risks. They don't really live. They merely exist, enduring life, and that is so sad.

God meant for us to celebrate life and to see each day as a precious gift. The psalmist put it like this: "This is the day that the LORD has made; let us rejoice and be glad in it."

Teach me, O Lord, how to celebrate each day. Help me be a good steward of each day you give me. Help me truly celebrate life. In Jesus' name. Amen.

JANUARY 8   THE LEAST OF THESE

"As you did it to one of the least of these . . . you did it to me."
(Matthew 25:40)

I have a good friend who is one of the most outgoing persons I've ever known. A former football player, he is strong and powerful; yet he has a teddy-bear personality. He expresses his love with hugs.

Once I heard him speak to a group of young people, and he said something that inspired them and touched me. He said: "When I first became a Christian, I was so grateful for the way God had turned my life around that I wanted to hug God, but I didn't know how. . . . Over the years, I have learned that the best way to hug God is to hug God's children; the best way to love God is to love God's children; the best way to serve God is to serve God's children."

That's what Jesus meant when he said, "As you did it to one of the least of these . . . you did it to me." Even the strongest of us men can hug God in this way!

Lord, enable me to reach out to others with love so that I might continue the ministry of Jesus Christ, in whose name I pray. Amen.

JANUARY 9   ARE YOU IN A PIT?

"For God so loved the world that he gave his only Son, that whoever believes in him should not perish but have eternal life."
(John 3:16 RSV)

One day a man took a shortcut across a field and fell into a deep pit. He tried to get out but couldn't; so he screamed for help. A pop psychologist passed by and said, "I feel your pain." A religious fanatic happened along and said, "Obviously, you have sinned greatly because only bad people fall into pits." A news reporter rushed up and asked, "Could I have an exclusive story on your experience in the pit?" A lawyer came and wanted to represent the man in a lawsuit. A neurotic came along and said, "You think *your* pit is bad; you should see *mine!*" But then someone else came along, saw the man's dilemma, and pulled the man out of the pit. Later, as the man told his story, people asked, "Who was the man?"

"It was Jesus!" he said.

"How do you know?" they asked.

"I know because he had nail prints in his hands!"

If you are in some kind of "pit" today, Jesus is waiting to help pull you out. Will you let him?

Thank you, Lord, for delivering me from those pits in life that imprison and enslave me. I pray in Christ's holy name. Amen.

JANUARY 10   EACH DAY IS A GIFT

Bless the LORD, O my soul, and do not forget all his benefits.
(Psalm 103:2)

A woman was cleaning her parakeet's birdcage when she accidentally sucked her parakeet, Chippie, into the vacuum. Horrified at what she had done, she frantically ripped open the vacuum bag. She found Chippie stunned and shaken but still alive. Chippie was covered with dust and dirt, so she grabbed him and ran to the sink, turned on the faucet, and held him under the cold water to clean him off. Then she ran with Chippie to the bathroom, turned on the hair dryer, and held him in front of the blast of hot air to dry him off. It was a traumatic morning for Chippie, to say the least. Later someone asked, "How's Chippie doing now?" She answered, "Well, Chippie doesn't sing much anymore. He just sits and stares."

We men are sometimes like Chippie. Sometimes we're so knocked around by life that we don't "sing" much anymore. We just exist. But we must remember that life is more than existing, more than coping. Life is a sacred gift from God. Each day is precious.

Look for the blessings in *your* life today.

Lord, teach me to celebrate each day as a sacred and precious gift from you. I pray in Christ's holy name. Amen.

JANUARY 11   TAKING UP THE TORCH OF KINDNESS

"A new command I give you: Love one another. As I have loved you, so you must love one another."   ***(John 13:34 NIV)***

I was only twelve when my father died. As we stood by his casket, scores of people came by. Some were rich and some were poor; some were young and some were old; some were professional people and some were laborers; some I knew quite well and some I had never seen before. But they all said the same thing: "Jim, your dad was kind to me."

I determined then and there that the best tribute I could pay to my dad was to take up his torch of kindness. From that moment, I have tried to be a kind person. I haven't always succeeded, but I have tried; and I am still trying to let my father's kindness live on in me.

Remember with me what a kind person Jesus was. We give up on people, but Jesus never did. Even on the cross, he was taking care of his mother and forgiving his executioners. To the very last, he was kind.

The best tribute we can pay him is to take up his torch of kindness.

O God, enable me to love other people in the spirit of Jesus, in whose name I pray. Amen.

JANUARY 12   TIME TO TURN AROUND

"The time is fulfilled, and the kingdom of God has come near; repent, and believe in the good news."   *(Mark 1:15)*

Some time ago there was a tragic story in the newspaper about the shooting death of a cabdriver. Several young people were being held as suspects in the brutal and senseless murder. One of them had confessed to firing the fatal shot. When asked whether the youth had expressed any remorse, one of the investigators reportedly said, "Well, they are really sorry they got caught!"

That is not what repentance is. Repentance means being so sorry for our sins that we want to change our ways. In the Old Testament, the Hebrew word for *repent* is *hashivenu*. It means literally "about-face, turn around, turn back and come this way." Repentance is a dramatic change, a radical turnabout. That's why we use such powerful images as new birth, new beginnings, and new life to talk about repentance. Repentance means being so sorry for our sins and wrongdoings that we want to turn around.

It's time to turn around.

O Lord, cleanse me of my sins; cleanse me from those enemies within—such as selfishness, arrogance, and jealousy—that poison my soul. Turn me around to head in your direction. In Christ's name. Amen.

JANUARY 13   LOVED AND FORGIVEN

"This son of mine was dead and is alive again; he was lost and is found!"   *(Luke 15:24)*

A young woman came to see me. She had been living a sordid lifestyle. She was penitent but haunted. "I've asked God to forgive me, but how could God ever forgive me for what I've done?"

I said, "Because Jesus told us that God is like a loving father." She didn't seem convinced, so this is what I said: "Imagine I'm your father and you just told me what you have done—with all the shady details. I could say: 'Get out of my sight. I don't ever want to see you again.' Or I could say, 'I'm so sorry this has happened, but I love you with all my heart. Let me help you make a new start.' Which do you think I would say if you were my daughter?"

She answered, "The second one."

"Why?" I asked.

"Because you are a father," she said, "and you love your children."

I said, "Listen! If I'm capable of that kind of forgiveness, how much more is our Father God?"

Jesus taught us that God is like a devoted, caring parent who loves us unconditionally and forgives us unreservedly.

Show me the way, O Lord, to come home to you through Jesus, in whose name I pray. Amen.

JANUARY 14   YOU CAN COME HOME NOW

"Father, forgive them; for they do not know what they are doing."
(Luke 23:34)

In the personal ads, a lot of people with initials tell unnamed persons that they are forgiven. "You can come home now; you are forgiven," they say. It occurs to me that this is what the cross means.

There's a story about a police officer who found a little boy sitting on the curb crying because he was lost. The officer said, "Don't worry. I'll help you! Glance around and see if you can see anything that looks familiar." The little boy looked around for a few moments and then suddenly his face brightened because off in the distance he could see a church with a cross on top. The little boy said, "There! Look! If you can get me to the cross, we can find the way home!" That says it all, doesn't it?

In Christ, God was reconciling the world to himself. On the cross, God was saying, "You can come home now; you are forgiven."

Perhaps you need to hear these words today—or perhaps you need to share them with someone else.

O God, empower me to live in the spirit of forgiveness. I pray in the name of Christ who gave his all for me. Amen.

JANUARY 15   PERMISSION TO FORGIVE

"Forgive us our debts, as we also have forgiven our debtors."
(Matthew 6:12)

A doctor inspecting the water on a farm found one pond with water that was unsafe to drink. He called all the farmhands together and told them, "Do not drink from this pond. The water is poisonous!" He put a big sign in the pond that read *Danger! Unsafe water! Do not drink!*

The next day the farmer's son got hot while working. Ignoring the doctor's sign, he drank from the condemned pond. Later that night he became deathly ill. They called the doctor and told him what had happened.

What did the doctor do? Did he say, "Don't blame me?" Did he refuse to come? No! He came and sat up all night with that sick young man and saved his life. Why? Because the doctor knew that he had permission to forgive. He had learned that from the Great Physician!

Those of us who know the Great Physician know that we, too, have permission and inspiration to live daily in the spirit of forgiveness. Who needs *your* forgiveness today?

God of Forgiveness, forgive me for my sins, my mixed-up priorities, my weaknesses, my harsh words, and my shortcomings. Give me the Christlike grace to be forgiving toward others. I pray in Christ's name. Amen.

JANUARY 16   TAKE YOUR OWN ATMOSPHERE
                                                    WITH YOU

Do not be overcome by evil, but overcome evil with good.
(Romans 12:21)

Not long ago, a television newsman was interviewing a group of
astronauts about the opportunities and dangers of travel in space. He
concluded the interview by asking this question: "What do you think
is the single most important key to successful space travel?" One of
the astronauts made an interesting response. He said: "The secret of
traveling in space is to take your own atmosphere with you!"

As I heard that, I realized that this is also true in our travels
through life. We don't have to be changed or altered or influenced
or destroyed by alien or even hostile environments in this life. We
can take our own atmosphere with us each day—at home, in the
workplace, and wherever else we may go.

Romans 12 puts it something like this: Don't let the world
around you squeeze you into its mold. In other words, give your
life totally to God and don't let anything choke the life out of that.
Or, put another way, you can take your own atmosphere with
you—the atmosphere of Christ.

Help me this day and every day, O God, to take the atmosphere
of Christ with me wherever I may go. Keep me strong and unwa-
vering in my commitment to you. In Jesus' name. Amen.

JANUARY 17   FOURTEEN-DAY CURE FOR
                                                    LONELINESS

"Love your enemies and pray for those who persecute you."
(Matthew 5:44)

A story circulates about noted psychologist Alfred Adler. It is
reported that he once put an ad in the paper that read: *Guaranteed:*
Fourteen-day Cure for Loneliness. A woman showed up at his office
and said, "It says here that you can cure my loneliness in fourteen
days. Is that true?"

"Absolutely," said Dr. Adler. "If you will do exactly what I tell you to do for fourteen days, you won't be lonely anymore."

"Tell me more," said the woman.

Dr. Adler said, "For fourteen consecutive days, I want you to do something kind for somebody else."

The woman said, "Why should I do something kind for somebody else?"

Dr. Adler is said to have replied: "In your case it might take twenty-one days."

When we live in the spirit of selfishness and resentment, we are likely to end up bitter or lonely. However, when we reach out to others in the loving spirit of Christ, we will end up filled with a sense of meaning and purpose and joy.

Lord, help me live from day to day in such a self-forgetful way that even when I kneel to pray, my prayer shall be for others. I pray in Christ's name. Amen.

JANUARY 18   LIVING YOUR FAITH

"But I say to you that listen, Love your enemies, do good to those who hate you."   *(Luke 6:27)*

In *Twelve Tests of Character*, Harry Emerson Fosdick gives an illustration about living our faith. During the atrocities in Armenia in the early 1900s, a Turkish soldier had chased a young woman and her brother down the street into a dead-end alley. The soldier killed the brother, but the young woman escaped. Later she was captured and, since she was a nurse, was put to work in a military hospital.

One day the same soldier who had killed her brother was brought into the hospital and placed in her ward. He was critically wounded, and the nurse knew that the slightest inattention would cause his death. One part of her cried out for vengeance, but the spirit of Christ won out. She conscientiously and tenderly nursed him back to health, and each evening she prayed for him.

Later he asked, "Why did you care for me so faithfully?" She replied, "Because I serve him who said, 'Love your enemies and do them good."' After a quiet moment, the Turkish soldier said, "Tell me more of your religion."

Do others want to know about your faith because of the way *you* live?

Help me, O Lord, to live my faith. In the name of Jesus Christ, my Lord. Amen.

JANUARY 19   WORKING WITH GOD

They left everything and followed him.   *(Luke 5:11)*

Does your faith give you a sense of partnership with God? If you will live each day saying within yourself, *I am a child of God,* your life will never be the same. No person can believe that and be the same as before!

A lawyer was on a trip to Korea and was being shown around by a missionary. The lawyer saw two Koreans working in the field with a rude hand plow. One was holding the handles, guiding it, and the other was pulling the plow. The missionary said, "They sold their ox so they could make a contribution toward building a new church, and this year they are taking turns pulling the plow themselves."

The lawyer was amazed and exclaimed, "What a sacrifice!" But the missionary replied, "They call it a privilege! They were glad they had an ox to sell and grateful they are strong enough to pull the plow. They actually believe they are working with God!"

Do you feel that you are working with God?

O Lord, give me a pure, humble heart of love and faith—a heart committed to serving you. Help me see each day as a new opportunity to share your love with others. I pray in Jesus' name. Amen.

JANUARY 20   STEP BY STEP

He opened his mouth and taught them, saying...
(Matthew 5:2 RSV)

In the Beatitudes, we have a step-by-step outline of the faith pilgrimage:

We are poor in spirit—that is, we humbly recognize how much we need God.

We mourn our sins.

In meekness, we commit our lives totally to God.

We want to learn the faith, to grow spiritually; we hunger and thirst for righteousness.

We go out into the world to live the faith in the spirit of mercy.

We go in the spirit of genuineness, being authentic rather than hypocritical—pure in heart.

Finally, we come to the height of spiritual maturity. In the spirit of God, we become peacemakers.

Then Jesus adds a P.S. "Oh, by the way," he says, "If you do these things—you may well be persecuted. People may give you a hard time, but don't be afraid because I am with you. I will protect you. I will see you through."

Walk with me step by step each day, O God, and take me along the paths you would have me to walk. In Jesus' name. Amen.

JANUARY 21   ARE YOU COMMITTED?

"If any want to become my followers, let them deny themselves and take up their cross and follow me."   ***(Mark 8:34)***

As Arabian stallions are trained, they are taught to obey the master, to trust him completely, and to always respond promptly to his call. When the master sounds his whistle, the stallions are trained to stop, no matter the circumstances, and come immediately.

As a final test, the stallions are placed in a corral in the desert midway up a hill. At the bottom of the hill is a beautiful oasis with crystal blue waters. The stallions stay in the corral for several hours under the blazing desert sun until they are frantic for water. The master stands at the top of the hill as they are released from the corral. Of course, they all head straight for the water. But just before they reach it, the master blows the whistle. The horses that ignore the master's call are considered not ready and must have further training; but the stallions who turn and go immediately to the master are considered well trained, and they are graduated. They are so committed that they put their master's will before their own.

Are you that committed to God?

O God, let my prayer each day be, "Thy will be done." In Jesus' name. Amen.

JANUARY 22 OBEDIENCE

He humbled himself and became obedient to the point of death—even death on a cross. *(Philippians 2:8)*

A young man wrote an enthusiastic love letter to his girlfriend. The letter read:

My darling, my love for you is so great that I would travel to the ends of the earth for you, dare the greatest dangers, fight my way to your side though giants should oppose me. Through storm, flood, or fire, I would persevere to reach you. Accept this letter as the expression of my undying love.
Yours forever,
John
  P.S. I'll be over to see you Saturday night . . . if it doesn't rain!

Halfhearted love is no good. Halfhearted obedience won't do. Someone has called it "sanctified stubbornness." Isn't that a great phrase? It makes me think of the faith of John Bunyan. Bunyan had been in prison for twelve years. He was offered his freedom if he would promise to stop preaching Christ, to which John Bunyan replied, "I am determined yet to suffer until moss grows over my eyebrows rather than to violate my faith!"

Do you know that kind of commitment? Do you know that kind of obedience to God's will?

O God, give me the strength and courage this day to recommit my life to you. I pray in my Savior's holy name. Amen.

JANUARY 23   WHY CAN'T WE JOIN HANDS?

Clothe yourselves with love, which binds everything together in perfect harmony.   *(Colossians 3:14)*

Some years ago a little girl was lost in the woods. It was winter-time—snowing, sleeting, and bitterly cold. Hundreds of people combed the forest, desperately searching for the little girl. Time was of the essence. They knew she couldn't survive long in that freezing weather. For hours they looked but had no luck. Finally, the searchers came up with the idea of joining hands so they could walk through the forest in a single line.

They tried it, and in less than fifteen minutes they found her! But it was too late. She had died from cold and exposure. In the hush of that awful moment, someone said, "Why, oh why, didn't we join hands sooner?"

Sometimes when I see the troubles and conflicts in the world, I think about that. Why, oh why, can't we join hands?

O God, you are Lord of Life and the Lord of Creation. Help me see other people not as adversaries but as sisters and brothers for whom Christ came and died. Teach us how to join hands and be your family. I pray in Jesus' name. Amen.

JANUARY 24   USING OUR STRESS

"Come to me, all you that are weary and are carrying heavy bur-dens, and I will give you rest. Take my yoke upon you, and learn from me."   *(Matthew 11:28-29)*

We men are under a lot of stress today. Jesus tells us he will give us rest if we will take his yoke upon us and learn from him. In a nutshell, *yoke* means service or ministry. Jesus is saying: Put ser-vice to God and others first in your life and everything else will fall into place. Redeeming the stress, using the stress, letting the stress stir us to creative service for God—that is a key to Christian living.

The apostle Paul had been beaten, flogged, imprisoned, and shipwrecked; stoned, robbed, scourged, and criticized. Yet through it all he could say, "I'm ready for anything, for Christ is my strength" (Philippians 4:13, author's paraphrase). In other words, "Whatever is thrown at me, I'm going to use it to serve my Christ."

May we do the same.

Teach me, O God, how to use my stress to serve you. I pray in Jesus' name. Amen.

JANUARY 25   MIRACLE WORKERS WITH OUR WORDS

In the beginning was the Word.   *(John 1:1)*

The first sermon I ever preached was at Saint Mark's Methodist Church in Memphis. I was sixteen years old and in tenth grade. I read the scripture lesson, preached all the way from Genesis to Revelation, and drank three glasses of water—all in four minutes!

Now, I know some people like four-minute sermons, but I felt awful—embarrassed, defeated, humiliated, and ashamed. During the last hymn, I thought, *This is not for me. I can't do this. I'll never try this again!*

After the service, one of the older saints of the church came up, shook my hand, and said with a warm smile, "Son, you did just fine! I'm so proud of you! I think you've got the makings of a minister, and I believe God's going to make a preacher out of you."

He probably was just feeling sorry for me, but I will always be grateful to him for giving me the right words at the right time. It was a miracle what those words did for me. They picked me up, inspired me, and made me want to try again.

We can be miracle workers with our words—in our homes, in our workplaces, and in our places of recreation. Will you be a miracle worker today?

O God, help me be a miracle worker with my words. I pray in the name of Jesus, the Word made flesh. Amen.

JANUARY 26   BE AN ENCOURAGER

So we, who are many, are one body in Christ, and individually we are members one of another.   *(Romans 12:5)*

On the evening of April 14, 1865, President Abraham Lincoln attended a performance of *Our American Cousin* at Ford's Theatre in Washington, D.C. A few minutes after 10:00 a gunshot rang through the crowded house. John Wilkes Booth, one of the best-known actors of the day, had shot the president. Lincoln was carried unconscious to a neighboring house. His family and high government officials surrounded him. At 7:22 the next morning, President Lincoln died.

At some point during that horrible night, a Secret Service man emptied the president's pockets and put the contents in a box labeled "Do not open." Many years later, the box was found and opened. It contained a pair of glasses, a little money, and the president's wallet with eight newspaper clippings, all highly complimentary of President Lincoln. Even a giant of a man like Abraham Lincoln needed words of encouragement. Don't we all?

There is something tremendously important that each of us can do. We can be encouragers!

Use me today, O Lord, as your minister of encouragement. In Christ's holy name. Amen.

JANUARY 27   LEAD WITH YOUR HEART

Prove me, O Lord, and try me; test my heart and mind.   *(Psalm 26:2)*

When our granddaughter, Sarah, was six years old, she went to the doctor for a checkup. As the doctor came into the examining room, Sarah held up both hands to get his attention and then said: "Dr. Ames, I know what you are going to do. You are going to do five things. You are going to check my eyes, my ears, my nose, my throat, and my heart."

Dr. Ames smiled and said, "Well, Sarah, that is exactly right. Is there any particular order I should go in?"

Sarah said, "You can go in any order you want to; but if I were you, I'd start with the heart!"

That's what Jesus did, isn't it? He started with the heart. He started with love, and that is precisely what he wants us to do!

O God, touch and cleanse my heart and make me the person and the servant of Christ you want me to be. Help me this day, O God, to lead with my heart. I pray in the name of Jesus Christ. Amen.

JANUARY 28   SERIOUS BUSINESS

What does the LORD require of you but to do justice, and to love kindness, and to walk humbly with your God?
(Micah 6:8)

A businessman announced to his office staff that he was going on a diet. The very next day he arrived at work with a large coffee cake in hand.

"What happened?" his colleagues asked. "We thought you were going on a diet."

"I was," the man replied, "but as I was on my way to the office this morning, I passed by a bakery and saw this incredibly sumptuous-looking coffee cake on display in the window. So I prayed, 'God, if you really want me to have that coffee cake for breakfast this morning, please find me a parking spot right in front of the bakery.' And sure enough, there it was—the eighth time around the block, there it was!"

We can laugh at that story—and for some of us who have a sweet tooth, it hits home. The truth is that too many of us treat our Christian faith the same way. We say we are committed to Christ, but we also want to go our own way, to keep on with our own lifestyle. But being a Christian is serious business. It is committing to Christ with every fiber of our being.

Enable me, O God, to live for you each day. In Christ's holy name. Amen.

JANUARY 29   THE FOUR-WAY TEST

"Do not judge, so that you may not be judged."
(Matthew 7:1)

When we were children, most of us learned a little rhyme that goes like this: "Sticks and stones may break my bones, but words will never hurt me!" There's just one thing wrong with that: it's just not true! Words *do* hurt! In fact, our worst hurts come not from sticks and stones but from words. Words can rip us apart and knock the very life out of us.

Rotary International strongly advocates what they call "The Four-way Test." It works like this. Before you say anything, you ask these four questions:

Is it true?

Is it fair to all concerned?

Will it build goodwill and better friendships?

Will it be beneficial to all concerned?

If you can't answer those four questions with a firm yes, then don't say it. This is the gracious spirit Jesus was calling for in Matthew 7 when he said, "Judge not."

O God of mercy and grace, put your gracious Spirit within me.
Help me not be so judgmental. Touch my heart and make me
more Christlike in all of my relationships. I pray this in Jesus'
name. Amen.

JANUARY 30   THE FUEL THAT EMPOWERS US

Be strong and take heart, all you who hope in the Lord.
(Psalm 31:24 NIV)

Jesus showed us that hope is better than despair. He planted the indomitable spirit of hope deep in our souls. Hope is the energy, the fuel, the power source that keeps us going.

The gas gauge on my car went haywire one day, moving back and forth like a miniature windshield wiper. On a trip to Buffalo, Texas, I knew that I was getting low on gas because I had driven more than three hundred miles since my last fill-up. But you know, we men seem to have two things in common when it comes to traveling. First, we don't like to stop to ask directions; second, we don't like to stop for gas. Anyway, as I came into Buffalo, my car began to knock and sputter. Fortunately, I was able to coast into a service station. Now, my car was in good shape—except that, like all cars, it will not run without fuel.

Our lives are like that, and hope in God is our only energy source. It's the fuel that empowers us. Take it away and we sputter and die.

Keep your "tank" filled with hope by spending time in God's Word each day.

O God, help me be filled with hope today. In the name of Jesus. Amen.

JANUARY 31   FLY, RUN, WALK

They shall mount up with wings like eagles.   ***(Isaiah 40:31)***

When I was quite a bit younger, I preached a sermon on this powerful text from Isaiah 40:

[We] shall mount up with wings like eagles,
[We] shall run and not be weary,
[We] shall walk and not faint. (v. 31)

In the sermon, I mentioned that this verse mystified me because it seemed out of sync—that we should fly, then run, and then walk.

After the sermon a good friend in her eighties came to me and in her gracious, humble way complimented my sermon. She said, "Jim, I'll tell you why that verse bothers you. It's because you are still young. When you get older, you will understand and appreciate it. Isaiah was right. That's the way it works in the faith pilgrimage. You fly, you run, and you walk. When you first have a faith experience, you are so excited you want to fly like an eagle. Then, you settle back after a while and run with perseverance like a marathoner. But the real test of faith is the test of time and

34

endurance, that daily humble walk with God. That's what it's all about."

Now that I am older, I understand.

Let's keep on walking....

Empower me, O Lord, to let each day be a humble walk with you. In Jesus' name. Amen.

FEBRUARY

A Man Named David

J. ELLSWORTH KALAS

[God] made David their king. In his testimony about him he said, "I have found David, son of Jesse, to be a man after my heart, who will carry out all my wishes." **(Acts 13:22)**

We humans want heroes, people we can look up to. Early in the biblical story we meet a hero named Nimrod: "He was the first on earth to become a mighty warrior.... Therefore it is said, 'Like Nimrod a mighty hunter before the LORD'" (Genesis 10:8-9). I doubt that Nimrod deserved such hero worship. I'm certain that Abel, Enoch, and Noah were more admirable, but they didn't catch the public fancy the way Nimrod did.

That's because *hero* is a hard word to define—especially in our day when it is the business of publicists and promoters to produce heroes. Is a person a hero because he hits home runs or amasses a billion dollars or wins an election? How do we measure a hero?

I invite you to think with me this month about a person who is still famous after some three thousand years. In a sense, anyone you know named David owes his name to this man. He wasn't a perfect man, but the Bible says that he was "a man after God's own heart." That's someone worth knowing.

Help me, dear Heavenly Father, learn how to be a hero to those who know me best. Amen.

FEBRUARY 2   INAUSPICIOUS BEGINNINGS

Samuel said to Jesse, "Are all your sons here?" And he said, "There remains yet the youngest, but he is keeping the sheep."
(1 Samuel 16:11)

If you're around teenagers—perhaps a teenager in a store or fast-food establishment is serving you—take a good look, because you may be in the presence of greatness. The greatness may be artfully disguised, in which case you'll need to mix your observations with faith and imagination, but don't let the disguise confuse you.

When King Saul failed tragically as Israel's leader, God sent the prophet Samuel to find a new king among the sons of a Bethlehem farmer named Jesse. Jesse introduced seven very impressive young men to Samuel, but God whispered no to each one. When Samuel asked if there was not yet another son, Jesse confessed, almost as if it were an afterthought, that there was another: "the youngest, but he is keeping the sheep."

The rest, as they say, is history. The overlooked boy was David, who ever after would be the standard by which Israel's kings would be judged, and whose star graces modern Israel's flag. Some greatness is easily discerned, but the most notable greatness is sometimes visible only to the eye of faith and love.

Help me, O Lord, to look at others with your eyes of faith and love. Amen.

FEBRUARY 3   THE CRUCIAL INGREDIENT

Then Samuel took the horn of oil, and anointed [David]. . . . and the spirit of the Lord came mightily upon David from that day forward.   *(1 Samuel 16:13)*

David may have been only a shepherd boy, but he had a great deal going for him. As the Ronald Knox translation puts it, he was "red-cheeked, fair of face, pleasant of mien" (1 Samuel 16:12). One wonders why his father Jesse had left him out in the fields in virtual anonymity when Samuel asked to see his sons.

As we trace David's career through the next few weeks, we will see the breadth of his talents. He was a natural athlete, a compelling leader, a military genius, a poet, and a musician; and he had the kind of personality that drew devotion from both men and women.

In truth, he had so much going for him that he was set up for self-destruction. Human history is strewn with the wreckage of highly talented individuals. Indeed, the more talent one has, the greater the peril.

That's where our scripture of the day comes in. The "spirit of the Lord" was "mightily upon David." Mind you, this didn't prevent him from falling at times, sometimes precipitously. But God's Spirit aided David's recovery.

Whatever my gifts, O Lord, grant me above all the gift of your Holy Spirit. Amen.

FEBRUARY 4   PERSUASIVE SPEECH

"The LORD, who saved me from the paw of the lion and from the paw of the bear, will save me from the hand of this Philistine."
(1 Samuel 17:37)

As a boy, I was impressed that the boy David could defeat the giant Goliath. Now, as a man, I am more impressed that he ever got the chance to do so.

Israel's traditional enemy, the Philistines, had a giant and, because of him, an idea. Why endanger the lives of hundreds or even thousands of soldiers? Why not have one representative from each nation fight and let the war be settled by the battle between these two men? If there must be war, here was a more humane way to handle it—especially if you had a giant to represent your side.

The men of Israel thought their cause was hopeless. But the shepherd boy, David, convinced King Saul that he could win the day.

What was it in this teenager that persuaded the king to trust him with the nation's future? I submit that you will find the secret of David's forty years as king not in the slingshot that slew Goliath, but in the personality that persuaded Saul to trust him.

O Lord, give me character that will lend power to my words. Amen.

FEBRUARY 5 ACID TEST

And the women sang to one another.... "Saul has killed his thousands, / and David his ten thousands." *(1 Samuel 18:7)*

David's victory over Goliath convinced King Saul to bring the young man into his royal retinue. But soon Saul was tested at the very core of his person. As the armies marched back to the capital, crowds of women along the way sang, "Saul has killed his thousands, / and David his ten thousands." Saul realized that the young shepherd was no longer his ally but also his competitor for the affection of the people.

One has to be very secure to be compared unfavorably with someone without thinking unkindly of that person. Unfortunately, Saul wasn't that secure. He should have been; after all, he was physically impressive, with many achievements of his own. More than that, he was king. But if you don't have a proper sense of your own worth before God, no amount of power, applause, or recognition will satisfy you.

The Bible says that the next day an evil spirit came upon Saul. I think the evil spirit was named Jealousy. It has destroyed millions. If it appears in your life, name it, flee from it, and ask God to deliver you.

Save me from the power of Jealousy, my God, by the power of your love. Amen.

FEBRUARY 6 PRICELESS FRIENDSHIP

The soul of Jonathan was bound to the soul of David, and Jonathan loved him as his own soul. *(1 Samuel 18:1)*

Next to our relationship with God, I know of no greater gift than the gift of friendship. Friendships can be long or short, sustained or intermittent, deep or casual; I have enjoyed the whole gamut, I think, and I am grateful for any form in which friendship comes and at whatever length or depth. But nothing can be compared with those friendships that bind persons together in heart and soul.

David and Jonathan had such a friendship. Jonathan died young, so the friendship was short; and because of the hatred Jonathan's father bore against David, the two men saw little of each other. But what the friendship lacked in length it made up for in depth. That kind of friendship has the ability to leap the boundaries of death, as I'm sure it did for David.

I testify to this because I have reached an age when so many of the people I have cherished most deeply have passed from this life. Still, by grace, they seem very close. I cherish such friendships for you.

Help me, O Lord, give of myself so generously and so sensitively that I will make someone (perhaps several) richer by my friendship. Amen.

FEBRUARY 7   TOUGH VICTORY

David had success in all his undertakings; for the Lord was with him.   *(1 Samuel 18:14)*

This verse is like a headline on the sports page: "Wildcats Victorious!" It's true, but it's only a headline; it doesn't reveal what went into the victory or how near defeat may have been.

"David had success in all his undertakings," but he had to work for them every day. Success wasn't delivered to his door each morning with the daily paper. Often his success came in spite of circumstances, not because of them. David's employer, King Saul, was hoping for his failure and sometimes working for his removal. But the Lord was with David.

I think David would have understood Abraham Lincoln when he

said, "Sir, my concern is not whether God is on our side, My great concern is to be on God's side, for God is always right."* David surely realized that he had to follow the Lord if the Lord was to be with him.

Nothing is so presumptuous as to think that God is obliged to bless us. We cannot walk in ways that are contrary to God's standards and expect that the Lord will bless us. The Lord was with David because David was in a place where God could be at home.

Help me, Father, to live where you are pleased to dwell. Amen.

* "Creative Quotations from Abraham Lincoln," www.creativequotations.com.

FEBRUARY 8   IMPERFECT OPPORTUNITY

"The LORD forbid that I should...raise my hand against him; for he is the LORD's anointed."   **(1 Samuel 24:6)**

King Saul's fear of David became psychotic. David's popularity and success convinced Saul that he must destroy the young man, so Saul set out with his army to apprehend David. Instead, by chance he fell into David's control. With one blow David could destroy Saul while he slept.

Some would say the circumstances were providential. David's men argued that the Lord had delivered Saul into his hands. Consider, too, that Saul was seeking David's life; thus David could reason that to kill Saul would be an act of self-defense. And, of course, perhaps David remembered that years earlier the prophet Samuel had anointed him for high office; David could have conjectured that the time had come for Samuel's action to be fulfilled.

But David chose the high road. Saul, David insisted, "is the LORD's anointed." God had installed Saul as king, so if Saul were to be removed it would have to be by God's action. David did not believe he could fulfill the will or purposes of God by violating the law of God.

Remind me every day, dear Lord, that the end does not justify the means. Give me a pure heart. Amen.

FEBRUARY 9   GOOD ADVICE

"When the LORD has . . . appointed you prince over Israel, my lord shall have no cause of grief, or pangs of conscience, for having shed blood without cause."   *(1 Samuel 25:30-31)*

No one is so smart or so successful that he or she can survive without good advice. David was a masterful leader. Having been exiled by King Saul, David gathered around himself a motley crew that a sociologist might call ne'er-do-wells, and he held this group together by the sheer power of his own personality and character. At times they acted as a kind of security agency, protecting wealthy farmers against roving bands of thieves.

In a particular instance they provided this service for a man named Nabal. Theirs was not a contractual service but one performed with payment negotiated afterward. Nabal refused payment and did so scornfully. David, in turn, was deeply offended. He vowed that Nabal would pay with blood.

But Nabal's wife, the wise and beautiful Abigail, appealed to David for mercy. She told David that someday he would be in high office and that he would hate then to be remembered for shedding innocent blood. David was wise enough and humble enough to take her advice. Incidentally, when Abigail became a widow, David married her.

Please make me smart enough to know when I am wrong. Amen.

FEBRUARY 10   NEW STRENGTH

But David strengthened himself in the LORD his God.
                                          (1 Samuel 30:6)

At this point in David's life he was working with some quite irresponsible people. Aggression was their daily fare, so at times of trouble they turned naturally to violence. When a band of Amalekites raided the city where the families of David and his men resided, destroying the city and taking the families captive, David's men wanted someone to blame. David was their leader, so they blamed him for their troubles even though he was as much a victim as they were. They began organizing to stone him.

What do you do in the face of irrational personal tragedy and even more irrational companions? If you look too long at the problem, at your enemies, and at your own soul, you're likely to become irrational yourself. You become part of the problem rather than part of the solution.

David knew enough to get outside himself and his problems. He needed a new vantage point from which to analyze the situation. He found it when he "strengthened himself in the LORD his God." Looking at God, he saw resources greater than his problems. When he inventoried the strength of God, he found new strength within himself.

Teach me, dear Savior, to find my strength in you. Amen.

FEBRUARY 11   FAIR DEAL

"For the share of the one who goes down into the battle shall be the same as the share of the one who stays by the baggage."
(1 Samuel 30:24)

When David and his six hundred men set out to regain their families from the Amalekite raiders, heat and weariness took their toll. Two hundred men were too exhausted to go on, so David left them guarding supplies while he led the larger group to victory.

In the ancient pattern of war, victory meant spoils. Some "corrupt and worthless fellows" (v. 22) among the four hundred argued that those who had stayed behind should get none of the booty. David insisted on a new principle: those who went into battle and those who stayed by the baggage should share alike. According to the biblical writer, this became "a statute and an ordinance for Israel" (v. 25).

Centuries later the great British poet John Milton dealt with the same issue at a personal level when he lost his sight while still in his middle years. He feared that God would condemn him for work left unfinished. It seemed to Milton, however, that God answered, "They also serve who only stand and wait."

We can trust the judgment and mercy of God.

Use me where and how you will, O Lord. Amen.

FEBRUARY 12   BAD NEWS

Tell it not in Gath, proclaim it not in the streets of Ashkelon.
(2 Samuel 1:20)

We sometimes complain that the media specialize in bad news. The media reply that they're giving the public what they want. I suspect that both opinions are right, and that the one feeds into the other.

David had a better way. When he received the tragic news of the deaths of King Saul and David's dearest friend, Jonathan, and with it the news of Israel's bitter defeat at the hands of the Philistines, he wrote a poem lamenting that the glory of the Lord had been "slain" by tragedy (2 Samuel 1:19). Then he made a dramatic appeal: Don't let this word get into the hands of the enemy. He wrote, "Tell it not in Gath, proclaim it not in the streets of Ashkelon."

Bad news is not to be ignored or denied, but neither should it control us. When we dwell on bad news, whether it is gossip or fact, we strengthen the enemy of our souls.

Despair enervates the soul. By concentrating on trouble rather than thinking on God, we put a barrier between God and ourselves and diminish our own emotional and mental resources.

David's enemy was the Philistines. Our enemy is often our own outlook.

Save me, O Lord, from selling out to the negative. Amen.

FEBRUARY 13   TIME TO WAIT

The time that David was king in Hebron over the house of Judah was seven years and six months.   *(2 Samuel 2:11)*

A good leader is decisive. He knows how to make up his mind.

David was decisive, but he wasn't in a hurry. When the people learned that King Saul was dead, Judah—David's tribe—anointed him king; but the rest of the nation accepted Ishbaal, Saul's son, as king. This arrangement lasted more than seven years. Considering David's popularity with all the people, it seems likely he easily could have effected a leadership coup. Or in a worse scenario, David had the military skill to overpower Israel's army. And, of course, David always could remind himself that he had already been anointed king, so why not step up and claim the title now that Saul was dead?

David resisted all such reasoning. He seemed content to bide his time. I submit that this patience was a sign of his decisiveness. He saw no need to hurry because he was confident of himself and of God's purposes. Centuries later the prophet Isaiah wrote, "One who trusts will not panic" (Isaiah 28:16). In the King James Version, it reads, "shall not make haste." The decisive person knows when to hurry and when to wait.

Give me the strength of character to be patient. Amen.

FEBRUARY 14   SHEPHERD KING

"The L*ORD**** said to you: It is you who shall be shepherd of my people Israel, you who shall be ruler over Israel."***
(2 Samuel 5:2)

P erhaps most people know David best as the author of Psalm 23, the Shepherd Psalm. Nevertheless, it seems strange to hear David's call to kingship in the same language. Kings and shepherds have quite different job descriptions. Come to think of it, I'm not sure that many postmodern people want to think of their political leader as a shepherd, since that implies that the people are like sheep.

But it's a good image for a king (or a president or prime minister) to keep in mind. It might help such persons to keep themselves and their work in perspective. Imagine a newspaper or television interviewer asking a government leader or a corporate CEO, "How would you characterize your job?" and having the person answer, "Well, it's a lot like being a shepherd."

There's little room in such an answer for pomposity or a sense of self-importance. In such an answer, the office is reduced to its primary, bedrock issue: this executive is responsible for the welfare of the people in his or her charge; which suggests that, in a very real sense, he or she is their servant.

Whatever my role, O Lord, make me a good shepherd. Amen.

FEBRUARY 15   DAVID DANCES

David danced before the LORD with all his might.
(2 Samuel 6:14)

Our culture is currently very casual, but most of us wouldn't be ready even in our time to see our chief executive be so unrestrained in a parade that his nakedness might be exposed. That's what David did, and his wife Michal was both humiliated and angry. Michal was the daughter of a king as well as wife to one, and she had a strong sense of how kings ought to conduct themselves. I suspect she felt that her husband was demonstrating his hill-country upbringing, and she was embarrassed to the point of contempt.

David saw it another way. For years Israel's most sacred object, the Ark of the Covenant—the very symbol of God's relationship to Israel—had been in the hands of their enemies, or at least outside the ordained place of worship. Now the ark was coming home with shouting and the sound of the trumpet (v. 15), and David was so happy he couldn't contain himself.

In the course of my life I have been in many exuberant celebrations—political, musical, and athletic. I've seen people do quite foolish things on such occasions. I confess that I like David for being so excited about God.

Help me, O Lord, know what is worth getting excited about. Amen.

FEBRUARY 16   DREAM POSTPONED

When your days are fulfilled and you lie down with your ances-
tors, I will raise up your offspring after you. . . . He shall build a
house for my name.   *(2 Samuel 7:12-13)*

David enjoyed so many accomplishments that his every step
seemed to lead to success. Military hero, musician and poet, king,
one adored by so many—but his greatest dream was not fulfilled
in his lifetime.

David wanted above everything to build a house of worship for
the Lord God. This man who danced in unrestrained exuberance
when the Ark of the Covenant was returned to Israel wanted now
to provide a place worthy of the ark and of the worship of God.

But pure as David's dream was, it was rejected. As he explained
to the son who succeeded him, God had denied his great wish, saying, "You have shed so much blood in my sight on the earth"
(1 Chronicles 22:8). God's house was to be built by a man of peace.

Robert Browning said that "a man's reach should exceed his
grasp, or what's a heaven for?"* We should dream so well that we
have to leave part of our dream to be fulfilled by those who follow
us—and so fully that we long for heaven.

Fill my heart, dear Lord, with dreams that please you. Amen.

* "Quotations by Author," Robert Browning, www.quotationspage.com.

FEBRUARY 17   GREAT KING

So David reigned over all Israel; and David administered jus-
tice and equity to all his people.   *(2 Samuel 8:15)*

How does one measure the greatness of a leader? Now and then
American historians rate the quality of past presidents, and now and
then historians rewrite history in ways that affect those evaluations.

Most of our evaluations have to do with matters of the economy
or issues of war and peace. Within the past several generations we
have become increasingly personality driven, often giving more

attention to style than to substance. The biblical writers could have given David high marks as a military leader; and when it came to style, he obviously had great natural public appeal.

But when the biblical writers summarized David's reign, they had a different scale of evaluation: Was the king faithful to God, and did he rule ethically? Here was David's score: he "administered justice and equity to all his people." In those few words the Scriptures provided the kind of standard that would unfold centuries later in documents such as the Magna Carta and the Bill of Rights. Justice and equity are beautiful words, easily spoken and sung. But they happen only when a nation cherishes unique principles of character and conduct.

Make me, dear Savior, an instrument of equity and justice. Amen.

FEBRUARY 18   A GOOD MEMORY

Mephibosheth lived in Jerusalem, for he always ate at the king's table.   (2 Samuel 9:13)

A great leader should have a good memory. One day David asked, "Is there still anyone left of the house of Saul to whom I may show kindness for Jonathan's sake?" (2 Samuel 9:1). Saul and Jonathan had been dead for years, but David remembered his vows of friendship with Jonathan and wanted, in honor of that friendship, to show kindness to anyone in Saul's family.

The one person remaining was a son of Jonathan, Mephibosheth. When fleeing the palace as a five-year-old, Mephibosheth had been dropped, leaving him lame in both feet. David brought him to Jerusalem so he could eat daily at the king's table as a member of the royal household.

David had a good memory. He remembered his long-ago friendship so he could fulfill its vows. He also knew how to forget. Saul had done David much harm, but David was ready to help any descendant of Saul in Jonathan's honor. Because of his good memory, David extended kindness to Mephibosheth as long as Mephibosheth lived.

A good memory is measured not by dates, addresses, lectures, and encyclopedic recalling, but by our loyalty to people—and sometimes by what we are willing to forget.

Quicken my memory, dear Father, for goodness and justice. Amen.

FEBRUARY 19   MISUSED POWER

So David sent messengers to get [Bathsheba], and she came to him, and he lay with her.   ***(2 Samuel 11:4)***

I wish I could say that David's conduct was always exemplary, but I can't say that and be true to the biblical story. In that ancient world, kings led their armies in battle. But a time came when "David remained at Jerusalem" (2 Samuel 11:1). One afternoon he saw from his palace a woman, Bathsheba, bathing on her roof. He discovered she was the wife of one of his army officers. David brought her to the palace where they committed adultery.

When the king learned that Bathsheba was pregnant, he tried at first to deceive her husband, Uriah; failing at that, David arranged for Uriah's death. Thus one sin led to another. David was confident no one knew, but the prophet Nathan confronted him with one of the most poignant sermons in all of history (see 2 Samuel 12:1-15). Rent by guilt, David repented.

Our world would call David's conduct sins of passion. I submit that they were also sins of power. I fear David had become so accustomed to his kingly prerogatives that he felt that whatever he wanted, he should get. He misused the power of his office, of his personality, and of his manliness.

Save me, dear Lord, from abusing your holy trust. Amen.

FEBRUARY 20   REPENTING

For I know my transgressions, / and my sin is ever before me.   ***(Psalm 51:3)***

David had sinned grievously and dramatically. So what shall he do with sin? Shrug it off by blaming circumstances or people? Flee guilt by drug or diversion? Go into a miasma of despair? David took the God remedy. He confessed, making no excuses. He faced the horror of what he had done and cast himself on the mercy of God. He realized that since God is the ultimate arbiter of sin, forgiveness and deliverance must come from God.

All of us sin. Some sins are more conspicuous and more socially condemned, but this is not to say that they are necessarily more reprehensible. Some of us do pretty well at a public level, but we'd hate to have the thoughts and intents of our hearts revealed. We are adept at finding synonyms for sin: "Bad choice. An unfortunate mistake. A psychological predisposition. An inherited tendency." The list is long and grows daily.

But since sin is our ultimate human sickness, it should be treated like any other sickness: recognize that it exists and accept the remedy. The remedy? Repentance, grace, and divine, redeeming forgiveness. It's really quite simple—and therefore hard to accept.

You know my heart; forgive me, please, and lead me to new life in your Son. Amen.

FEBRUARY 21   TOUGH GRIEF

"But now he is dead; why should I fast? Can I bring him back again?" *(2 Samuel 12:23)*

The prophet Nathan told David that the child he and Bathsheba had conceived in adultery would die. When the child became ill, David pleaded with God, fasted, and lay night after night on the ground before God. David's closest counselors pleaded with him to rise up, but he refused to do so.

On the seventh day, the child died. The king's servants were afraid to tell him; if he had been so passionate in the child's illness, what would he do in his death? But when David learned that the child was dead, he rose, washed himself, put on bathing ointment, dressed, and went to the house of God to worship. From there he went to his home to eat and begin life anew.

David's reasoning was tough and simple. As long as the child was alive, he would fast and weep for his life; but when the boy died, he could do no more and thus would go on with his life. To paraphrase Reinhold Niebuhr: Change what you can, accept with serenity what you cannot change, and be wise enough to know the difference.

Dear Lord, help me work, pray, and move on. Amen.

FEBRUARY 22   FAMILY PROBLEMS

But Absalom sent secret messengers throughout all the tribes of Israel, saying, "As soon as you hear the sound of the trumpet, then shout: Absalom has become king at Hebron!"
(2 Samuel 15:10)

Our deeds have their consequences even though our sins may be forgiven. David suffered a series of family tragedies following his sin with Bathsheba. One of David's sons raped a half sister, Tamar. Eventually Tamar's brother, Absalom, got revenge for his sister by killing the sibling who had violated her. The murder made Absalom, who was a favorite of his father, a fugitive from the family.

One can imagine what scandal magazines would do with such a story today. I suspect that ordinary gossip did the same in David's day. Eventually David tried cautiously to reconcile with Absalom, but by then the rupture between the two had grown too deep. Slowly but effectively, Absalom developed a circle of supporters until he was able to cause David and his remaining followers to flee from the palace. The man who was once the object of national adoration was now running for his life, driven out by his own son and some of his most trusted associates.

Even when we repent of the seed we've sown, we may have to deal with its inevitable harvest.

Have mercy on me, dear Savior, when I violate your will. Amen.

FEBRUARY 23   A VICTORY THAT COST TOO MUCH

"O my son Absalom, my son, my son Absalom! Would I had died instead of you, O Absalom, my son, my son!" (2 Samuel 18:33)

David, the old warrior, knew how to win the battle, but he lost what he wanted most. He had asked of his generals only one thing: that they "deal gently for my sake with the young man Absalom" (2 Samuel 18:5). Instead, Joab took Absalom's life.

David's grief at the death of his son was so great that victory meant nothing to him. Indeed, his grief was so great that it brought a pall over David's army, because his sorrow seemed to bring shame on the army's service. Only after Joab warned David that he was in danger of revolt did David put aside his grief and resume his role of leadership.

But David had learned that some victories cost too much. When we gain our end—whether in business, politics, or sports; whether in career or in reputation—at the price of our family, our integrity, or our relationship with God, we have paid too much. Unfortunately, we often don't see the price tag on our victories until it is too late.

Dear Lord, help me see the price of my pursuits before I close the deal. Amen.

FEBRUARY 24   ROCK AND FORTRESS

The LORD is my rock, my fortress, and my deliverer, / my God, my rock, in whom I take refuge.   (2 Samuel 22:2-3)

As David approached death, he summarized his life in a song celebrating God's deliverance "from the hand of all his enemies" (2 Samuel 22:1). David was a man of many achievements in many fields, but his life was virtually in continual conflict.

When the prophet Samuel came to anoint a chosen son of Jesse, David was in the fields; he had not even been invited to the family dinner. Some kind of sibling rivalry is surely implied here. When David sought the chance to fight Goliath, he explained that he had conquered wild animals while tending his flocks. Soon after his victory over Goliath, David was thrust into years of conflict with Saul.

On the throne, he secured Israel's borders by becoming a man of blood. The security that followed was soon destroyed by the revolt of Absalom and then Sheba's rebellion. On his deathbed, David arbitrated a crisis between two of his sons.

David's grand life was, in truth, a life of almost unceasing struggle. No wonder, then, that he began his song by naming the Lord his rock, fortress, and deliverer.

My battles may not be as many as David's, dear Lord, but I am grateful for your care. Amen.

FEBRUARY 25   SAD WORDS

"There is also with you Shimei. . . . You must bring his gray head down with blood to Sheol."   *(1 Kings 2:8a, 9b)*

I promised myself as I began this month that I would be as true in telling David's story as the Bible is. The Bible, you see, is a painfully honest book. It never tries to fool us about its characters, because it doesn't want us to fool ourselves.

David was at his noblest and best in dealing with a man named Shimei. When David was fleeing from Absalom's revolt, Shimei stood by the roadside showering David with dust and stones and mocking him. David restrained the bodyguards who wanted to kill him. A few days later, when David was restored to his throne, Shimei returned sheepishly to beg for mercy. Again, David restrained the soldiers who wanted Shimei to suffer for his arrogance.

This was David at his best. But apparently the incident festered in David's memory. Now, almost ready to die, he tells his son to give Shimei the judgment deferred.

It hurts to see this pettiness in a great soul. The story reminds us, however, what meanness we can nurture in our souls unless God's Spirit constantly redeems us.

Deliver me, dear Savior, from hateful memories. Amen.

FEBRUARY 26   HIGHEST PRAISE

[God] said, "I have found David, son of Jesse, to be a man after my heart, who will carry out all my wishes."   *(Acts 13:22)*

We first met David when Samuel came to the household of Jesse to find Israel's king-to-be. When Samuel was impressed with the eldest son, God not only rejected his choice but also corrected his standard of judgment: "For the LORD does not see as mortals see; they look on the outward appearance, but the LORD looks on the heart" (1 Samuel 16:7). Many centuries later a New Testament writer affirmed that judgment, telling us that David was a man after God's own heart (see Acts 13:22).

We know full well that David wasn't a perfect man. Not only was he sometimes impetuous and petty; he was both an adulterer and an accomplice in murder, and he seems often to have been a poor husband and father. How is it, then, that he had such standing with God?

Quite simply, because he so passionately wanted God. His relationship with God was more important to him than anything; so when he sinned, he repented. The fact that David cried, "Do not cast me away from your presence" (Psalm 51:11) tells us how much he wanted God.

Give me a longing for you, dear Savior, such as marked your servant David. Amen.

FEBRUARY 27   LONELY SONG

O LORD, how many are my foes! / Many are rising against me.
(Psalm 3:1)

We call David the sweet singer of Israel, and the book of Psalms is often referred to as the psalms of David; so it wouldn't be right to leave David's story without looking at some of the psalms attributed to him. Tradition says that Psalm 3 was written when David was fleeing from his son Absalom. It is a lonely song, with an inventory of David's enemies, many of whom were saying, "There is no help for you in God" (3:2).

I suspect that the number of the enemies was not really as significant as their makeup—his own son and some of his former confidants. Few experiences are more devastating than to be betrayed by those we trust or for whom we have great affection.

In the depths, however, David was reassured: "But you, O LORD, are a shield around me" (3:3). And in that knowledge he could "lie down and sleep," even if there were "ten thousands" against him (vv. 5-6). The former census of despair was no longer a controlling statistic.

When trouble tries to write the end of our sentences, faith interrupts with a "but": "but God."

Teach me to stay in your care, O Lord, by living with faith and integrity. Amen.

FEBRUARY 28   THE SHEPHERD

The LORD is my shepherd, I shall not want.   ***(Psalm 23:1)***

We don't know when David wrote this psalm. Your imagination, colored by your own experiences, can supply a likely time. Personally, I see this psalm written not by the shepherd boy but by the mature man, who in the midst of some crisis goes into the reservoir of memory to recall boyhood days.

We do that, you know. That's why it's so important to fill our lives with good memories. And there's still time to begin. Get some material today for good, new memories that can effectively crowd out the old, bad ones. And do what you can to bless some children or young people you know with good memories, so that they will have a healthy store in later years.

David must have been a good shepherd in order to describe so well the way a good shepherd works. We know the quality of his walk with God by the way he imagined himself in the role of the sheep.

And when David speaks of walking through the "darkest valley" (v. 4)—"the valley of the shadow of death" (KJV)—we realize again the fierce struggles that marked his life and the faith that sustained him.

Thank you for being my shepherd; may I never leave your fold. Amen.

FEBRUARY 29   DAVID'S GREATER SON

[Bartimaeus] began to shout out and say, "Jesus, Son of David, have mercy on me!"   *(Mark 10:47)*

In the years following David's reign, Israel's historians made him the standard by which all other rulers were judged. Israel's poets and prophets began to declare that someday a descendant of David would come as king to the whole world as the Messiah, the Christ.

Centuries later when a baby was born in Bethlehem, the angel announced "good news of great joy for all the people: to you is born this day in the city of David a Savior, who is the Messiah, the Lord" (Luke 2:10). The first chapter of Matthew's Gospel is a genealogy of Jesus, beginning with these key words: "Jesus the Messiah, *the son of David*, the son of Abraham" (Matthew 1:1, emphasis added).

And here and there, as the story of Jesus' ministry unfolded throughout the Gospels, surprising and unlikely people identified Jesus not simply as teacher, man of Nazareth, or miracle worker, but as "the son of David." So it was one day outside Jericho when a blind beggar, Bartimaeus, heard that Jesus was passing by. His call for healing began, "Jesus, Son of David." And the Son of David answered by restoring the man's sight.

Jesus, promised Son of David, I renew my pledge of love for you. Amen.

MARCH

Roles of a Lifetime

RAMON PRESSON

MARCH 1   "READY, AND . . . ACTION!"

But you are a chosen people, a royal priesthood, a holy nation, a people belonging to God, that you may declare the praises of [God].   *(1 Peter 2:9 NIV)*

The Bible is a very visual book, filled from Genesis to Revelation with symbols, analogies, metaphors, and word pictures. To help us understand who we are in relationship to God, Scripture invites us to role-play an extensive cast of characters that includes occupations, animals, and common objects. The inspired authors urge us to think of ourselves as athletes, soldiers, trees, sheep, builders, salt and light, conquerors, artwork, account managers, vine branches, aliens, ambassadors, children, shining stars, and prize-fighters, just to name a few.

The biblical writers thrust us on stage to act out multiple roles in a production that resembles a school play more than a Broadway show. The point is not to impress an audience but to become and learn from each character. Professional actors call it "getting into the role."

Each day this month you'll be ushered backstage to get into costume. There are no lines to memorize but, rather, lessons to be learned from both positive and negative examples of the character. Are you ready? The curtain is going up.

Dear God, help me this month to see and embrace the rich meanings of what it means to be a follower of Christ. Amen.

MARCH 2   A NEW CREATION

Therefore, if anyone is in Christ, he is a new creation; the old has gone, the new has come!   *(2 Corinthians 5:17 NIV)*

I was walking a few steps behind a Korean family of five, each holding a small American flag, outside the Greenville County courthouse. I had just led the benediction during the naturalization ceremony where fifty-seven people born in nineteen different countries had been newly pronounced U.S. citizens. The youngest of the Korean family was waving her new flag with gusto. She paused, looked up at her father, and said, "Daddy, are we *really* Americans now?"

I was stopped in my tracks. This little girl had grasped and was celebrating the bestowing of her new identity, an identity and citizenship with corresponding rights and privileges I take for granted.

We live out of a sense of our identity. Our sense of identity may come from our careers, celebrity, relationships, appearance, and our abilities, or from our faults, losses, and failures. Ultimately, who we believe we *are* exerts substantial influence on what we *do*.

Neil Anderson insists that understanding the profound implications of our identity in Christ is the key to spiritual victory and the abundant life Christ promised those who carry a new flag.

God, help me grasp who I am and whose I am. Amen.

MARCH 3   ALIENS AND STRANGERS

I urge you, as aliens and strangers in the world, to abstain from sinful desires, which war against your soul. (1 Peter 2:11 NIV)

Aliens and strangers? Oh yeah, that sounds like something exciting to strive for. Where do we sign up? Actually, there's no additional registration required. If you are a follower of Christ, you already are an alien (not like E.T., although sometimes people will think you're talking like someone from another planet). To the world you are a foreigner in their land, a stranger to their cultural norms, philosophies, obsessions, and moral standards.

Whenever you're a tourist, you typically try to be discreet about it. Blend in as much as possible. Don't make it so obvious that you're an outsider. Peter reminds us that as Christians, we're tourists here in this world. We're not home yet. We're renting a room in Hotel Earth. But Peter doesn't tell us to blend in with the crowd. On the contrary, there should be something peculiar about our behavior, distinctive about our integrity, different about our relationships that would provoke someone to say, "Hey, buddy, you ain't from around here, are ya?"

Father, I confess that I have the capacity to blend in with my surroundings like a chameleon. Help me be an oddball in the most positive way. Amen.

MARCH 4   APPOINTED AMBASSADOR

We are therefore Christ's ambassadors, as though God were making his appeal through us.   (2 Corinthians 5:20 NIV)

The United States has more than three hundred embassies throughout the world from Austria to Zaire. The embassy is a place of refuge and assistance for U.S. citizens and the residence of the American ambassador to the host country. An ambassador represents U.S. interests and concerns to that country. For the sake of international relations, Washington desires that its ambassadors not only accurately represent U.S. policy and positions, but also build bridges of goodwill to the leaders and citizens of the host country.

We are ambassadors of Christ, representatives of his Kingdom to those outside it and unfamiliar with it. We are trusted carriers of Christ's message and empowered reflectors of his character. An ambassador does not seek to impose American rule in the host country. Likewise, being an ambassador of Christ does not call for an overly aggressive stance or subversive approach with unbelievers. We're not spies or undercover agents plotting a coup.

In this world we are citizens of another Kingdom with orders to so accurately represent our King that it makes others desire to emigrate to its borders.

Lord Jesus, help me represent you well in my home, my neighborhood, my workplace, and my community. Amen.

MARCH 5   RELUCTANT JUDGE

"Do not judge, or you too will be judged."   *(Matthew 7:1 NIV)*

How would you know if your brake lights were out? Someone else would have to tell you, right? When you're driving, you obviously can't see your taillights.

How do you respond to someone who points out to you a spiritual, emotional, relational, behavioral, attitudinal, or moral "brake light" that's gone dim? Do you get defensive, make excuses, or counter with criticism of *their* faults?

In the book *Leadership and Self-Deception*, the authors note our susceptibility to faulty self-diagnosis. We often fail to realize that our attitude or behavior is the problem, shifting the critique and blame upon others.

Jesus cautioned, "It's hard to see clearly enough to extract a speck of sawdust from your wife's eye when you have a fishing pier protruding from your own." Some mistakenly think that Jesus' command to resist judging means to avoid making personal evaluations. Truthfully, you cannot help but interpret and evaluate the actions of others. What Jesus is cautioning against is the feature of judging that includes condemnation. The problem is that it's much more fun to profess someone else's sins than it is to confess our own.

Holy Spirit, remind me to take self-inventory before I ring someone else up, and help me evaluate myself more accurately. Amen.

MARCH 6   WEDDING CRASHER

"But when the king came in to see the guests, he noticed a man there who was not wearing wedding clothes."
(Matthew 22:11 NIV)

You're a last-minute wedding guest. You didn't have time to rent a tux, and your navy blazer is at the cleaners. You're not wearing a leisure suit, so why are they making such a fuss over your clothes?

For a royal wedding such as this, the guests are given a wedding garment, an expensive covering worthy of the event. But you're not wearing one. The host didn't run out of your size. You just decided that you didn't need it. "I look good just as I am," you said to the greeter.

The parable symbolizes grace offered and grace rejected. You reject the covering because you presume that your common decency puts you on the front row. You don't need Jesus' redemptive work on the cross. How you're living is good enough. So naturally you're offended when the bouncer tosses you out. Doesn't he know who you are? You feel the hardness of the street and the cold of the black night as you hear unnatural sounds getting closer. Then you wake up from your nightmare, relieved it was only a bad dream.

Lord, as I get dressed today, I thank you for the robe of righteousness (Isaiah 61:10), the cloak of grace given to me through Christ. Amen.

MARCH 7   NEAR-SIGHTED BUSINESSMAN

"This is how it will be with anyone who stores up things for himself but is not rich toward God."   *(Luke 12:21 NIV)*

In Matthew 6, Jesus reassures the poor who have no stocks, mutual funds, or retirement accounts to fall back on. They don't live paycheck to paycheck but day to day. Jesus speaks to them about responding in faith in the face of scarcity.

In contrast, the Luke 12:16-21 parable addresses our response to abundance. Jesus tells a story about a successful businessman who has more product than he can store in his current warehouse, more profit than he can put in his Roth IRA.

With no thought of gratitude to anyone beyond himself, with no consideration of human need beyond his own wish list, the businessman builds a bigger warehouse and opens a Swiss bank account.

But the excess stashed away is not hidden from God, and in heaven an accountant closes the books. A rich man surrounded by his wealth enters the afterlife empty-handed.

Do you have a copy of *GQ*? No, not the magazine. Your *Gratitude Quotient*. Your *Generosity Quotient*. Both are qualities evident in the life of the man who knows he's been blessed. With God, your GQ is more important than your IQ.

God, help me increasingly display gratitude and generosity, qualities that Jesus exhibited in abundance. Amen.

MARCH 8   INTENTIONAL INVESTOR

"To one he gave five talents of money, to another two talents, and to another one talent, each according to his ability."
(Matthew 25:15 NIV)

Have you ever been to your high-school reunion? There's a standard question that makes the rounds during every conversation at every reunion: "So, what are you doing now?" Here's a paraphrase: "We've had the same 3,650 days of opportunity since graduation ten years ago. What did you do with your 3,650?"

Imagine those 3,650 days are like the daily blocks on a wall calendar. There's a lot you can build with almost four thousand blocks.

In Jesus' parable, the master gives his servants an investment opportunity or responsibility. Note that there's not an equal distribution of investment capital; it is based on the master's assessment of ability—differing amounts but the same assignment—grow what I have entrusted to you.

What financial resources have been entrusted to you? What spiritual gifts has God given you? What special talents do you possess? What investment capital of life-shaping experiences do you hold? Now here's the rubber-meets-the-road question: How are you going to invest that spiritual treasure? It's not really yours, you know. It's on loan.

God, help me seize the privilege of expanding your Kingdom through what you have entrusted to me. Amen.

MARCH 9   PURCHASED PROPERTY

You are not your own; you were bought at a price.
(1 Corinthians 6:19b-20 NIV)

I was thrilled to be having dinner with author Calvin Miller. We were discussing one of his books in depth when he asked the hostess if she had a copy on hand. She did, indeed. He said, "May I impose upon you to give that copy to our young friend, and I'll buy you a replacement copy and send it to you." The woman was glad to bless me with the book, but she resisted Miller's intent to pay for a replacement. Miller insisted as he inscribed the inside cover to me.

Miller, the creator and author of the book, insisted on buying a copy of his own book in order to give it as a gift. What humility and generosity!

Friend, God created you. He has always owned you. But through Christ's death, he paid the price and purchased you *again*. He paid for something he already owned! Why? So he could give you the gift of abundant and eternal life.

I treasure Miller's book to this day, not only as a gift from a favorite author, but also as a reminder that God owned me, bought me again, and gave me life and himself as a gift.

God, I am humbled by your grace and generosity. Thank you. Amen.

MARCH 10   WISE BUILDER

"Everyone who hears these words of mine and puts them into practice is like a wise man who built his house on the rock."
(Matthew 7:24 NIV)

Regardless of your handyman skills, you *are* a builder. The only question, according to Jesus, is what kind. The parable in Matthew 7:24-27 is not a distinction between religious and nonreligious people; it actually divides religious folk into two camps. Jesus describes two similarities and two differences among all life-builders.

Similarities: (1) Both builders "hear" the teachings of Christ. (2) Both homeowners get the same weather report.

Distinctions: (1) The wise man considers the message and implements it in his daily life. The foolish builder hears the same message, takes copious notes, buys the entire tape series, but stops short of actual application. (2) The implementer's home weathers the storm, but the note taker's construction project caves in against the wind and downpour.

Is there an area of the Christian life where your knowledge far exceeds your action?

Think about these words written by Larry Crabb: "To be a genuine follower of Christ is not to live in a land with no storms but to live in a home that no storm can destroy."

Lord, help me do today what I know to be right and true. Amen.

MARCH 11   MASTERPIECE

For we are God's workmanship, created in Christ Jesus to do good works. *(Ephesians 2:10 NIV)*

Workmanship: a good masculine word evoking images of unshaven guys surrounded by tools in their garages, completing do-it-yourself projects with admiring onlookers shaking their heads in amazement. The problem is that the origin of the word translated "workmanship" is the Greek word *poema*. Fast-forward to the future and it becomes the English word *poem*.

How do you feel about being God's poem? Hold on. Remember that King David was a warrior poet who wrote most of the psalms. God likes poetry. In fact, the Creator apparently has a special fondness for creativity and art of all kinds.

Great poets don't take kindly to other people editing their work. When God crafts a poem, he likes it just as he wrote it. The warning to would-be critics and wannabe correctors: "Don't mess with my masterpiece." Don't misinterpret God's delight with you as your right to deflect all advice and reject all constructive critique. The paradox here is that you're always a work in progress; but regardless of the stage you're in, God displays the priceless you in a magnificent frame. So wake up, Mr. Poem. Rhyme and shine.

God, I seldom feel like a work of art. Help me embrace my true identity in Christ. Amen.

MARCH 12   SECURE SON

For you did not receive a spirit that makes you a slave again to fear, but you received the Spirit of sonship. And by him we cry, "Abba, Father."   (Romans 8:15 NIV)

March Madness is my favorite time of the year in sports. I grew up in North Carolina, where college basketball rules as king over all athletic domain. I fill out my brackets, make my predictions, and then sit on the edge of my seat as sixty-four teams become thirty-two, sixteen, eight, four, and then two. Davids pelt Goliaths. Players, coaches, and fans display emotions of elation and agony. Finally, a champion is crowned.

I tend to forget that these incredible athletes who are twice my size are still boys—boys with mothers and fathers who are so proud of their sons that they can't see straight.

Sir, have you noticed that despite your age there is still a boy inside you wishing to make your daddy proud? How hard is it for you to imagine that your Heavenly Father is pleased with you and glad you are his son? How well do you think you have to perform to gain his approval or secure his love?

Father, thank you for treating me like a beloved son. Help me understand and live in my sonship. Amen.

MARCH 13   BIG CHILD

"I tell you the truth, anyone who will not receive the kingdom of God like a little child will never enter it." (Mark 10:15 NIV)

Jesus said that if we're to come to God, we must become like children. However, the apostle Paul frequently exhorted his churches to grow up and put away their childish ways. So, are we supposed to be children or not?

There is marked difference between being *childish* and being *childlike*. Children are dependent, and they're secure in their dependency. They are trusting, hopeful. They are imaginative, creative, and playful; and they don't take themselves so seriously. They are climbers, explorers, and daredevils. Children have yet to learn they cannot sing, dance, or draw well enough. They do it all with delight and confidence.

In the comedy *Big* starring Tom Hanks, Josh is a boy who is magically aged to adulthood. He awakens to find himself with the body of a thirty-year-old in need of a shave. Others are fascinated by adult Josh's childlike innocence and enthusiasm. Josh is just being himself, albeit in a grownup's body.

Jesus doesn't call us to be immature, but to be mature without pretense—clown saints, not stuffy Pharisees. So, come to Jesus in your railroad footy pajamas or your little-league uniform. He's laughing with his arms open.

Lord, help me come to you like a big child, trusting and hopeful, reverent but unpretentious. Amen.

MARCH 14   ROOMMATE

Jesus replied, "If anyone loves me, he will obey my teaching. My Father will love him, and we will come to him and make our home with him." (John 14:23 NIV)

John wrote, "The Word became flesh and made his dwelling among us" (1:14 NIV). The paraphrase from *The Message* says that "the Word . . . moved into the neighborhood." The good news of the Incarnation is that Christ indeed put on an earth suit and lived among us—God with us.

But Jesus offers to go from being a resident in your town or a neighbor in your subdivision to being your roommate! Jesus wants to move in and bring the Father with him.

Where would you prefer Jesus to live—down the street or in the next room? Close quarters will likely require some adjustments on your part. Maybe you'd be more comfortable with Jesus at a safe distance yet close enough in case of emergency.

What does anyone look for in a roommate? Compatibility. Jesus makes the lease agreement conditional upon obeying his teaching because that says something about relational compatibility between you two.

Would you knowingly select a roommate whose beliefs, attitudes, values, behavior, and lifestyle were quite contrary to yours?

So, where do you want Jesus to live?

Father, I want you and Jesus to move in; help me do some housecleaning. Amen.

MARCH 15   ACTOR

"Woe to you, teachers of the law and Pharisees, you hypocrites!"   ***(Matthew 23:13 NIV)***

Show-offs, dirty cups, blind guides, white-washed tombs. Those are just some of the word pictures Jesus employs in Matthew 23 to describe the Pharisees. The descriptive word Jesus most often used for the religious police was "hypocrite."

We think we know what *hypocrite* means—someone who professes one thing and does the opposite; someone who doesn't practice what he or she preaches; someone who doesn't walk the talk. However, *hypocrite* means something more than incongruence between belief, verbal profession, and action.

A hypocrite is a form of the word *actor*. An actor is playing a role, reciting a script someone else wrote. An actor doesn't have to believe his or her lines; he or she has only to speak them convincingly. Actors love the stage and crave applause.

Spiritual hypocrisy exceeds mere inconsistencies in our behavior; it is making an external show of something with little internal conviction. Acting more committed or pious than we really are is playing to the crowd for approval.

When we "stage our faith" for human accolades, we'll hear Jesus say, "That's the extent of your reward, so enjoy it" (Matthew 6:5, *author's paraphrase*).

When do you catch yourself "performing"?

God, help me grow a genuine faith and seek your rewards over the fleeting applause of men. Amen.

MARCH 16   SHOOTING STAR

Do everything without complaining or arguing, so that you may become blameless and pure, children of God without fault in a crooked and depraved generation, in which you shine like stars in the universe. **(Philippians 2:14-15 NIV)**

Reality shows like *American Idol* and *Survivor* give people with no agents or Hollywood connections a chance to become celebrities and stars. I live outside of Nashville, a mecca for aspiring musicians who hope to be discovered, land a record deal, and become a star.

Paul says that you can become a star right now, right where you are—not a celebrity but a bright light against a contrasting canvas of spiritual darkness. Against the cultural din of cynicism, sarcasm, bitterness and blaming, accusations and mudslinging, Paul exhorts you to stand out by being radically different: cooperative, grateful, peacemaking, blameless, and pure.

If your coworkers, business associates, customers or clients, neighbors, and friends were asked to name a "true gentleman" they know, would it be you? How do you speak, act, and react in a way that would label you a "Christian gentleman" in your workplace and social network? God is doing his own version of *Star Search,* and he welcomes your audition.

God, help me be different from the inside out, so that the authentic change inside may shine brightly. Amen.

MARCH 17   SALTSHAKER

"You are the salt of the earth."   *(Matthew 5:13 NIV)*

Whereas nutritionists advise us to take in less sodium, Jesus exhorts us to pour it out. We view salt as a seasoning, an enhancer of flavor. Jesus' audience utilized salt as a preservative.

Jesus is calling us to be cultural preservatives in a world that, left to itself, will rot in its own depravity. But being cultural salt doesn't mean being an angry, fuming condemner of all things secular.

America's unchurched majority view Christians as angry, narrow-minded judges known primarily for what we are *against.* Combine this with the fact that they see little of the difference that Christ makes in our character, the way we do business, or the way we love our wives, and you can understand their suspicion and disinterest.

Being salt in a crazed world does mean upholding a standard, but more importantly it means living out an authentic Christlikeness in the midst of people and systems deprived of a visual aid of Jesus' life and teachings. The world needs you to get your salt out of the shaker...and be sweet about it. It doesn't need more salt in its wounds.

God, help me sprinkle salt this week in a redemptive way. Amen.

MARCH 18   LIGHT BULB

"You are the light of the world....Let your light shine before men, that they may see your good deeds and praise your Father in heaven."   *(Matthew 5:14, 16 NIV)*

By imitating the life of Christ, occasionally you'll be persecuted. Jesus promised that his followers would be vilified by some, just as he was. But quite frankly, the imitation of Jesus is so infrequently attempted that the world fails to get much of a chance to respond to the exhibit. They're more desperate for a genuine display than you may realize.

Jesus calls you to be a lighthouse in the storm, a flashlight in the dark, a candle during someone's power failure, a porch light to the outcasts, headlights to the aimless, sunlight that dispels the gloom and warms the bones, a red light and siren signaling that help is on the way.

"Imitate me and do good deeds," Jesus urges. But it's not an act to impress people, attract applause, or garner awards. It's merely an honest glow that radiates because of a greater light source, like the moon that shines neon because of the absorbed and refracted rays of the sun. That's why you are called to be a light. You're a Son reflector.

Father, help me be alert and responsive to the kind of light you need me to be today. Amen.

MARCH 19 AVID COLLECTOR

For if you possess these qualities in increasing measure, they will keep you from being ineffective and unproductive in your knowledge of our Lord Jesus Christ. **(2 Peter 1:8 NIV)**

Capitalism thrives on our felt need to add to our collections—collections of tools, golf clubs, books, electronics, CDs, DVDs, fishing lures, and various trophies from our eBay victories.

Peter exhorts us to get the faith starter kit and regularly add to the collection of godly character qualities found in verses 5-7. Then, in the context of presenting the benefits of accumulating these qualities, verse 8 offers a sobering reality: It's quite possible, even common, to be "ineffective and unproductive in your knowledge of Christ." My brain's hard drive can be filled to capacity with truthful and helpful knowledge from the Scriptures and great Christian books; but ultimately it begs the question asked by G. K. Chesterton: "How is your theology transforming your biography?"

It takes time to add to a collection of rare eighteenth-century coins. You develop an appreciation of their value and then you become a hunter, scouting and searching to find their trail. Transforming your character requires that you value the outcome enough to constantly stalk the qualities of Christlikeness. It's a life-long journey. When would you like to start?

God, help me be an avid collector of godly qualities. Amen.

MARCH 20   GOOD SOIL

"Still other seed fell on good soil, where it produced a crop."
(Matthew 13:8 NIV)

The small town of Clewiston is in the heart of sugarcane country in south Florida. As you enter the town you see a sign proudly displayed that reads *Clewiston: Her Soil Is Her Fortune*.

The soil is rich, soft, and darker than coffee grounds. So valuable is the soil that you also see signs prohibiting opportunists from looting the soil for their gardens. Police confront many an out-of-town motorist slinging shovels of the magic dirt into the trunk of a car strategically parked on the side of a back road. The fines are stiff because the soil is valuable.

In this parable, Jesus creates an analogy with four variables and one constant: four different soil types; one brand of good seed. Result: three crop failures and one success story.

How's *your* dirt? God's word is always good seed. What kind of reception does it find in your mind and heart? What would a soil analysis of your heart reveal? What's currently growing in your field?

Now think long term. What kind of legacy do you want to leave? If you wish to grow a flourishing example, you must start with the dirt, because your soil is your fortune.

Lord, help me condition my soil to receive your truth. Amen.

MARCH 21   THRIVING TREE

He is like a tree planted by streams of water, / which yields its fruit in season / and whose leaf does not wither.

(Psalm 1:3 NIV)

The summer of 2007 brought drought conditions to much of the country, including Middle Tennessee. Seeing that a Japanese maple in the backyard was sporting some wilting leaves, I asked my youngest son, Cameron, to give the tree a drink with the hose. Moments later I spotted him giving the branches a shower. When I instructed him to aim the water at the tree base in order to let the water get down to the roots, he informed me that his method was getting water to the dehydrated leaves more quickly.

I explained that the hidden roots are like straws through which the tree drinks.

The leaves have no mouths to slurp the rainfall. When offering water to a thirsty tree, there is a major difference between giving it a bath and giving it a drink.

The psalmist declares that the man who grounds himself in the truths of God becomes like a tree planted next to an ever-present and reliable water source that aims its nourishment right at the roots. Favorable circumstances are as fickle as the weather, but the river keeps flowing, providing, and hydrating a tree that responds with a sprouting of fruit.

Where are you planted?

God, help me transplant myself closer to the river. Amen.

MARCH 22   FRUITFUL BRANCH

"I am the vine; you are the branches. If a man remains in me and I in him, he will bear much fruit."   *(John 15:5 NIV)*

Consider a V-8 engine with enough torque and horsepower to lift a house. Now raise the hood and loosen the battery cable on either pole, and you have just rendered a monstrous masterpiece of engineering absolutely powerless. The connection between the engine, the cable, and the battery is vital.

Jesus says he is the vine. You're a branch. You have one job description as a branch in God's vineyard: stay connected. If the vine is healthy and there's a healthy connection between the vine and branches, there will be fruit. Since Jesus is the vine, we know the vine itself is healthy.

So how do you become and remain spiritually healthy? Stay connected. Your task is not to force fruit out of your limbs but to focus on your connection to Jesus, the Vine.

This means you can't just hook up to the big vine on Sunday mornings. Remember the fruit of the Spirit in Galatians 5:22-23? Well, there's a crop failure if you're not connected.

How can you remain connected to Christ? How will your life be noticeably different?

Jesus, show me what it means to hold on to you, to do this thing called "abiding." Amen.

MARCH 23   A FUNNY SMELL

We are to God the aroma of Christ among those who are being saved and those who are perishing.   (2 Corinthians 2:15 NIV)

Aromatherapy? That's the smell of beef and pepperoni seeping out from the pizza box. It's the aroma of coffee brewing and bacon frying. It's the smell of a new baseball glove and the interior of a new car. It's the breeze bringing you a whiff of steaks on a charcoal grill. It's the smell of a small-town hardware store.

Do you remember when men's cologne was called "aftershave" and had various masculine names? Those aftershaves smelled like wood chips dipped in rubbing alcohol, but at least it was a manly odor. My grandfather wore a particular brand, the bottle of which reminded me of a grenade with a pin in it. Very manly. To this day, whenever I smell that scent I think of Granddad Presson.

We are to be the aroma that makes people pause, twitch their nose, sniff, and say, "That fragrance reminds me of Jesus." We all give off a smell. The only variable is what kind.

What do you smell like?

Jesus, help me draw so close to you that your fragrance rubs off on me. Help me be an "air freshener" in places that are stale. Amen.

MARCH 24   SHEEP AND GOATS

"He will separate the people from one another as a shepherd separates the sheep from the goats." **(Matthew 25:32 NIV)**

Choosing between being a sheep or a goat doesn't initially excite me. But this parable is not about the endearing qualities of farm animals. Jesus isn't casting for a sequel to *Charlotte's Web*.

This parable is about what a shepherd favors. Shepherds are partial to sheep. If Jesus is a shepherd, then the best animal you could possibly be is a sheep. Jesus even tells you how to transform yourself into a highly favored wooly mammal: notice and respond to people in need.

Jesus has always had a tender spot for the needy, the hurting, the oppressed, the forgotten ones. If we want to be like him, we must notice what he notices and reach out to people who'll never get their picture in the society pages of Sunday's newspaper. And when we show compassion and generosity to these who cannot reimburse us, Jesus claims to register the deed as though the kindness was shown directly to him. In a way, there's a costume party going on here. Jesus often disguises himself as a single mom on food stamps. He invites us to put on the caring sheep outfit.

Jesus, help me see what you see, notice who you notice, and respond as you would. Amen.

MARCH 25   LION TAMER

Be self-controlled and alert. Your enemy the devil prowls around like a roaring lion looking for someone to devour.
(1 Peter 5:8 NIV)

If the devil is your enemy, then guess who the devil's enemy is? Yeah, it's you.

Let that sink in. You're not just an escaped captive or an irritant to the devil. You're not a competitive rival. You're the enemy because you are an ally of God, Satan's supreme enemy. There's a bull's-eye on your chest, dear brother.

Be alert lest you think the visible world is all there is. Be alert with your antenna up for sounds of stalking. Be self-controlled lest your complacency or a lack of self-discipline make the lion salivate. Few men seem to recognize the threat, whereas some even seem to chirp, "Here, kitty, kitty." They open themselves up for attack and then act surprised by the massacre of their lives and testimony. In verse 9, Peter doesn't tell you to outrun the lion but to "resist" and "stand firm." Bare your teeth and, in Jesus' name, roar back. In the pivotal moments and spontaneous decisions you make in the jungle, you often have only seconds to decide whether to pray or to be prey.

Lord, help me be alert, uncompromising, and victorious against the lion. Amen.

MARCH 26   EXPERT FISHERMAN

"Come, follow me," Jesus said, "and I will make you fishers of men." (Mark 1:17 NIV)

In 1983 when Apple Computer was in its adolescent years as a company, its founder, Steve Jobs, pursued John Sculley to join the team. As president of PepsiCo since 1977, Sculley had held the top office of one of the richest food and beverage companies in the world. Why should Sculley risk his secure position for an upstart computer company? Jobs famously asked Sculley: "Do you want to make sugar water for the rest of your life, or do you want to change the world?"* Sculley soon joined the Mac revolution.

There is no intent in this illustration to minimize or criticize the value of your current job. Jesus had been a carpenter most of his life. He wasn't mocking the fishing trade.

He was offering a promotion. Most likely, Jesus is not calling you to leave your job for full-time ministry. But what if he is inviting you to make a difference, not just a living? What if Christ is asking you to meet the needs of hurting people instead of just meeting sales quotas? What if he is calling you not to just address envelopes but to address the spiritual condition of those you work with or live near?

God, help me upgrade the vision for my life. Amen.

* http://en.wikipedia.org/wiki/John_Sculley

MARCH 27   RUNNER AND FIGHTER

I do not run like a man running aimlessly; I do not fight like a man beating the air.   ***(1 Corinthians 9:26 NIV)***

The other day I said to the great apostle, "Hey, Paul, wanna jog around the neighborhood?"

He frowned. "You mean running just to run? No goal, no competition, no cheering crowd, no finish line, no prize?"

"Well, uh . . . never mind."

Paul would be the first to say that, like athletics, success in the spiritual life requires training. However, that training—the early morning runs, the hours in the weight room—is all done with a grander purpose.

Does that mean that you can't ever just relax and enjoy life? Of course not. It is vital for your emotional, spiritual, physical, and relational health to make time for recreation, hobbies, socializing, and play. Even those activities all funnel into a purpose: a healthier you.

Rick Warren and the apostle Paul are advocates of the same vision: the purpose-filled life.

Regardless of your occupation, are you a *visioneer*? Do you have a vision and mission for your life—a sense of purpose beyond going to work for a paycheck to pay the mortgage so you have a place to sleep before you go to work to get a paycheck?

God, help me recognize and grab hold of the great purposes for which you created me. Amen.

MARCH 28   CONFIRMED CHAMPION

I beat my body and make it my slave so that after I have preached to others, I myself will not be disqualified for the prize.   *(1 Corinthians 9:27 NIV)*

Cheating scandals and disqualifications have plagued almost every sport. Winners have been stripped of victories, records, and medals, and banned from competing. Who are some such athletes who come to your mind?

Winning at all costs has often meant compromise. For the apostle Paul, there was no room for compromise, regardless of the personal price he had to pay. In the arena where character is everything, Paul disciplined his fleshly nature in order to be a true champion.

Paul wanted to finish well, to cross the line of his earthly life with his conscience clear. The thought of working so hard only to blow it near the end reinforced his resolve to stand strong. He would not disgrace his testimony and invite easy mockery of Christ and his church.

How about you? Are there any areas of compromise that you need to address? Is there compromise for pleasure or for a shortcut to immediate and temporary success? What is your outlook—short-term or long-term, temporal or eternal? Upon what is your focus—your pleasure and success or your influence on others?

Lord, for my sake, your glory, and the impact on others, help me be a qualified champion. Amen.

MARCH 29   FAITHFUL SOLDIER

Endure hardship with us like a good soldier of Christ Jesus.
(2 Timothy 2:3 NIV)

Robert E. Lee said, "It is well that war is so terrible, lest we should grow too fond of it." Recruitment commercials and advertisements for branches of the military emphasize the challenge and adventure of military service. Absent are images of hardship and boredom, graphic scenes of actual combat, or disturbing images of death. This is not meant to disparage military service. On the contrary, it is a noble endeavor; but it is not glamorous.

War is brutal, and the apostle Paul knew it; so he urged the young pastor Timothy to persevere despite unfavorable conditions, stressful situations, and difficult people. When Paul called Timothy to endure hardship "with us," it was a reminder that Timothy was not alone.

What unfavorable conditions are you facing? What stressful situations? Who are the difficult people?

Do you feel alone in your striving to endure? If not, give God thanks for the brother(s) who support you. If you do feel alone, what is a manageable first step to enlisting support, to inviting or creating the needed brotherhood?

God, help me endure and remain faithful regardless of my current disappointments, frustrations, or pressure points. Help me remember that I've been called into battle not as a solo fighter but as part of a brotherhood. Amen.

MARCH 30   FOCUSED SOLDIER

No one serving as a soldier gets involved in civilian affairs—he wants to please his commanding officer.   (2 Timothy 2:4 NIV)

Bode Miller, a star skier on the 2004 U.S. Winter Olympic team, left Athens with no medals but plenty of criticism that his interest in the Athens nightlife exceeded his devotion to his sport. In his selfish lack of discipline, he forgot or ignored that he represented more than just Bode.

The apostle Paul, like a general, called Timothy to be faithful despite adversity (v. 3) and focused despite distractions and temptations (v. 4). A true soldier on mission doesn't get drunk at the neighborhood bar or engage in promiscuous behavior with the locals. Even when "on leave," he or she doesn't leave behind his or her identity as a soldier.

We regularly make decisions, speak, and take actions based on our sense of identity. Are you a man who just happens to be a

Christian, or does your primary identity as a Christian determine your choices and your behavior as a man? There is a spacious difference between the two—about the size of a battlefield.

Dear God, help me think like a soldier, being aware of who I am and focused on the mission. Help me increasingly want to obey the orders of my Commanding Officer instead of ignoring them and making up my own. Amen.

MARCH 31   CONQUEROR

In all these things we are more than conquerors through him who loved us.   *(Romans 8:37 NIV)*

Think of the irony. Paul was writing to Christians in Rome about being "more than conquerors." These were residents in the hub of the vast Roman Empire, whose territory was acquired through military conquests.

To these citizens immersed in the reality of "conquer or be conquered," Paul said that the arsenal and army of Christ's love for us subdues all opponents that would threaten our security in him.

In Romans 8:35-39, Paul summarized everything imaginable that we might think casts a shadow of doubt over the love of God for us. Yet, no human experience or supernatural force can loosen the grip of God's love.

Since the world judges success by fame, power, and wealth, the jury may return a verdict that you are a loser. Don't believe it. The evaluations, the critics, and the afflictions of this world cannot hold you captive because the shackles can never fit the man who knows he is loved. Being furiously loved has made you a conqueror. Are you approaching this day with the attitude of one who is defeated or one who is victorious?

God, most days I don't feel much like a conqueror. Help me live out of my identity instead of my circumstances, conditions, and feelings. Amen.

APRIL

Connections

TIM GOSSETT

APRIL 1   MAKE SOME CONNECTIONS

Think over what I say, for the Lord will give you understanding in all things.   (2 Timothy 2:7)

People find God's guidance in many places—in scripture, during conversations, through prayer, while reading, and in many other situations. I often receive God's guidance when I make connections between two or more people, ideas, stories, or scriptures. For example, I hear God's voice when I discover a connection between two random ideas, or between a news story I read and a conversation with a friend that spurs me into action. This connection-making process is so foundational to my faith that I named a young adult Sunday school class at my church "Connections."

In the days that follow, I reflect on fifteen different topics; yet the topics also connect—in my mind and, I hope, in yours—to the ones before and after. To some extent, they also connect with the liturgical seasons of Lent and Easter. As you read them, ponder the connections in them and in your own life, for there you too may find God's guidance for your day.

God, my life is a series of connections—missed, discovered, and experienced. Guide me as I look for you in unexpected places. Amen.

APRIL 2   CHOOSE AND CHOOSE AGAIN

*Barricade the road that goes Nowhere. . . . I choose the true road
to Somewhere, I post your road signs at every curve and corner.
(Psalm 119:29a, 30 The Message)*

In Western Christianity, the season of Lent is the 40 days—not
counting Sundays—before Easter, which can fall anywhere
between March 22 to April 25. Thus, today may not fall within
Lent, but it likely does. Lent is a season for preparing ourselves for
Easter, but it's also about walking with Jesus in his final journey.

In Lent, we say we are going to choose *this* over *that*. We're
going to leave behind *that* "land of the dead" we've been in, and we
are going to "die" to all that hinders us from *this* participatory life
with God. On Ash Wednesday, the start of Lent, we remember we
are dust and ashes, which is about more than reflecting on our
mortality. The path of death to self is one of transformation, of
being born again to something new and better again and again in
our life. Are you ready for your own journey from Galilee to
Jerusalem?

*Walk with me, Jesus, as I walk with you toward the cross. Stay
with me, Jesus, as I stay with you on the journey of faith. Amen.*

APRIL 3   CHOOSE GOD, NOT EMPIRE

*Now after John was arrested, Jesus came to Galilee, proclaim-
ing the good news of God, and saying, "The time is fulfilled, and
the kingdom of God has come near; repent, and believe in the
good news."   (Mark 1:14-15)*

In the Gospels, most stories and teachings related to Jesus' life
appear just once or twice. This scripture is one of a handful that
appear in all four Gospels, indicating its centrality to Jesus' message. To repent is to literally turn around and go in the other direction. Which one? For Jesus, it was toward God's kingdom and not
Caesar's.

Many terms we associate with Jesus were also used for Caesar

Augustus—Lord, Son of God, Savior, Redeemer, and others. To hear this scripture as solely personal is to miss the profoundly political message of Jesus: God's kingdom is not like Rome's. Reject empire and embrace a new reality, the good news.

In an age when one country spends more on its military than all other countries combined, we would do well to hear Jesus' message anew.

Savior of the world, help me live in a way that brings forth the kingdom of God, not the empires of business, politics, and media. Amen.

APRIL 4   RESOLUTIONS ARE FOR EVERY DAY

Keep your eyes open, hold tight to your convictions, give it all you've got, be resolute, and love without stopping.
                              (1 Corinthians 16:13-14 **The Message)**

According to one source, the top ten resolutions typically made at the start of a new year are spending more time with family or friends, exercising, losing weight, quitting smoking, writing a book, quitting drinking, getting out of debt, learning something new, helping others, and getting organized.* Sound familiar?

So how are you doing on your resolutions for the new year? If you're like most people, you have forgotten what they were, given up on pursuing your goal, or simply never bothered to make any resolutions because of past years' experience.

Each day is a gift from God, a new opportunity to do the best with the time, talents, and resources we have. Whatever your resolution was, resolve each day to be perfected in love, strengthened in the faith, and filled with hope. Those are resolutions worth remembering—and keeping! (And give your other resolutions another shot. They're likely worth pursuing, too!)

O God, whose promises are always faithful, be with me today when my resolve to serve you weakens and I feel ready to quit. Amen.

* "Top 10 New Year's Resolutions," Kimberly and Albrecht Powell, http://pitts burgh.about.com/od/holidays/tp/resolutions.htm

APRIL 5   WHAT ARE YOUR WORK HABITS?

Whatever your hand finds to do, do it with all your might, for in the grave, where you are going, there is neither working nor planning nor knowledge nor wisdom.
                                    (Ecclesiastes 9:10 NIV)

A survey conducted by the Herman Group found that about a quarter of workers in white-collar jobs admit to playing computer games during work.* Not a gamer? Maybe you spend time surfing the Web for personal reasons, or you simply find excuses to visit with coworkers. Few of us can truly claim we work all day long.

Our time wasters are a symptom of larger problems. First, we easily lose sight of our spiritual call to serve others in all we do. Time wasters such as eBay, Facebook, and solitaire are generally self-centered activities. It is dishonest to spend our time on things that are solely for personal gain when we should be working for others.

Second, we may not be clear about how our job is a way of utilizing the gifts we have been given by God. When we have a sense of passion for our work, knowing we are following God's call in our own life, we are far more likely to be focused.

Today, consider whether your time and your sense of God's call are in sync.

My time is a gift from you, God. Help me use it wisely and honestly. Amen.

* Herman Trend Alert, Dec. 5, 2007, "Computer Gaming Costs Employees," www.hermangroup.com/archive.html

APRIL 6   I AM NOT MY SPAM

For the grace of God has appeared, bringing salvation to all, training us to renounce impiety and worldly passions, and in the present age to live lives that are self-controlled, upright, and godly.   *(Titus 2:11-12)*

It wouldn't surprise me if you have stopped using an e-mail account because of the amount of spam you were getting. I checked one of my old accounts before writing these words and discovered my last fifty messages were for various cheap pharmaceuticals, penis enhancement products, adult Web sites, knockoff "bling," and assorted worthless stock offerings.

Spam experts tell us the only way to end the madness is for *everyone* to delete these messages unopened. Yet a tiny percentage of people do open them, convinced that the promises are real and a better life just might be possible. So, the spammers keep on making money and sending more spam. It's a vicious, offensive, and depressing reality.

I'm not buying in to their hype. I am more than my hormones, my wealth, my apparel, or my anxieties. I'm a child of God, and I'm actually crazy enough to believe that with my whole heart.

Pure and holy God, when I'm confronted by so much that tells me I'm not good enough, enable me to see the shallowness of those worldly messages. Amen.

APRIL 7   WHERE'S YOUR IDENTITY ROOTED?

What marvelous love the Father has extended to us! Just look at it—we're called children of God! That's who we really are.
                              (1 John 3:1a **The Message)**

We live in a time of amazing technological advances, yet they frequently happen faster than we can deal with the ethical, social, moral, and environmental challenges associated with them. What does it mean, for example, when a Google-funded company, 23andMe, is providing genetic profiles for approximately $1,000? Reflecting on this particular development, one trend watcher said, "Up to now we have not been able to segment the population by the genetic factors. In the future, we will be able to do just that."*

As Christians, when our technological advances affect our sense of identity, statements like this should give us pause. Our gadgets, genetic profiles, or surgically enhanced bodies should not blind us to this truth: we are, first and foremost, children of God. Our value and sense of worth should be rooted in God's grace and love, not in our technology.

I am your beloved, creator God. Remind me of that when I think I'm somehow less than others. Amen.

* Herman Trend Alert, Nov. 27, 2007, "Genetic Testing Now Within Reach," www.hermangroup.com/archive.html

APRIL 8   TIME FOR A DIET?

"We are the clay, and you are our potter; we are all the work of your hand."   *(Isaiah 64:8b)*

A lot of the men I know need to go on a diet. Some need to lose a few pounds, or more than a few. Others need to de-clutter their homes, dumping all that paper they're "saving to read someday" in the recycle bin. A few would benefit greatly from spending less time on their collection of (name an item found on eBay) and more time with their family.

Still other men need to let go of emotional or spiritual baggage they've been carrying around with them for decades—ideas about themselves or God or the church that are just plain useless.

We often find it hard to succeed with these "diets" because we try to do them alone, attempting to mold ourselves into something new. Yet scripture reminds us that God is the potter, shaping and reshaping us when we allow ourselves to be changed.

Have thine own way, Lord, have thine own way. You are the potter; I am your clay. Amen.

APRIL 9   THE UNCERTAINTY PRINCIPLE

By faith Abraham obeyed when he was called to set out for a place that he was to receive as an inheritance; and he set out, not knowing where he was going.   *(Hebrews 11:8)*

Life is full of uncertainties, and questions about these uncertainties fill our minds. Will I get the raise? What will the test results mean for my child? Should I get pasta or steak? Does God really hear my prayers?

Whatever the uncertainty we face, men typically desire control, conviction, and competence. We want things to turn out our way, we want our decisions to be right, and we want to avoid looking stupid. In times of uncertainty, we may fear that we'll lose something we value greatly, or we may forget that we are not all-powerful.

Anyone who has read the slightest bit of quantum physics is familiar with the concept of Heisenberg's Uncertainty Principle: you cannot simultaneously know both a molecule's exact position and its exact velocity. In layman's terms, uncertainty is pretty much built into the fabric of the cosmos, into our DNA.

Since uncertainty is a given, let God be in control. Trust God's wisdom rather than relying on your own convictions, and remember that you are the person God created most qualified to be uniquely you.

My mind is often filled with doubts, questions, and a lack of trust in you. Grant me the certainty that you do indeed hold the world in your hands, Lord. Amen.

APRIL 10   BEAUTY IN THE DESERT

The grass withers, the flower fades; but the word of our God will stand forever.   *(Isaiah 40:8)*

The youth group and I gazed out from the top of an Arizona mountain, awestruck. I reflected on the timelessness of the rocks and the unchanging vistas. Of course, they weren't actually unchanging, a fact that dawned on me as I shielded my eyes from the swirling sands. The rock was some sort of sandstone, a towering pillar of compressed yet slowly eroding minerals. Every day it was a different rock.

My eyes welled with tears as I thought about those seemingly permanent things in my own life that were in reality constantly changing—relationships, jobs, health, spiritual life. I yearned for a few things that could simply remain the same.

Then I realized that although these rocks were changing, their beauty and ability to communicate the love of God was not. The view next year would be just as indescribable as the one I was privileged to be enjoying now. Likewise, there was great beauty and grace waiting for me to behold in my present situation, if only I was willing to stop, see, and acknowledge it.

O God, my Rock, with change comes great beauty, if we allow ourselves to see it. Help me remember your promises are timeless and unchanging. Amen.

APRIL 11   FOLLOW THE LEAD OF PAUL POTTS

He said to me, "My grace is sufficient for you, for power is made perfect in weakness."   *(2 Corinthians 12:9)*

When an ordinary-looking man with a chip in his front tooth stood on the stage of "Britain's Got Talent," the "American Idol" clone, and said he was going to sing opera, the judges could barely hide their smirks. Yet Paul's dream was to be a singer, and his voice was resonant and powerful. The audience jumped to their feet, moved by his performance, and ultimately Paul went on to win the entire contest. His humility, story, and voice all contributed to his victory.

Long ago, another Paul—of Tarsus—had a profound impact on the early church. He too apparently was a pretty ordinary man with some "thorn . . . in the flesh" (2 Corinthians 12:7) that could have easily stopped him from sharing his good news, but instead he boasted of his weaknesses.

What weakness of yours keeps you from stepping out boldly in faith? What thorn makes you feel ordinary and useless for God? If you're willing to be used by God, God's promise is that your weaknesses are God's strength!

Surprising God, I offer all of myself to you—even my weaknesses—that you might use me for the sake of Christ. Amen.

APRIL 12   BREATHE IN, BREATHE OUT

Then the LORD God formed man from the dust of the ground, and breathed into his nostrils the breath of life; and the man became a living being.   (Genesis 2:7)

In Hebrew, the word for spirit, breath, and wind is the same: *ruach*. Thus, for example, when in Genesis God breathes life into Adam, God's breath/spirit brings Adam to life.

Physicists have somehow determined that with each breath we breathe, we take in or breathe out a quadrillion atoms, a number my brain can't even fathom. But here's the really spooky part: those same atoms have been breathed by hundreds, probably thousands, of people and other living things before us. When we breathe, we literally take into ourselves our neighbors, our enemies, and persons we'll never meet—even people of the Bible.

This thought gives me a whole new way to contemplate what it is to be a spiritual person. My spirit, my very breath, connects me to God, to others, and to creation. Perhaps that's why my favorite kind of prayer is the "breath prayer," a way of praying in which you repetitively say to yourself part of a prayer while inhaling and part of it while exhaling. Try it with the phrase below.

[Inhale] God, live in me. [Exhale] God, love through me. [Repeat slowly several times.]

APRIL 13   NOT SOJOURNERS, BUT CO-JOURNERS

Two of them were going to a village called Emmaus, . . . talking with each other about all these things that had happened. While they were talking . . . , Jesus himself came near and went with them.   (Luke 24:14-15)

As a Christian educator, I'm convinced it's time for congregations and individuals to move to a pilgrimage model of Christian formation. In a pilgrimage ministry, the emphasis is upon relationships—friendships—between two pilgrims on a journey of faith. You are not just "raw material" for a teacher to dump his or her knowledge into, nor are you a "seed" that needs nurturing by the gardener/teacher. Instead, people of faith are pilgrims. We grow and learn from one another as we share our life of faith together.

Christian education, then, is about critical reflection in community on our experience of participating in and practicing a way of life. Like the Pilgrims of old, we travel together to places unknown and strange, but we do so together.

I hope you'll give some thought this week to some ways you could intentionally enter into a pilgrimage relationship with others in your congregation. What persons have invited you into a deeper relationship with God alongside them? Who might you invite to "co-journ" with you?

Connecting God, I'm grateful for [name three people who have been instrumental in your faith formation], who have walked with me on my faith journey. Amen.

APRIL 14   THE WOMB-LIKE LIFE

"Be as compassionate as your Father is."
                                    (Luke 6:36 **Scholar's Version***)*

Many translations of the verse above instruct, "Be perfect as your Father is perfect." Um, what? Is that even remotely possible? How can I possibly be perfect when I can't even remember to change the oil in my car regularly?

Perplexed by this verse, I started digging. Scholars have noted the verse has various translations and versions, but the word "compassion" is probably closest to Jesus' intent, as compassion is completely central to his teachings. In Hebrew and Aramaic (Jesus' languages), compassion is closely related to the word for womb. Because God is womb-like, be womb-like. In English, compassion literally means "with passion."

So what does that mean? We are to be life-giving, nourishing, and tender toward others, yet having the passion and intensity of a mother who guards her children. It means having a heart for those the Bible continually calls us to remember and protect—those who are most vulnerable in society. In essence, it means we are to live with a passion for justice, the social form of compassion. Tough? Yes. Possible? Definitely.

Compassionate God, fill me with your love, and show me how I may serve the neighbors you have placed in my life. Amen.

APRIL 15   THE NEVER-STAGNANT LIFE

But let justice roll down like waters, and righteousness like an ever-flowing stream.   *(Amos 5:24)*

Amos, a sheepherder, lived in a part of Israel that was very dry, with lots of closely spaced, rocky hills. There were few rivers or streams nearby. During the rainy season, the rains fell hard, forming wadis—stagnant pools of water—in the ravines. The water would dry up quickly and was available only part of the year.

Imagine, then, what it would have been like for Amos to live near an everflowing stream! This is the image Amos wanted to communicate. Justice and righteousness were synonyms for a world as God intends it, a way of living in which the poor would not experience economic exploitation.

Our call is to work for that kind of world today too. Our spending habits, the ways we vote, the work we do, the investments we make—all should help ensure that oppression and injustice cease for people everywhere on earth. That's not at all an easy task, and it definitely requires a radically different way of living, a way that brings wholeness to all of creation.

Living God, you desire shalom, wholeness, for your creation. Let me be used today for all that is good and just in the world. Amen.

APRIL 16   A COMMANDMENT FOR ADULTS

Honor your father and your mother, so that your days may be long in the land that the LORD your God is giving you.
                                                    (Exodus 20:12)

Parents like to think this scripture is directed to children, a pleasing verse that is helpful for controlling unruly kids. But in reality, it was directed equally (or even more so) to adults, who were reminded to honor their adult parents (living or not).

The Hebrews remembered or knew the story of their slavery in Egypt, and this story became their central metaphor. Their instructions often began, "Remember that once you were slaves in Egypt. . . ." They were to remember the stories of God's faithfulness and pass them on to their children, who would, in turn, remember and tell the stories to others. (The Exodus couldn't be repeated in each generation, after all.) To do so was to honor your parents.

Honor can also mean "give weight to" something or someone; that is, the verse isn't about obedience but about living your life in a way that shows you treat your parents with an appropriate seriousness.

How does your life honor your parents? If you have children, how are you sharing your stories of faith?

Loving Parent of us all, may my day—my life—honor you for all you have done for me. Amen.

APRIL 17   THE OTHER FIRST COMMANDMENT

The LORD God took the man and put him in the garden of Eden to till it and keep it.   *(Genesis 2:15)*

Husband. Captain. Boss. Friend. Brother. Fixer-of-broken-things. Men in today's world hold many roles, and all of these are important. Yet among the most basic roles we all share is one that might surprise you: gardener!

The first commandment of scripture is the one God gave to Adam—which literally means "earth man"—the literary representative for half of humanity. Eden, God's perfect creation, was to be kept by Adam. Biblically, it's really not a stretch to say that our most basic role is to be earth-keepers.

Now, I could kill a plastic plant! And if I did plant a garden, my dogs would no doubt destroy it. But that's OK, because being God's gardener has to do with every act we do. We are to tend to the amount of natural resources we use, to keep in check our impact on the environment, to "till" our lives through simplicity and frugality. In this time when global warming threatens our habitat—God's creation—the world needs men to proudly claim their commission to be gardeners.

Creator God, I am awed by the responsibility you have entrusted to humanity. Inspire me with a passion for your creation at all times. Amen.

APRIL 18   CONNECTED

God said, "See, I have given you every plant yielding seed that is upon the face of all the earth, and every tree with seed in its fruit; you shall have them for food." **(Genesis 1:29)**

In recent years, one of the major food trends has been the growth of the "locavore" movement. A locavore tries to eat, as much as possible, food that was grown close to home—say, within 100 miles. The environmental and health benefits of such a diet are tremendous, but equally important is the fact that this habit connects you to the land, to the farmer, and to the food that grows best where you are.

Our food habits say a lot about who we are and what we do or do not value. Too many of us have become completely disconnected from the food we (and others) eat. In the sacraments of baptism and communion, ordinary, simple elements become a means of grace for us. Likewise, each forkful of our favorite dish connects us to literally hundreds of people and places—a tiny opportunity for thankfulness, for remembering that God has created us to be dependent on one another.

Creator, when I overeat, eat without thinking, waste food, or fill my body with junk, remind me to be a wise user of your abundant creation. Amen.

APRIL 19   LOST?

By the rivers of Babylon—
  there we sat down and there we wept
  when we remembered Zion.   *(Psalm 137:1)*

One of my favorite TV shows is *Lost,* a drama about a group of plane crash survivors who end up on a very strange island. I think one of the reasons *Lost* speaks to many people is that its themes of being rootless, wrestling with one's past, and struggling to form community are common experiences of many people today.

One primary "meta-theme" of scripture is that of Exile, referring to the time when the people of Israel were carted off to Assyria and Babylon. Away from their land and from the temple, they couldn't imagine how they could go on or how they could worship. Yet, in time, their theology changed: they came to realize that God was present while they were "lost," and they developed whole new communities and ways of learning scripture because they were away from the temple.

You may experience exile in times of change and life transitions, or when you feel alienated, doubtful, and alone. These times are ripe with possibility and opportunities for great learning—if you're patient, hopeful, and trusting.

God, in times of deepest doubt and despair, when I yearn for what I've lost, guide me to a new understanding of your presence. Amen.

APRIL 20   GOOD > EVIL

Surely goodness and mercy shall follow me / all the days of my life, / and I shall dwell in the house of the Lord / my whole life long.   *(Psalm 23:6)*

Newscasts lead with stories of violence because the producers know that unthinkable acts draw in "eyeballs" and hook the viewer. Newspaper headlines frequently offer plenty of bad news about the economy, disasters, scandal, and global crises.

Advertisers know their products sell better when they offer them as a solution to some personal fear we hold. It surely can seem that goodness and mercy are in short supply.

Each line of the well-known Twenty-third Psalm describes the goodness a "sheep" experiences from the shepherd. The psalmist acknowledges plenty of danger and evil in the world—darkest valleys, enemies, injury requiring an application of oil—but declares that the Shepherd who leads the sheep is good, merciful, compassionate, and trustworthy.

Truth be told, there really is—on balance—more goodness in the world than evil. Every day, the people present in our lives offer us small acts of kindness, words that heal, guidance and instruction, restoration of our souls. In these small and big ways, God's goodness and mercy both lead us and follow us.

Shepherding God, lead me today in paths of righteousness, and help me see the good I can do with my words and actions. Amen.

APRIL 21   ECONOMICS 102: SIMPLICITY AND FRUGALITY

Better is a little with the fear of the LORD / than great treasure and trouble with it.   **(Proverbs 15:16)**

Almost no topic in the Bible is more common than money. Though "prosperity gospel" preachers have attempted to convince the public that the Bible wants us to be wealthy, the truth of the matter is that scripture constantly admonishes us to share our wealth with the poor, to be wise stewards of our resources, and to be mindful that our riches can harm our relationships with God and neighbor.

Many, perhaps most, Christians in developed countries need

to learn the value of simplicity and frugality. A simple lifestyle draws us close to the poor, those for whom God has a special heart. Having less "stuff" means we have more time and space for relationships and more money to share with others. It also is a way of reducing our "carbon footprint," our impact on the environment. We need to learn a new *oikonomos*—a way of thinking about economics that always takes into account the well-being of all. If you truly wish to be loving and compassionate toward all, tend to your household economics.

God of all earth's people—rich and poor, citizen and immigrant, elderly and newborn—help me show care and compassion through my spending. Amen.

APRIL 22   WHEN *YOU* REALLY MEANS *Y'ALL*

"You are the salt of the earth; but if salt has lost its taste, how can its saltiness be restored? It is no longer good for anything, but is thrown out and trampled under foot."
(Matthew 5:13)

Contemporary Christians tend to personalize the messages of scripture: what does this mean for me, personally? Much less thought is given to the way a particular text might apply to a whole community of believers.

In part, this is a logical consequence of the hyper-emphasis upon the individual that is so prevalent today. A second reason has to do with language. English doesn't truly have a plural "you." There's "you all" and it's shorter cousin "y'all," but if we hear the word "you" as the scripture is read from the pulpit, it's hard to know if the author meant "hey, you, sir" or "hey, everyone." Other languages, biblical Greek and Hebrew, do have separate words for the singular and plural form of the word.

Oftentimes "you" in scripture is indeed plural, like the "you" in today's passage. Ask yourself when you come across "you" in scripture, *How will I understand this differently if I hear it as a message to the whole community of believers, rather than just to me?*

God, your word speaks both to individuals and to communities. Help me hear the ways my faith community is to live and act in the world. Amen.

APRIL 23   ARE YOU LIVING YOUR DREAMS?

Pure and lasting religion in the sight of God...means that we must care for orphans and widows in their troubles, and refuse to let the world corrupt us.   *(James 1:27 NLT)*

In biblical times, orphans and widows were among Judea's most vulnerable people because they had no land or power. Today, James might instead mention the uninsured, the homeless, and the two billion people who live on $2 a day or less.

A close friend of mine makes it his life's mission to do everything in his power to end world hunger by 2015. He truly believes that's his purpose, and he lives like it too. Ask him how he's doing, and he'll always say, "I'm living my dreams!"

When we have lunch together, we dream about and work on ways we're going to make that vision a reality. More important, we're reminded that we need each other, that it takes community to tackle really large problems like world hunger. Imagine what could happen if every reader of this devotion committed himself to this vision!

James reminds us, though, that the world can easily corrupt our vision, our "pure and lasting religion" marked by acts of service. In my experience, community is the cure for corrupted vision.

Gathering God, give me your heart for the poor and oppressed. Guide me to a community of friends who are committed to serving others. Amen.

APRIL 24   ARE YOU A FOLLOWER?

Then he said to them all, "If any want to become my followers, let them deny themselves and take up their cross daily and follow me."   *(Luke 9:23)*

One of the strangest experiences of my life happened at a rest stop between Cincinnati and Chicago. Two things dominated the scene: red and rainbows. The red was worn by the "Red Heads," two or three buses worth of fans of the Cincinnati Reds baseball team. These older adults had stopped there to have lunch. The rainbows were everywhere else, worn by "Dead Heads," fans of the rock band the Grateful Dead. These young people were on their way to a Chicago concert, and they were using this rest stop as, well, a place to wash, cook, party, and relax.

I smiled and laughed as I watched them interact, and as I drove away I thought about whom I was following—or said I was. Would I be willing to drive all over the country to follow Jesus? Was my faith as rabidly passionate as that of these devotees of a sports team and a musical group? What about me would say to the world that I claim the name Christian? How would you answer these questions?

With each step of my life, Jesus, I want to follow you. So with each step of my day, Jesus, I'll try to follow you. Amen.

APRIL 25   NON-SECRET AGENTS

And whatever you do, in word or deed, do everything in the name of the Lord Jesus, giving thanks to God the Father through him.   *(Colossians 3:17)*

A church exists for mission and ministry in the world, not just within its walls. The "worship service" is a not an hour in our week but a helpful way for us to think about our lives. We gather weekly for worship, for a communal recognition of our need for God and one another—a common time to re-experience the body of Christ in its fullness. We leave for service in the world, a forgiven and reconciled people to offer forgiveness and reconciliation to everyone we meet. In short, we leave to engage in ministry and mission.

Like Zacchaeus, we find ourselves—sometimes unexpectedly—to be God's change agents in the world. We no longer need to sit in a tree, waiting for a glimpse of Jesus. If we want to see Jesus, he's right there waiting for us in the homeless shelter, the restaurant around the corner, the battered women's shelter, the mission field we had never heard of before, and the person sitting next to us in the worship service.

May "worship-service" be the pattern that guides my days, and may I remember your command to share your love with others. Amen.

APRIL 26   SHOCK AND AWE

So they went out and fled from the tomb, for terror and amazement had seized them; and they said nothing to anyone, for they were afraid.   *(Mark 16:8)*

The earliest manuscripts of the earliest Gospel—Mark—have a shocking ending: they include no resurrection appearance. Instead, they conclude with three women finding the stone rolled away, and a man in white telling them that Jesus has been raised—end of story. Most biblical scholars believe that the later verses of Mark 16, starting at verse 9, were added by later scribes, probably because this abrupt ending was simply unacceptable.

What are we to make of this strange ending? Scholars have offered many suggestions, enough to literally fill a book. Whatever the reason, we're left with questions, and perhaps that's the point. What would we believe if this were the only account we had? What would we do if our faith were so tested? Why do we still look for Jesus in the land of the dead? What will we do now with the news that God has vindicated Jesus?

Awesome God, there are many times I can't comprehend your word and your grace. Fill me with the confidence to proclaim my Easter faith boldly! Amen.

APRIL 27   LIVING BY STORY

The unfoldling of our words gives light;
    it imparts understanding to the simple.

                               (Psalm 119:130)

Until I was eighteen, as near as I can recall, I was a biblical literalist. It hadn't occurred to me to read the stories of scripture in any way other than as historical truth. Although there was a developmental aspect to my literalism, more important was the fact that no one had ever taught me how to "live by story." I had never really grasped that "their" story (the people of scripture) was my story too.

Eventually, I discovered I was invited to claim and be claimed by this book, to see my story both in the text and as a continuation of the text. I now see myself as connected to a Greater Story, to a people who span many generations, and to the God who was their God too. Living by Story is quite different than Living by Fact, Living by Fear, or even Living by Faith, all of which can become "closed" ways of living—closed to mystery, hope, and the power of metaphor.

In this Easter season, hear this word of wisdom: Look for more—more depth, more interpretations, more life, more hope, more possibilities.

You are so much more than I know, God. Fill me with greater insight for you and your Story. Amen.

APRIL 28   THE CHURCH IS LIKE A HOME

Happy are those who live in your house, ever singing your praise. *(Psalm 84:4)*

One of my favorite hymns is a little-known song by John Thornburg called "The Church Is Like a Home." The first verse talks about how the family's book is the Bible, and the family's table welcomes anyone who might come to eat. We are told that the doors of the home are always open. The last two lines of this verse read:

and Christ, the host, invites us in.
The church is like a home.*

In my own denomination, everyone is welcome at the communion table. It's a meaningful experience when I serve communion, placing the piece of pita bread in open hands and saying, "Bread for the journey." Everyone comes forward—young and old, persons with mental and physical disabilities, those with more doubts than beliefs, friends and guests, even persons with gluten allergies (we also have rice cakes). Christ's table is the place where we rediscover what it is to be unconditionally welcomed and where hospitality is offered to all.

For me, the church is like a home. If it is for you too, I hope you're doing your part to welcome all to dine.

Welcoming God, fill my heart with unconditional regard for others so that they would feel welcome in my church home. Amen.

* "The Church Is Like a Home," John Thornburg, © 2003 by Wayne Leupold Editions, Inc.

APRIL 29   THE CHURCH IS SHARING LIFE

For where two or three are gathered in my name, I am there among them.   ***(Matthew 18:20)***

Yesterday I wrote about one of my favorite hymns, "The Church Is Like a Home." The second verse of the hymn talks about how we share life together as the church—births, deaths, dreams and milestones, and even disagreements. And the songwriter affirms that through it all, God draws us close.

My favorite moments of each week are usually the times when the participants in whatever group I'm with simply spend a little time sharing what's happening in our lives—the first ten minutes of the Connections (young adult) Sunday school class, teatime on Wednesdays with the volunteers in the Media Resource Center, the moments before bell choir rehearsal begins when I can chat with the people next to me, and joys and concerns time at the close of youth group.

These are not insignificant times at all—they are in fact holy moments, times when we allow one another to catch a glimpse of our "real" selves. The sharing of our lives is the glue that holds a congregation together, I think, and in those moments Christ is present among us.

Help me trust your promise, Christ, that you are present whenever two or more of your church are gathered together. Amen.

APRIL 30   AND NOW WE LOOK AHEAD

Teach them to your children, talking about them when you are at home and when you are away, when you lie down and when you rise.   *(Deuteronomy 11:19)*

The last verse of "The Church Is Like a Home" declares that the church must now look ahead so that children will be cared for, youth can grow, and we can reach beyond ourselves in service, viewing the world as holy ground.

In ancient days, passing on the stories and practices of faith was done in many ways, most frequently within families. Memory aids such as the *mezzuzah* and *tefillin* brought scripture to mind frequently. A pile of rocks, created at a place of significance, ensured it would be remembered as holy ground. It was an oral culture, so storytelling, not writing, was the primary way of sharing faith.

Today, too many families lack the knowledge of the Bible to pass on its stories, relegating this task to the church. But as the saying goes, faith is caught more than taught. An hour a week of Sunday school isn't enough. What are you doing to tell your faith stories to your children, grandchildren, or youth at your church?

I have heard your call to teach your children, Lord. Help me as I live and share your word with others. Amen.

MAY

Lessons from Surprising People

RUSSELL T. MONTFORT

MAY 1   ABRAHAM

Now the LORD said to Abram, "Go from your country and your kindred and your father's house to the land that I will show you."   *(Genesis 12:1)*

In the Bible, God chose to help some surprising people—people like you and me. Some of these people responded positively to God, while others turned and walked away. Some simply didn't get it. This month we will take a look at some of these "surprising people" and consider what we can learn from them.

Let's begin with Abraham. He was seventy-five years old when God told him to go to a new place and begin a new nation—the Hebrews. It is difficult to begin a new life in a new place doing a new thing under the best of circumstances. Being seventy-five years old compounds the degree of difficulty—not to mention the fact that Abraham didn't even know where he was going. Abraham, however, said yes.

Why Abraham? Why not someone with a quicker step and a stronger back? Because God was going into business with a nation of people yet to be, and God was looking for a co-creator of this nation—someone willing to step out in faith and take risks. I believe Abraham would have agreed with this statement: It is better to do something doubtful or overbold—and therefore in need of forgiveness—than to do nothing at all.

God, it's better to try something really big for you than to try nothing at all for you. Help me act boldly in faith. Amen.

MAY 2   RICH MAN, POOR MAN

"There was a rich man who was dressed in purple and fine linen and who feasted sumptuously every day. And at his gate lay a poor man named Lazarus, covered with sores, who longed to satisfy his hunger with what fell from the rich man's table."
(Luke 16:19-21)

Upon reading these verses, we visualize a man whose self-indulgence knew no bounds. Whatever he wanted, he requested it and received it. In his closet were more garments than he could wear in a lifetime. The waste from his table would have been a feast in a normal household. However, his self-indulgence was just a symptom of deeper problems. He passionately loved the only thing that could not love him back. He loved himself.

As we learn later in the story, the poor man went to heaven and the rich man went to Hades. The rich man was forever separated from God not because of cashmere sweaters, a luxury car, or filet mignon—or even because of beluga caviar. The rich man went to Hades because he didn't even know Lazarus was out there. He had no idea that someone needed him; that someone was dying of starvation at his own door. All he cared about was himself.

God, help me look beyond my own needs and wants to see the needs of others and respond in love. Amen.

MAY 3   DIETRICH BONHOEFFER

To all who received him ... he gave power to become children of God, who were born, not of blood or of the will of the flesh or of the will of man, but of God.   *(John 1:12-13)*

Dietrich Bonhoeffer said that "to be a Christian does not mean to be religious in a particular way ... but to be a man—not a type of man, but the man that Christ creates in us."*

That last phrase is crucial: "the man that Christ creates in us." Having chosen Christ as the center of all that is important to me, not only do I act; he acts upon me. This living Christ is not passive. He goads me to do my best; he haunts me at my worst; he summons me to be what I could be; he forgives me what I am. He calls me into the lives of the unlovable; he enables me to get along without their love. He is at the center of all I do, and I am grateful for his presence.

I will never fulfill the burden of becoming all that God means for me to be; but because of Jesus, I know what it would be like to be truly and fully alive. And I want that.

God, I want to be your son—truly and fully alive. Amen.

* www.christianitytoday.com/history/special/131christians/bonhoeffer.html

MAY 4   THE PRODIGAL SON

"Father, I have sinned. . . . I am no longer worthy to be called your son."   *(Luke 15:21)*

When the man whom we have learned to call "the prodigal son" said these words to his father, he wasn't referring to the wild parties he went to or the way he had wasted his money. His sin was that he never wrote a letter home; that he broke all of his ties with the past; that he disavowed his previous commitments. It was a deliberate attempt to separate himself from those who had given him his life.

Sin is not climbing on a chair to steal a cookie, nor is it breaking and entering. Sin is not gambling or drinking or lying, nor does it have sexual implications. Those are all symptoms of sin, just as a boil is symptomatic of diseased blood.

Sin is leaving home without caring, cutting yourself off from the cradle of your existence. Sin manifests itself in different ways: sometimes in pride; sometimes in lust; sometimes in indifference. Sin is when you try to live as though you have nobody but yourself to be responsible to or for.

God, whose name is Love, I have lived irresponsibly, because I have lived a self-absorbed life. Amen.

MAY 5   BISHOP HANS LILJE

How long, O LORD? Will you forget me forever? How long will you hide your face from me?   *(Psalm 13:1)*

There are times when everything goes well, and there are times when nothing seems to go well. There is sunshine and rain; there is joy and sorrow. Even Jesus felt abandoned by God when he cried out that Friday on the cross, "My God, my God, why have you forsaken me?" (Matthew 27:46).

This is not an uncommon experience at all, even for the most deeply religious people. Ups and downs in life are to be expected as a normal part of our sense of awareness of the presence and power and love of God.

Bishop Hans Lilje of Germany told of the dark days when the Nazis had thrown him into prison, stripping him of all his possessions, including his Bible. All he had to encourage and comfort him were the things he remembered in Scripture and prayers.

The same thing in less dramatic form is also true of us when we repeat the Twenty-third Psalm in days of depression and loneliness and grief: "The LORD is my shepherd." "The LORD is my shepherd."

Memory. Memory helps us see our present situation in perspective.

God, I know that remembering, I shall again praise you! Amen.

MAY 6   TWO MOTHERS AND TWO FATHERS

We must always give thanks to God for you,...because God chose you.   *(2 Thessalonians 2:13)*

It is obvious that we can't choose many of the circumstances of our lives. Someone we love no longer loves us, and there is nothing we can do about it. Death comes into the circle of our love; calamity and tragedy immobilize us. It is easy to feel desolate. But there is another response, and it is the recognition that in every set of circumstances, we can choose our attitudes and our responses.

In a community where once I lived, there were two sets of parents—two mothers and two fathers—who had children with developmental disabilities. They refused to give in to the awful circumstances of their lives. They became instrumental in organizing a school in the community for other developmentally challenged children so that all the children would have the best opportunities for life that were possible.

They chose their own way; I thank God for them and for you.

God, you have honored us by refusing to conduct the affairs of our lives. We cherish the thought that our decisions, moment by moment, determine whether or not you are glorified in our lives. Amen.

MAY 7   ZEBEDEE

[Jesus] saw two other brothers, James son of Zebedee and his brother John, in the boat with their father Zebedee, mending their nets, and he called them. Immediately they left the boat and their father, and followed him.   (Matthew 4:21-22)

I have wondered how Zebedee, a fisherman, felt about his sons James and John taking off after an itinerant preacher. It is probable that Jesus broke the hearts of many families in his part of the world. In Roman society, family was among the most cherished community values. As a matter of fact, one of the chief Roman criticisms of Christianity was that it destroyed families.

In our day, churches advertise that they are family churches. They organize family nights and family camps and build family life centers. But nuclear families also can do a lot of damage to their individual members by demanding so much from them that they crack under the strain.

One of the greatest gifts a parent can give a child is the reassurance that not all of the parent's hopes and dreams and aspirations are resting on that child. When a parent complains to the child that "I gave you" or "you owe me," then that family has failed.

God, we pray for every family, that they may be circles of love and affirmation. Amen.

MAY 8   THE APOSTLE PAUL: IMITATE ME

Brothers and sisters, join in imitating me.   (Philippians 3:17)

One can't really imitate someone else; be someone else. But there is today's peculiar text. "Be imitators of me," says Paul. In other words, "You have an example in us." He said it often: "Become as I am."

He goes on to talk about the enemies of Christ, worldly people who he identifies by saying, "Their god is the belly" (Philippians 3:19). It's not clear what he means; it sounds as though he is speaking to people whose tables are extravagantly laden with exotic food and drink, or people who are ruled by their libido or other basic urges. Too much, too costly, too selfish!

People who ask us to be as they are turn us off. We wouldn't want them to think that we are boasting. But Paul wasn't calling us to engage in this or that behavior of his; he was talking about an entire life commitment.

When Jesus told us to be kind and do good works, there was no body of ethical teaching to be appropriated. He called us to discipleship. He wanted followers, not admirers. He said, "Follow me!" Paul took him seriously and asked the Philippians to fall in behind him.

God, may I be an imitator of Paul, who was a follower of our Lord, our Savior, Jesus. Amen.

MAY 9   THE APOSTLE PAUL: GRACE

Where sin increased, grace abounded all the more.
(Romans 5:20)

There is something healing about every new morning. But for some of us, there is also something depressing in every new day. If things in your life are pretty much running on their own steam in a kind of downward spiral, then morning will probably not be inspiring to you. Just a few years ago, there was a popular bumper sticker that declared "S _ _ t Happens!" meaning that bad stuff just happens in life. It said in effect that we not only cannot avoid it, we might as well expect it. And that's true, but that is only half the story, because grace happens too. Grace happens all the time. You didn't do anything to bring it about. You don't deserve it. It's the way life is.

Choose to focus on the grace rather than on the tough stuff that happens. It will not only comfort you through hard times; it will instruct you and sensitize you to the renewing possibilities of each new day. It makes the morning a positive time to anticipate—wondering just where grace will break through.

God of grace, accompany me throughout this day and help me identify that grace that is greater than all my sin. Amen.

MAY 10   THE APOSTLE PAUL: CHOOSE TO REJOICE

Rejoice in the Lord always.... The Lord is near. Do not worry about anything.... And the peace of God... will guard your hearts and your minds in Christ Jesus.   (Philippians 4:4-7)

"All life is suffering" says the first and truest of the Buddha's four noble truths, by which he means that sorrow, loss, and death await us and everybody we love. Yet Paul says, "The Lord is near. Do not worry about anything." He was probably in prison at the time. He had every good reason to be worried.

He doesn't deny that the worst things will happen to all of us, as no doubt he suspected they were soon to happen to him. He doesn't try to minimize them. He doesn't promise the Philippians that as a result they will be delivered from the worst things any more than Jesus was delivered. The worst things will happen, no matter what; but beyond our power to understand, we will have peace both in heart and mind.

It is no joke when he says, "Do not worry about anything," or as he puts it a few lines earlier, "Rejoice in the Lord always; again I will say, Rejoice."

Father God, in the darkness of my own worrying, I say, "I will rejoice. I know I will!" Amen.

MAY 11   A MAN AND HIS BARNS

"The land of a rich man produced abundantly.... [And the man said to himself], 'Soul, you have ample goods laid up for many years; relax, eat, drink, be merry.'"   *(Luke 12:16, 19)*

Jesus told this story. The point of the story is not that there is something wrong with amassing wealth, but that the man was intending to store it all by building bigger barns, and that by storing it, it would be lost. He was called foolish because he didn't recognize that his wealth had brought him happiness and that it could do the same for others, but only if it were not locked up. His sin was not that he had become wealthy but that he wanted to keep it all.

The Bible puts before us a radical concept of stewardship because it claims that any hungry person has as much right to the food in my pantry as I do. Perhaps any shirt hanging in my closet unworn belongs to the man who needs it.

God, I pray for the whole world—the created world, from which we take our livelihood—and I thank you for the family of humanity that populates it. We are brothers and sisters. Keep me mindful that I must share the good things of my life. Amen.

MAY 12   THE APOSTLE PAUL: THIS PRESENT
                                                        DARKNESS

Our struggle is not against enemies of blood and flesh, but against ... the cosmic powers of this present darkness.
                                                        (Ephesians 6:12)

Paul identifies this enemy as the devil. Many modern men may have trouble with that word—devil. Maybe Paul's word, darkness, will do. That's what we need to be set free from—the darkness in ourselves that we never fully see, never completely understand, and for which we never feel fully responsible.

Paul says it clearly: "I do not do the good I want, but the evil I do not want is what I do" (Romans 7:19). Nations of us do that too. It is also the evil in this world that the world does not want. We say that only someone who is insane wants war, but we have discovered that there are people who love war, who are drawn to it like a moth to a flame. So war goes on, and now we have instantaneous video coverage to show us the carnage of every day's battles.

Call it what you will—the evil in this world is greater than the evil we choose, and that is big enough by itself. This is the darkness from which we need to be liberated.

Holy God, we pray for nothing less than the salvation of this world. Amen.

MAY 13   THE APOSTLE PAUL: AN END TO
CHILDISH WAYS

When I was a child, . . . I reasoned like a child; when I became an adult, I put an end to childish ways.   ***(1 Corinthians 13:11)***

In this famous letter to the Corinthians, Paul is saying that to love as a Christian loves, you have to be grown up. Jesus once said, "Unless you change and become like children, you will never enter the kingdom of heaven" (Matthew 18:3). Whatever Jesus and Paul meant about becoming little children, they didn't mean that we are to become childish. Saying a man has a childlike faith is often a nice way of saying that the man is dangerously naive about life and has an inherent tendency not to think. Jesus gave us a strong and muscular example of a courageous life; there was nothing childish about it.

Paul is saying that faith has to do with independence. He is daring us to stand on our feet with boldness and to risk on behalf of others. Christian faith has a maturity; a balance; a responsible, reasonable, bold, unselfish quality to it.

Some Christians want to substitute rules for faith; like children, they have an excessive need to be right. Part of the pain of growing up is finding out that life and life's decisions are not easy.

God, it is childish of us to try to remove uncertainty and risk from our lives; true faith involves trust. Amen.

MAY 14   THE APOSTLE PAUL: PRAY WITHOUT CEASING

Always seek to do good to one another. . . . Rejoice always, pray without ceasing.   (1 Thessalonians 5:15-17)

To pray without ceasing is not to be forever on bended knee before some absentee God, but in every moment to know that God is met, praised, and served as we love one another and take care of one another. Prayer is not so much what we say to God but what we do on behalf of one another.

This means, then, that worship is more than what happens when hymns are sung, scriptures are read, and prayers are offered. It is not something you can "get over with" on a Sunday morning. Wherever you find yourself and another person is a temple. Christ is present as you really give your soul to that person—to enable him to stand, to hold him up, and to do whatever it is he needs to do. It is the only real holy ground you will ever know. Every such moment is one in which you may be engaged in the saving action that was going on in Christ.

There is worship—and your life is the liturgy, the most authentic liturgy ever offered to God.

God, if indeed my life is liturgy, I have much to be about today as my life intersects with others. Keep me alert to their needs. Amen.

MAY 15   A LITTLE GIRL

*The L*ORD *is our God, the L*ORD *alone. You shall love the L*ORD *your God with all your heart, and with all your soul, and with all your might.   (Deuteronomy 6:4-5)*

If we are to raise modern Christians, it might be important to talk as little as possible in "religious terms." A child's capacity for abstraction is not yet developed.

One night our daughter, then about four, was preparing for bed. She and her mother were talking about the presence of God—how God is always with us. Our daughter volunteered, "God was with us today when we went to the store." Her mother replied, "Yes."

"And God is with us right now, isn't he?" she asked. "Certainly," claimed her delighted mother. Having said that, the four-year-old leaned forward and said almost in a whisper, "I see him. He's standing in the corner. He has a bird in his hand."

It is beyond the conceptualization of a child to think of God as everywhere, but she could think of God being in Jesus. That is somewhere.

When teaching our children about God, it is crucial that we begin with life experiences, not creedal explanations of life.

God, imbue me with a life characterized by love, courage, good manners, loyalty, truth, and integrity, and in so doing lead little ones to you. Amen.

MAY 16   JESUS' DISCIPLES

Then Jesus summoned his twelve disciples.   *(Matthew 10:1)*

These disciples were the people who Matthew says started the church. We know little about them with the exception of Simon Peter and his brother Andrew, and perhaps John and Matthew, the keeper of their purse. And of course we know Judas Iscariot, who betrayed Jesus. And though they aren't mentioned here, we know that some of Jesus' closest associates were women—Mary Magdalene and Joanna, and the other Mary and her sister Martha, to cite just a few.

The disciples have had a sorry reputation over the centuries. They all ran away, except the women, when Jesus was arrested. The main reason for the disciples' bad reputation is that they never seemed to understand what Jesus was saying.

Jesus made his church out of human beings with more or less the same mixture of cowardice and guts as you would find in any church today. Just as he called those imperfect disciples and left them in the world as his body, so also we are called to love one another—the way Jesus says God loves us. We are called by the good God to be the hands and feet and heart of Christ to one another.

Empower us, God, to be the hands and feet and heart of Christ to one another. Amen.

MAY 17   ADAM AND EVE

Therefore a man leaves his father and his mother and clings to his wife, and they become one flesh.   *(Genesis 2:24)*

After the creation of heaven and earth, God created Adam. Then, declaring that Adam needed a helper, God started forming all the animals and birds. After Adam named them all, there was still no helper for him. So God created Eve, to which Adam responded, "Now, that's more like it!"

Here in poetic narrative is the premise that God has provided man and woman for each other. But to this premise, a man and woman are invited to bring a promise. Their relationship is not to be based just on feelings or affection—those wane from time to time. It is not to be based on mutual needs—those can lead to exploitation.

Love is not a feeling; it is an intention. A marriage centers on the promise of oneself to another self. Marriage is the place you go to be fully known, to give yourself away.

The love that is affirmed at a wedding is not just a condition of the heart but an act of the will, and the promise that love makes is to will the other's good even at the expense of our own good. And that is quite a promise.

Be present, God, with my beloved and me. Amen.

MAY 18   THE WOMAN WHO ANOINTED JESUS

The Word became flesh and lived among us, and we have seen his glory, the glory as of a father's only son, full of grace and truth.   *(John 1:14)*

That is to say, we saw him, we touched him, and we experienced him with our senses. We experienced carnally this man of grace who was the very Word of God in our midst. We were treated to real, honest-to-God knowledge of God in that man, Jesus. Ours is a sensuous God. Jesus is the Son of this God.

Picture this: Jesus is a guest in a house, and a woman arrives uninvited. We know she is uninvited because the host is outraged at what she does, which is to touch Jesus' feet. Then, weeping tears on his feet, she wipes his feet with her hair and pours perfumed ointment on them (see Luke 7:36-50).

The host is miffed not at her but at Jesus because he does not rebuke her. Not only that, Jesus just sits there accepting and enjoying the delicious sensations of the scent filling the room, of the coolness of the ointment on his feet. He savors it.

I think the record is clear. If Jesus is Emmanuel—"God with us"—then we must affirm that ours is a scandalous God who enjoys sensuous experience.

Thank you, God, for that grace that comes to us through our bodies and our senses. Amen.

MAY 19   A HUMBLE MAN

Then Jesus said, "Father, forgive them."   *(Luke 23:34)*

A man came to see me often when I was pastor of a church in Bonn, Germany. He left his home in Sri Lanka in order to find work that would support his wife and children plus his younger, unmarried sisters—all who were back home.

He worked as a houseman in the home of a diplomat. He cooked, washed, ironed, and kept the yard. He was embarrassed at having to do "women's work." As a devout Hindu, he ate no meat and, at times, did not get enough protein. It was frustrating to me to see how his socialization had boxed him in. I tried to give him a little assertiveness training to use on an employer who was not only insensitive but also unfair. "But I cannot do that, Father," he would answer. "My religion calls for me to remain humble and accept authority."

People like this man make nervous wrecks out of Christians. We really like the Jesus who took the whip and cleared the Temple. The Jesus who accepted his death and forgave his torturers seems strange. He taught also about the blessedness of those who are meek and those who hunger and thirst for righteousness.

Father God, give me the gift of humility. Amen.

MAY 20   JOE CARL

"In fact, the kingdom of God is among you."   (Luke 17:21)

How would you feel about a friend who did all the talking and never let you get a word in edgewise? That's pretty much how many of us structure our prayer life. The theological implication is that either God has nothing to say or God is disinterested. It must get tiresome for God.

There are other ways of praying than using words. The head is a good place to start in prayer, but if we don't move out of the head and into the heart, our prayer life will be sterile. We must consider the possibilities in silence.

Joe Carl was an ebullient sixteen-year-old who died one night in an automobile crash. Family and friends gathered in the home, waiting for the parents to return from the hospital. When they came, no one said anything. In the entire room no one said anything. There were no empty words of sympathy; it was a graceful silence punctuated with embraces and sighs. They received great support that no words could have given them—but the silence of yearning love and concern did. The silence was eloquent and powerful.

Jesus spoke of God's kingdom as a domain within.

God, meet me in the sequestered throne room of your kingdom within my heart. Amen.

MAY 21   A DYING PATIENT

So teach us to count our days that we may gain a wise heart.
(Psalm 90:12)

A pastor was talking with a terminally ill patient in a hospital. She said to him very candidly, "I am dying and I don't know how to act." And why would she? We take very good care of one another as we are dying, but we hardly ever talk it through. Sometimes we even pretend in order not to upset others. But the fact of the matter is that we will die. Death was a reality for Jesus, the Christ; he actually died.

If Jesus had to take death seriously, so do we. After the faith healings, after the remarkable brushes with death, after the seeming comeback from a serious illness—after all that comes the final will of God: we will die. If we are to live, we must understand ourselves as limited and finite creatures. Death becomes the event that forces us to confront the meaning of our days. Sophocles is said to have remarked: "We must come to the end of the day to say how wonderful was the day." Death is what gives meaning to life. Our lives are created so as to create a worthwhile memory.

We Christians have the hope of heaven, but for now we must take seriously the life that is to be lived here.

God, teach me to count my days that I may gain a wise heart. Amen.

MAY 22   WORSHIPERS

I was glad when they said to me, "Let us go to the house of the LORD!"   *(Psalm 122:1)*

Worship isn't something to be watched and appropriated the way one responds to a lecture or even a play. Probably a more apt metaphor is that it is like going to the circus, where you can't possibly experience everything that is going on because it keeps changing and spinning out of your vision the way a kaleidoscope does. What you come away with is a montage of images, sounds, and smells, and you know that you have been to "The Greatest Show on Earth." The circus is actually experienced more at the feeling level than as an exercise of the mind.

But real worship is not mindless, because we should be engaged at the intellectual level too—along with experiencing expectation, joy, excitement, anxiety, hope, repentance, and sacrifice.

More than what seems to be happening is happening because God's Spirit is there, working God's way among the people.

Lord, I come gladly to your house. May I find peace within your walls and joy among my relatives and friends. Amen.

MAY 23   THE MAN WHO KILLED HIS BROTHER

Cain rose up against his brother Abel, and killed him. Then the Lord said to Cain, "Where is your brother Abel?" He said, "I do not know; am I my brother's keeper?"   ***(Genesis 4:8, 9)***

Cain killed his brother Abel and hid Abel's body. When God inquired about Abel, Cain shouted, "Am I my brother's keeper?" Just before this awful thing happened, the Bible says that we were made in God's image—not meaning that we look like God, but that we are endowed with God's characteristics. These God qualities are buried deep in all of us as a source of wisdom, strength, and healing. We have access to this source, but we also have the freedom to choose not to draw upon it.

Later in the Bible, Jesus says of us, "What can they give in return for their life?" (Mark 8:37). He is pointing out that there are no second chances. We have only a few years to make this planet a better place. The lesson to be learned is that we need not be actively evil to miss being with God. We need only be inactively indifferent to miss it. We can simply miss it by failing to keep up with our brothers and sisters.

God, I choose to be a keeper of my brothers and sisters. Amen.

MAY 24   JOB

"Oh, that I knew where I might find [God]."   *(Job 23:3)*

Though the Bible witnesses to those moments in which people experience God's presence, it is equally careful to report those in which people experience God's absence. Job, a faithful devotee of God who was reeling from multiple disasters, bawled, "Oh, that I knew where I might find [God]." Remember, too, that cry in Psalm 22, where the writer felt abandoned by God; it was also shouted out by Jesus as he died: "Why have you forsaken me?"

One thing that causes us to experience God's absence is the misconception we hold of God's presence. We expect God while on our knees at prayer, but God more often appears when we stand erect and confident before a challenge. God is not absent; it's just that we are blind to the mysterious and ordinary ways in which God comes.

How else are we to understand the man we call Christ? To the entire world he appeared to be no more than a man—born in a barn, the child of working parents. Yet, God was there in him. God took on the form of a man because God was determined to be with us.

God, that was a terrible risk you took, and it cost you your Son. But now we know you. Thanks. Amen.

MAY 25   A CHILD

[Jesus] said to them, "Let the little children come to me; do not stop them; for it is to such as these that the kingdom of God belongs."   *(Mark 10:14)*

All through the account of the public ministry of Jesus, he speaks of certain surprising people as being dear to him. We shouldn't be startled, then, to hear this thing he said about children.

Centuries before Jesus lived, a man named Isaiah prophesied something we have learned to call "the peaceable kingdom." Poets, preachers, and painters have restated Isaiah's words: "The wolf shall live with the lamb, the leopard shall lie down with the kid, the calf and the lion and the fatling together, and a little child shall lead them" (11:6).

Jesus picked up that metaphor about a little child leading us, and audaciously he said as he gathered a child into his arms that the greatest among those present was that child.

What could Jesus and Isaiah have meant? Maybe, for starters, they meant that peacemaking is for the politically naive, and that the beginning of a new order that does not include war as one of its options will require a reassessment of values that will not be unlike being born again.

God, I need a new way of thinking about things. I pray that world leaders will make decisions that will bring us a peaceable kingdom. Amen.

MAY 26   THE NEWS JUNKIE

Hear, O Israel: The LORD is our God, the LORD alone.
(Deuteronomy 6:4)

It is possible to get too much information—a lot of it unsolicited. It is possible to become a "news junkie." We are assaulted by images of brutality, murder, and mayhem in the media. Some of it is misinformation and untrue. We often want to turn our heads and withdraw from the world.

What can assist us in learning to live in this world? Worship can; but not worship as a specialized activity, indulged behind closed doors. We mustn't pull the blinds and seek God in abstraction from the life of the world around us.

Worship is a matter, rather, of seeing the scenes of everyday life more clearly in the light of the eternal; it is a matter of hearing the sounds of today more acutely because in them we hear the voice of God.

Worship doesn't mean stopping our ears so we cannot hear. It does mean that through the noises of a rattling, jolting, challenging world, we may hear the call of the world unseen: "Hear, O Israel: The LORD is our God, the LORD alone."

God, this day I shall love you with all my heart, and with all my soul, and with all my strength. And I shall love my neighbor as myself. Amen.

MAY 27   A MAN OF MISFORTUNES

He who keeps you will not slumber. He who keeps Israel will neither slumber nor sleep.   (Psalm 121:3b-4)

There is a Yiddish story about a man to whom all kinds of misfortunes fell. He pleaded to the Lord, "Why me, I who have so consistently and conscientiously fulfilled every one of the 613 laws of the Pentateuch? Why me?" A still, small voice from heaven replied, "Because you're such a bore."

I believe God would rather we be creative than right. A twenty-first-century theologian said, "It is better to do something doubtful—and therefore in need of forgiveness—than to do nothing at all."

God is constantly trying to make things better for us. Too often we picture God as an immovable rock, when it is God and God alone who refuses to rest. Listen to the psalmist: God neither slumbers nor sleeps. It is better to do something doubtful or over-bold on our part, and therefore in need of forgiveness, than to do nothing at all. If we choose, we are sometimes wrong; but if we never choose, we are always wrong.

God, life is grand and beautiful and sweeping and full of grace—never boring! Thank you. Amen.

MAY 28   A FARMER

The kingdom of God is as if someone would scatter seed on the ground, and would sleep and rise night and day, and the seed would sprout and grow, he does not know how. (Mark 4:26-27)

A farmer went to his field and sowed his seeds. He never returned to that field during the day or night. He trusted that in his absence, even while he was asleep, the seed would grow. It did.

Jesus sowed his seed in our hearts, and then off he went like the farmer in the story. Of course, the farmer knew that things would not be ideal. There were the birds and droughts, the weeds and insects, the parasites and blights; but there was also the power of the seed itself, maturing and growing in divine power.

Jesus sowed his seed in us and went away knowing that one day we would find that seed growing in us through all the weeds, all the dangers, all the droughts.

The world is a dark place, but it is not all dark. The outcome is sure. Whether or not you will be a part of that outcome depends on the growth of the seed in you. You could miss out on the harvest.

God, bring the seed to life in me! Amen.

MAY 29   A GRIEVING MOTHER

Whether we live or whether we die, we are the Lord's.
                                        (Romans 14:8)

I went to the hospital late one night to see about a young man who had suffered burns over much of his body. I sat with his wife in a dimly lit waiting room. We talked for a while, and then we prayed together. Just as we lifted our heads, a soft voice said, "He'll be OK; he'll be OK."

We looked toward the sound of the voice, and seated in the half dark alone was a middle-aged woman whom we had not previously noticed. I thanked her for her encouragement and asked why she was there. She said that her son and his wife had been in an automobile accident two days previous, and that very day her son had died. Now she was there to spend the night with her daughter-in-law because "she ought not to be by herself tonight."

Then she looked directly at the young wife with whom I was visiting and said again, "He'll be OK. My boy's OK. He belongs to the Lord!"

The young wife got up and moved to the seat beside the other woman. They embraced. It was a highly charged, and sacred moment—an exchange of love and peace.

Loving God, we affirm it! You are present everywhere. Amen.

MAY 30   THE STRING SAVER

In the beginning . . . God created [everything]. . . . [And] God saw
everything that he had made, and indeed, it was very good.
(Genesis 1:1, 31)

There was a lady who was frugal beyond imagining. When she
died, her family went through her accumulated treasures and
found there a box labeled "pieces of string too short for anything,"
which was full of pieces of string too short for anything.

That sounds eccentric in a consumer society. We have of late
become ecologically concerned, but we aren't bona fide, hardcore
savers like the string lady. I grew up in a home of occasional short-
ages. Even our water supply had to be carefully reserved. The same
food showed up on the table more than once, and at last the leftovers
fed some animal. Outgrown clothes were passed on to someone else.

Time passes, affluence sets in, and attitudes adjust. Even leftovers go down the disposal because most dogs don't eat leftovers
anymore.

But we must get very serious about having been appointed by
God as keepers of the good earth.

Great God of everything, you have made us and put us in this
good place with enough of everything. We will be responsible.
Amen.

MAY 31   THE MIDDLE-CLASS MAN

[God] has told you . . . what is good; and what does the LORD
require of you but to do justice, and to love kindness, and to
walk humbly.   *(Micah 6:8)*

The man asked his pastor if it is possible to "be in, but not of the
middle class." He wondered if he could live in affluence without
becoming immune to those who don't. The question he raised was
this: "Can we live in a world of cashmere wool, 100 percent cotton,
silk scarves, and luxury SUVs without our values being a copy of
those who do?"

I think we can transcend our environment when we recognize that the systems and the institutions of our time do not work as well for others as they do for us. The systems may need reformation. It is not important how we do it; what matters is that we begin to understand people and conditions outside our social niche.

God, guide me to be just, kind, and wise. Amen.

JUNE

Old Testament Men

ANDY LANGFORD

JUNE 1 OLD TESTAMENT MEN

In the beginning God created... **(Genesis 1:1a TNIV)**

The Old Testament covers more than two thousand years of history and dozens of different lands. In thirty-nine books, the Old Testament includes the names and stories of thousands of men from Adam to Malachi (the last man named in the Old Testament). How can we possibly know, let alone understand, these men from millennia ago?

We cannot discuss them all, but during this month we will discover that many of these men were just like us. They faced struggles in their families; difficulties in their relationships with women; anxieties about their children; conflicts with other men; concerns about their nation; and even some major battles with floods, giants, great fish, and lions. Each man, however, knew the presence of God.

Throughout the ages, men have told the stories of these Old Testament characters to other men. First told around campfires, then on scraps of parchment, and finally in complete books, all of these stories were so important that these men could not be forgotten. As we journey with them, may we not only remember their stories but also discover anew God in our own lives.

Creator God, open my ears to hear new stories, enlighten my mind that I may understand, and enlarge my heart that I might feel your presence. Amen.

JUNE 2   BORN OUT OF DUST

Then the L   *God formed a man from the dust of the ground and breathed into his nostrils the breath of life, and the man became a living being.*   *(Genesis 2:7 TNIV)*

God was lonely and yearned to have someone to talk to. In response, God created Adam, the Hebrew word for "man," the pinnacle of God's creation. In all creation, Adam alone was made in the very image of God.

The most famous scene in Rome's great Sistine Chapel is a finger of God reaching out to touch a finger of Adam. The artist Michelangelo through his fresco shows us how God yearns to be in communion with us, and how we yearn to touch the One who made us. But in this work of art, the fingers of God and man do not quite touch.

The truth, however, is that in our own creation God has touched us. God formed each of us in our mother's womb. God breathed into us the breath of life. And God is reaching out to us, even if we cannot see God's hand.

Life-breathing God, blow your presence into my life, and today may I feel your touch. Amen.

JUNE 3   ADAM AND THAT FORBIDDEN FRUIT

When the woman saw that the fruit of the tree was good for food...and also desirable for gaining wisdom, she took some and ate it. She also gave some to her husband, who was with her, and he ate it.   *(Genesis 3:6 TNIV)*

Who introduced sin into the world? Some place all the blame on the serpent. Other people give credit to Eve, the first woman who took the first bite. But what about Adam, the first man, "who was with her"? Shifting blame is not a new experience.

In his letter to the Romans, Paul said that "sin entered the world through one man" (5:12 TNIV). That one man was Adam. And Adam's fall became a pattern that every man after him followed.

Paul was unwilling to let Adam pass the blame. Adam could not blame the serpent or Eve but had to claim his own culpability.

One of the first steps in being faithful men is acknowledging our own failures. Ultimately, a man cannot shift responsibility for his own wrong actions. We may blame other people, our culture, our situation, our families, and a whole host of others when we turn away from God. Yet being a man requires naming our own failures.

Judging God, you know my failures. Help me name them honestly; but then, forgiving God, set me free! Amen.

JUNE 4   NOAH AND THE ARK

The LORD then said to Noah, "Go into the ark, you and your whole family, because I have found you righteous in this generation."   (Genesis 7:1 TNIV)

Following in the footsteps of Adam, every man and everything else in all creation disappointed God. Cain, son of Adam, killed his brother Abel (Genesis 4). Then, "the earth was corrupt in God's sight and was full of violence" (Genesis 6:11 TNIV). What was God to do?

God chose one man who was holier than all others, and he commanded this man, Noah, to build a great boat. If Noah responded affirmatively, then when the rains came down and the floods came up, he, his family, and breeding stock of all creation would float upon the waters.

Can you imagine the ridicule Noah suffered for following God? His friends laughed at him for building a yacht while not a drop of rain appeared in the sky. Neighbors chuckled when Noah bought food supplies for elephants and parakeets. Yet Noah followed the word of God, and thanks to him, all the creatures of God, including humankind, survived. Thanks, Noah, for listening to God.

God of the skies and rain, help me listen when you speak. Enable me to take up my tools and build whatever you call me to create this day. Amen.

JUNE 5   ABRAM LEAVES HOME

The LORD came to Abram in a vision: "Do not be afraid, Abram. I am your shield, your very great reward." (Genesis 15:1 TNIV)

When Abram was seventy-five years old, God told him to take his family and belongings, leave the land of his birth, and travel to an unknown land. If Abram followed, God would bless him and make him a blessing for every nation. Abram, who would later be known as Abraham, was the second most important man (following only Moses) in the Old Testament.

When Harland Sanders of Kentucky was sixty-five years old, the two-lane highway in front of his family's hotel and restaurant closed when the state built a new interstate highway several miles west. What was Sanders to do? Retire? Bemoan his loss? Sue? Die? Sanders took to the road with his family recipes and began an enterprise known today as Kentucky Fried Chicken, with its finger-licking-good food.

Wherever we are in our own life journey, God has plans for us. Whatever age we are, we still have opportunities for change. We are the spiritual children of an elderly wanderer whose journey blessed all creation.

God of the journey, do not let me become too settled in my life, however old I am. Open my eyes to see new destinations that will bless the people I love and me. Amen.

JUNE 6   ABRAM AND HIS NEPHEW

So Abram went up from Egypt to the Negev, with his wife and everything he had, and Lot went with him. (Genesis 13:1 TNIV)

Lot was Abram's nephew. Lot's father, Haran, died, and Abram became responsible for the young man. Lot had traveled with Abram all the way from the land of Ur to the land God had promised. There Abram and Lot began to quarrel over who possessed what. Lot went one way, and Abram went another; yet Abram still felt responsible for his younger relative. Abram saved Lot when

Lot lost a battle to a local king, and Abram even delivered Lot (but not his wife) out of the cities of Sodom and Gomorrah before their destruction. Eventually, Lot's family became a set of foreign nations that fought against the people of God.

We can choose our friends but not our family. Some days family members are close; and other times they lead us into conflict. We cannot choose how someone else will act, but we can choose how we will act; and we can choose to show them the love of God.

Abram models for us steadfast loyalty to family.

Father God, help me be faithful to my family—the "good" relatives and those family members who have offended—for we all are your children and one family. Amen.

JUNE 7   ABRAM AND HIS ILLEGITIMATE SON

So Hagar bore Abram a son, and Abram gave the name Ishmael to the son she had borne.   *(Genesis 16:15 TNIV)*

After Abram's tempestuous relationship with Lot, God promised Abram his own son. Unfortunately, Abram's wife, Sarah, had no luck becoming pregnant. In response, Sarah encouraged Abram to impregnate her slave Hagar, who then gave birth to Ishmael. No one bothered to solicit Hagar's opinion about this arrangement. And Ishmael shared no blame at all in his birth.

Hagar liked being the mother of Abram's child and dreamed that Ishmael would inherit Abram's estate. Sarah, however, who proposed this course of action, resented Hagar and Ishmael. Eventually, at Sarah's insistence, Abram expelled both Hagar and Ishmael out of his camp. In the desert, this mother and child might have died. Yet God did not abandon them, and they survived. Ishmael married a woman from Egypt and became the father of all Arabs.

Many fathers today have children from more than one woman. Divided families, mixed loyalties, and conflicts are not new. Some of these conflicts last for generations. In this story and in our stories, however, God remains faithful to all parties and brings good out of awkward situations.

God of Abram and Sarah and Hagar and Ishmael, build bridges in my broken family, and may I never blame children for the sins of their parents. Amen.

JUNE 8   ABRAHAM AND HIS BELOVED SON

Sarah became pregnant and bore a son to Abraham in his old age, at the very time God had promised him.
                                        (Genesis 21:2 TNIV)

Finally, Sarah conceived Abraham's child. As had been foretold by three strangers—and despite Sarah's response of laughter—Isaac was born when Abraham was one hundred years old. Isaac, the shining glory of his father, would inherit Abraham's name, property, and blessing from God.

Yet God had one more test for Abraham. God instructed Abraham to take Isaac to the top of a mountain and offer him as a human sacrifice to God. God could not ask for a more precious gift. Without questioning, Abraham traveled to the mountain and prepared his son for death. At the last moment, seeing Abraham's absolute faith, God spared Isaac's life. God said to Abraham, "Because you have done this and have not withheld your son, your only son, I will surely bless you and make your descendants as numerous as the stars in the sky" (Genesis 22:16-17). On that very mountain, two millennia later, God offered up for us God's only Son, Jesus Christ, to die for us.

Simply put, what are we willing to offer God to show our faithfulness? Can we follow Abraham's example of faithfulness?

God of Abraham and Isaac, give me the strength to offer to you whatever or whoever is most precious to me. Amen.

JUNE 9   JACOB WRESTLING WITH GOD

So Jacob was left alone, and a man wrestled with him till daybreak.   *(Genesis 32:24 TNIV)*

Abraham begot Isaac, who begot the twins Esau and Jacob. Esau, the older son, loved the outdoors and hunting. Jacob, the pampered mother's boy, would rather sit by the tent and scheme how to inherit his father's wealth.

Jacob stole his elder brother's inheritance and fled for his life. He then misappropriated his father-in-law's flocks and again had to flee back home for safety. When Jacob drew near his home, he heard that his wronged brother was coming to meet him with armed men. All Jacob's tricks had finally caught up with him.

Scared and weary, Jacob fell asleep beside the Jabbok stream until God appeared. All night long, Jacob wrestled with God. Finally, Jacob released God when God blessed him and gave Jacob a new name: Israel, one who "struggled with God and with human beings and . . . [overcame]" (Genesis 32:28 TNIV).

For all of us, there comes a day when all our schemes, ploys, and tricks catch up with us. On those dark days of the soul, may God wrestle with us until we turn the corner and become the men God calls us to be.

Wrestling God, see through my tricks and discover who I am and what you call me to be. Amen.

JUNE 10   JOSEPH AND HIS BROTHERS

Now Israel loved Joseph more than any of his other sons.
(Genesis 37:3 TNIV)

The old man Jacob, renamed Israel, had twelve sons, and the most beloved son was Joseph. Unable to learn from his own disastrous relationship with his brother Esau, Israel favored one son above all the others. Naturally, Joseph's brothers hated him because of his father's focused love.

Joseph's brothers sold him into slavery and told Israel that Joseph had died. Yet Joseph was taken to Egypt and became a prized advisor to the pharaoh of Egypt. When famine came across the region, Joseph provided for his family and brought his father and the entire household to Egypt for protection.

All brothers fight with one another. We struggle to gain ascendancy, denigrate our siblings to our parents, and take advantage whenever possible. Both parents and brothers are to blame. But God used the conflict between Joseph and his brothers to save the people of Israel. Out of conflict came salvation. May the same be true of our own family conflicts.

Providential God, see me through my struggles with my own family to find your way of reconciliation. Amen.

JUNE 11   BIRTH OF MOSES

Now a man of the house of Levi married a Levite woman, and she became pregnant and gave birth to a son.
(Exodus 2:1-2a TNIV)

Moses was the deliverer from slavery, the divider of the sea, the giver of the law, the leader in the wilderness, and the author of the first five books of the Old Testament. His life journey began in conflict with Egypt, the greatest power in the ancient world—a conflict that defined the rest of his days.

When Pharaoh declared that every son born to the Hebrews should be put to death, Jewish midwives saved the boys. Moses' mother hid him for three months until she placed him in a basket in the Nile River. Pharaoh's daughter discovered him and raised him in her home. Moses was a prince of Egypt until the day he murdered an Egyptian soldier.

Our lives begin in a common way: a man and a woman come together to create life. After our birth, our parents try to the best of their ability to provide for our safety and nurture. Yet could any parent have dreamed of what each of us has become? Usually, we can see the hand of God in our lives only in retrospect.

Birth-giving God, I give thanks for my own parents and first days; in retrospect, may I remember the first glimpses of your presence in my own life. Amen.

JUNE 12   CALL OF MOSES

God called to [Moses] from within the [burning] bush, "Moses! Moses!" And Moses said, "Here I am."   *(Exodus 3:4 TNIV)*

As a convicted killer, Moses had fled from the land of Egypt and found refuge with the family of Jethro in the Sinai desert. For years, this former prince of Egypt served as a shepherd to the flocks of his father-in-law. Moses expected that he would never again return to the land of his birth and his people held in slavery.

But then, in the shadow of God's mountain, Moses saw a bush that was burning but not consumed by the fire. On that holy ground, after a strenuous debate, Moses accepted God's command: "I am sending you to Pharaoh to bring my people the Israelites out of Egypt" (Exodus 3:10 TNIV).

God has a mission for each of us. The voice of God may come through a burning bush, a gentle voice, a newspaper article, a conversation with a friend, or a prompting in our heart. We may resist God's call, yet God is persistent. God's call cannot be ignored.

Mission-calling God, open my eyes, ears, heart, and feet to receive and obey your call so that I may fulfill the task you have for me. Amen.

JUNE 13   MOSES AND HIS FATHER-IN-LAW

Then Moses went back to Jethro his father-in-law and said to him, "Let me return to my own people in Egypt. . . ." Jethro said, "Go, and I wish you well."   *(Exodus 4:18 TNIV)*

After fleeing Egypt and rescuing Jethro's daughters from shepherds, Moses was welcomed into Jethro's family. Jethro understood his need to repay the wandering Egyptian prince.

Later Jethro presented to Moses his daughter Zipporah in marriage (see Exodus 2:21). Zipporah gave birth to children, and so Jethro became a grandfather. Immediately after speaking to God in the burning bush, Moses asked Jethro for advice. And after Moses delivered the people out of Egypt, he brought them to

Jethro for a blessing and further advice. Clearly, the two men were bound to each other not by blood but by marriage and by respect for each other.

Many satires and jokes have been made about men and their in-laws. Yet in many cases, marriage extends the bonds of family and provides even greater resources for wisdom and strength. May we give thanks to God for the gifts of extended family—especially for wise, older men gifted to us through marriage.

God, may I receive the love, strength, and wisdom that come to me through men who are not of my blood but are still my family. Amen.

JUNE 14   MOSES DIVIDES THE SEA

Then the LORD said to Moses, "Why are you crying out to me? Tell the Israelites to move on. Raise your staff and stretch out your hand over the sea to divide the water."
(Exodus 14:15-16 TNIV)

Moses felt challenged by God at every step in his life. Yet perhaps no challenge was as difficult as when he and his people stood beside the Red Sea with the Egyptian army closing in behind them. Moses asked the Lord what to do. God's answer: "Divide the water."

How do we respond to the major hurdles in our own lives? When faced with a career change, a serious economic challenge, or any other great task, our way is to solve our problems by ourselves—to show that we are men!

Moses learned how *not* to do it alone. He solicited the support of family, and most of all he appealed to God. And Moses always received the answers he needed.

When crushed between two impossible forces, may we also pray to God for support and the power to pass over whatever obstructs us.

Sea-dividing God, show me a way to face that problem in my life that seems to have no answer. Help me remember that if you can divide the sea, you can also guide me in a safe direction. Amen.

JUNE 15   MOSES AND THE TEN COMMANDMENTS

So Moses . . . summoned the elders of the people and set before them all the words the LORD had commanded him to speak.
(Exodus 19:7 TNIV)

Moses faced the problem of creating a new nation from a motley assortment of former slaves. He returned to the mountain where he had first seen the burning bush, and there God gave Moses what we know as the Ten Commandments. In response to God's mighty acts of freedom, the people would organize their common life by observing ten basic laws of relationship with God and all people. Jesus later summed up these laws by simply asking his followers to love God and love their neighbors.

Many years ago I climbed to the top of Mount Moses in the southern Sinai desert. After a three-hour hike in the darkness, I witnessed the sun rising across the desert mountains. This experience was truly a mountaintop moment. Understanding anew how mighty God is and how insignificant I am, I committed again to follow not my own desires but, with God's help, to keep God's law.

Law-giving God, take me to the top of the mountain and help me keep your laws. Let every moment of my life be an opportunity to love you and all people. Amen.

JUNE 16   JOSHUA AND JERICHO

Joshua commanded the army, "Shout! For the LORD has given you the city! The city and all that is in it are to be devoted to the LORD."   *(Joshua 6:16-17a TNIV)*

When Moses died, Joshua took command of the people. He prepared to enter the land God promised Abraham by sending out spies and assessing his people's enemies. Their largest obstacle was the city of Jericho, whose walls appeared impregnable.

Like Moses before him, Joshua appealed to God for wisdom, and God told Joshua what to do. For six days the men of Israel marched around the city blowing horns and shouting. On the seventh day, after they had marched around the city blowing horns and shouting, the walls of Jericho came tumbling down. The whole of the Holy Land lay before them.

When faced with foes too great to conquer, the wise men of the Old Testament appealed to God, and God responded. Men like Joshua did not rely on military weapons or their own cleverness or strength; they relied on God. And when they did, God never failed them.

Conqueror of Jericho, whenever I am tempted to trust in my own wisdom or power, teach me to trust first in you. Before you, no walls are too strong and no enemy is too overpowering. Amen.

JUNE 17   SAMSON'S STRENGTH AND WEAKNESS

Samson said, "Let me die with the Philistines!" Then he pushed with all his might, and down came the temple on the rulers and all the people in it.   (Judges 16:30 TNIV)

Samson was a muscular man who never cut his hair and had a bad tendency to fall in love with women who abused him. In their struggles with the Philistines, the people of God relied on Samson to defeat their foes with his strong arm and cruel pranks. Against the strength of Samson, the Philistines had no defense. But Delilah, with her sexual wiles, learned Samson's secret, cut his hair, and turned him over to the Philistines as a slave. Only at the end of his life, with his hair and strength restored, did Samson finally call upon God. Samson and his enemies died together.

Sometimes we trust too much in our physical strength or stamina to overcome our enemies. The greater strength, which Samson discovered too late to save himself, is the power that comes only from God.

May we keep our bodies strong, but even more so, may we strengthen our relationship with God.

God of the judges, judge me when I trust too much in my body and myself. Help me use my body not as my god but as a temple for you. Amen.

JUNE 18   BOAZ AND RUTH

When Boaz had finished eating and drinking and was in good
spirits, he went over to lie down at the far end of the grain pile.
Ruth approached quietly, uncovered his feet and lay down.
                                           (Ruth 3:7 TNIV)

The book of Ruth contains the story of the great-grandparents of
King David. A non-Jewish woman from Moab (whose ancient
ancestor was Lot, the nephew of Abraham) played a critical role in
Jewish history.

Boaz, a wealthy landowner, found himself infatuated with the
lovely Moabite woman who had arrived in Bethlehem. Ruth's husband, a man from Bethlehem, had died and left her a widow
responsible for her mother-in-law, Naomi, and herself.

Boaz secretly provided additional food for the women; and after
he had been seduced by Ruth, he married her in an honorable
fashion.

Although many lessons may be learned from this story, Boaz
appears to be an upstanding man who fell in love with an outcast
woman. Rather than abuse the relationship, he did the honorable thing. He did not allow age, race, or religion to separate him
from the woman who needed his assistance and love; and their
love for each other became the fountainhead of the greatest king
of Israel.

God of Ruth and Boaz, when I am placed in awkward or even
immoral situations, help me act justly and do what is right.
Amen.

JUNE 19   SAMUEL AND SAUL

When Samuel heard all that the people said, he repeated it
before the LORD. The LORD answered, "Listen to them and give
them a king."   *(1 Samuel 8:21-22a TNIV)*

Samuel was a great spokesman for God who reminded the people of Israel to trust in God alone; yet the people wanted a king like the nations around them. Finally God gave them a king who unified the twelve tribes, a man named Saul.

Yet the message of Saul's story continues to be one of the hardest for us to hear. When our society faces a tragedy or problem, we believe that strong political leaders, decisive military officers, or a new government program will solve the crisis. Samuel, however, knew that Saul would fail. When the people put their trust in one man, that man went mad, created wars, and fostered even more social inequity.

We need in our society men and women who speak the word of God, challenge each of us to do what is right, and call us again and again to put our trust first and foremost in God alone.

Lord of the prophets, when I hear anew the lessons of the past, help me not to repeat them but to learn from them. Let me put my trust today not in some strong leader but in you alone. Amen.

JUNE 20   DAVID AND GOLIATH

So David triumphed over the Philistine with a sling and a stone; without a sword in his hand he struck down the Philistine and killed him. *(1 Samuel 17:50 TNIV)*

David, the youngest son of Jesse and the great-grandson of Boaz and Ruth, kept his father's sheep flocks. When David went to visit his brothers in Saul's army, he saw and heard the giant Goliath, who stood more than nine feet tall. Neither Saul nor any other man would fight against this man from Gath.

David, however, knew the power of God. Without armor or metal weapons, he ran toward Goliath with only a sling and a smooth stone. With one throw, David dropped Goliath and then cut off Goliath's head with the giant's own sword.

David spoke truthfully when he declared to the giant: "You come against me with sword and spear and javelin, but I come against you in the name of the LORD Almighty" (1 Samuel 17:45 TNIV).

When faced with any giant in our own lives, may we also fight in the name of God.

God of sling and rock, guide my aim so that whichever foe I face today, I will defeat my enemy. Amen.

JUNE 21   DAVID AND BATHSHEBA

One evening David got up from his bed and walked around on the roof of the palace. From the roof he saw a woman bathing. The woman was very beautiful, and David sent someone to find out about her.   (2 Samuel 11:2-3a TNIV)

As king of Israel, David was the most powerful man in the nation. Nothing David desired could be denied him. When he looked down on Bathsheba, the wife of one of his soldiers, he wanted her. And so David impregnated Bathsheba, killed her husband, and married the new widow.

Sometimes we are placed in situations where we can take advantage of our position to use other people. Although none of us may be as unjust as David was in this instance, each of us may be tempted to use our power, money, or authority to force other people to do our will—even when our actions hurt ourselves, injure other people, or transgress against our God.

David, however, did not fool God—nor do we.

God of David, enable me this day to use my power, not for my own gain or needs, but for your sake alone. Amen.

JUNE 22   SOLOMON'S WISDOM

[Solomon said,] "So give your servant a discerning heart to govern your people and to distinguish between right and wrong."
(1 Kings 3:9 TNIV)

Solomon, second child of David and Bathsheba, ascended the throne of his father, David. At that moment, God asked Solomon what he wanted. Solomon simply replied that all he needed was wisdom, the ability to choose between right and wrong. Quite probably, Solomon saw that the major character flaw of his father was a lack of wisdom.

Wisdom is a very precious quality. The ability to discern between good and evil and to understand the difference between truth and falsehood eludes far too many people. Many of us have a great deal of knowledge. Too few of us are wise.

Every day, as we are bombarded with information and asked to make quick decisions, may we pause for a moment, take a deep breath, and seek what God would have us do.

God of all wisdom, help me today to know the difference between right and wrong and then act faithfully. Amen.

JUNE 23   SOLOMON BUILDS THE TEMPLE

[Solomon said,] "I intend, therefore, to build a temple for the Name of the LORD my God."   *(1 Kings 5:5a TNIV)*

Solomon's greatest achievement was building a great temple in which to worship God. Because of David's affair with Bathsheba, God never allowed David to bring the ark of the covenant into a permanent building in Jerusalem. Solomon achieved the task David was denied.

The temple was a glorious building—ninety feet long, thirty feet wide, forty-five feet high, and made out of cedar, juniper, olive wood, and gold. Within the temple, the people of God finally provided a true sanctuary for God's presence.

God gives each of us the ability to create in our lifetimes. Our creations may include an invention, a home, a building, or a company. These creations may also be more intangible: a good marriage, a strong family, or a strong friendship. Are the things and the relationships we have created worthy of God? Can God be found in them? Have we invested our creative power in ways that honor God?

*God of all creation, may I see you today in all you have cre-
ated, from the heavens above to the buildings below to all your
creatures on earth. Enable me to create monuments in my own
life that honor you. Amen.*

JUNE 24   JOB AND HIS FRIENDS

*When Job's three friends, Eliphaz the Temanite, Bildad the
Shuhite and Zophar the Naamathite, heard about all the troubles that had come upon [Job], they set out from their homes
and met together by agreement to go and sympathize with him
and comfort him.*   *(Job 2:11 TNIV)*

Job was a righteous man who loved God and amassed great fortune and power. Yet in a wager with Satan, God allowed Job to
lose his property, suffer the death of his children, and be afflicted
with sores. Job cursed the day of his birth (Job 3:1) and basically
asked, "Why should a good man suffer evil?"

Three of Job's friends came to stand by him. Much of the book
of Job centers on the conversations between Job and his friends as
they tried to make sense of his loss and see God's hand in his suffering. More important, his friends were simply there for him.

Illness, economic loss, job crises, and family struggles will
afflict all of us. Do we have friends who will stand with us? Will we
stand with our friends? Life without close male friends is truly
insufferable.

*O God, my Friend, stand by me when storms rage. Enable me to
stand by my friends when they suffer, and provide friends for
me when I seem to stand alone. Amen.*

JUNE 25   JOB AND HIS GOD

*Then the LORD spoke to Job out of the storm. He said: "Who is
this that obscures my plans with words without knowledge?
Prepare to defend yourself."*   *(Job 38:1-3a TNIV)*

Job did not suffer quietly. He argued with his wife, complained to his friends, and challenged God to provide answers to why he or any person suffers. Neither his wife nor his friends provided satisfactory answers, but God heard Job's lament and responded strongly.

Essentially, God challenged Job to be silent in the midst of struggles he could never fully understand. For many of the challenges of life, God never provides simple answers explaining why things happen the way they do. Sometimes being a man simply means dealing with our own crises without finding answers or solutions.

God, however, also praised Job for asking the hard questions and refusing to accept easy answers. As men who are just a little less than angels, we have the right and responsibility to speak honestly with God. We should never shy away from questioning God and demanding serious answers. God does not want patsies but men who are willing to engage in serious debate about the most serious questions of life.

God of the storm, speak to me in the midst of the storms of my life. Help me challenge you and be ready to hear you speak. Amen.

JUNE 26   AMOS AND HIS PEOPLE

The words of Amos, one of the shepherds of Tekoa—the vision he saw concerning Israel.   (Amos 1:1 TNIV)

A hundred years after the time of Solomon, Amos spoke God's word to the people in the northern kingdom of the holy land. A farmer, a shepherd, and an educated rural man, Amos traveled to the political and religious elite to indict their waste and idolatry: "I hate, I despise your religious festivals; I cannot stand your assemblies" (Amos 5:21 TNIV).

Whistle-blowers, constant complainers, and aggravating men are never loved. Most of us prefer men who get along, are good old boys, and run with the crowd. When someone from outside our group intervenes and challenges a specific belief or behavior, we have a tendency to dismiss them, reject them, and push them out.

The book of Amos simply ends without any resolution; did he offend one powerful person too many times?

Being faithful to God requires an openness to hear unpleasant truths. Sometimes gadflies speak the truth. Instead of fighting back or engaging in argument when we are challenged with hard words or challenging statements, maybe we should listen carefully for a word from God.

Truth-speaking God, open my ears to listen to your prophets today, especially when they speak words that challenge who I am and how I live. Amen.

JUNE 27   HOSEA AND HIS WIFE

When the LORD began to speak through Hosea, the LORD said to him, "Go, marry a promiscuous woman and have children with her, for like an adulterous wife this land is guilty of unfaithfulness to the LORD." **(Hosea 1:2 TNIV)**

Like Amos, Hosea also spoke the word of God to God's people and criticized the political, religious, and social culture around him. More important than his words, however, was the primary action he took. Hosea's relationship with his wife, Gomer, represented the relationship between God and God's people. She was a promiscuous woman. Hosea was not the father of her children, and thus he desired to break their marriage. As a sign of Hosea's faithfulness, however, he ultimately took Gomer back into his home. Although Israel would fall to the Assyrians, God would never completely abandon God's people.

None of our relationships with our significant others, and especially with our wives, is without stress. We hurt each other and place our own desires ahead of our covenantal relationship; and almost always, hurt and pain follow. We are fortunate, however, that God's love for us, like Hosea's love for Gomer, is vastly superior to our love for others.

145

God of the harlot and saint, thank you for your forgiving love. Empower me to imitate your compassionate behavior and not pursue my own selfish passions. Amen.

JUNE 28   JONAH AND THE GREAT FISH

Now the Lord provided a huge fish to swallow Jonah.
(Jonah 1:17, TNIV)

The forty-eight verses of Jonah tell the story of a man just like us. When God gave directions to Jonah, he ran in the opposite direction. When sailors on Jonah's boat prayed for deliverance from a great storm, Jonah slept through the crisis. When the sailors gambled, Jonah lost. Finally, Jonah owned up to his attempt to escape God. The great fish provided uncomfortable transportation back to land.

Jonah reluctantly accepted God's call. He preached one of the shortest sermons in the Bible: "Forty more days and Nineveh will be overthrown" (Jonah 3:4b TNIV). And because of Jonah's obedience, God provided salvation to 120,000 people!

When God wants us, we cannot escape. When God gives instructions, God expects us to listen. God has great plans for the people we are sent to serve and us, if we will only obey. If we spent less time running away and more time listening, how many lives could we change?

Inescapable God, break through my deafness and my desire to run in the wrong direction. Point me in the right direction today and let me speak your word of salvation. Amen.

JUNE 29   DANIEL AND THE LIONS

[King Nebuchadnezzar said,] "Daniel, servant of the living God, has your God, whom you serve continually, been able to rescue you from the lions?"   *(Daniel 6:20 TNIV)*

When the nation of Judah fell, the spiritual and political elite of God's chosen people were taken into exile to the land of Babylon. The words of the prophets came true, and God punished the Israelites for forgetting the Lord and all that God had done for them.

Daniel was one of the best and the brightest "young men without any physical defect, handsome, showing aptitude for every kind of learning, well informed, quick to understand, and qualified to serve in the king's palace" (Daniel 1:4 TNIV). These young men were expected also to worship the Babylonian gods. Daniel refused to capitulate to foreign gods and was thrown into a lions' den to die. Yet the lions ignored Daniel, and the king recognized Daniel as a man to whom he should listen.

Often in our own lives, we are offered advancement, honor, and rewards if we forget our God, act like everyone else, and worship at the idols of money, power, or position. Would we be willing to be thrown to the lions for our faith?

Fearsome God, may I honor you more than the expectations of the people around me. Amen.

JUNE 30   NEHEMIAH REBUILDS JERUSALEM

[Nehemiah said,] "Send me to the city in Judah where my ancestors are buried so that I can rebuild it."
(Nehemiah 2:5b TNIV)

At the end of the Babylonian exile, two men, Ezra and Nehemiah, were allowed by King Cyrus to return to Jerusalem, rebuild the walls of the city, and construct a new temple to the God of Abraham, Isaac, and Jacob. Despite much opposition, they reconstructed Jerusalem and erected the temple that Jesus would come to know five hundred years later.

Our journey this month with these twenty-four Old Testament men is now over, but our own journey with God is not. What kind of walls are we building in our own lives? What monuments to our God will last five hundred years? Will our names be remembered in generations yet to come?

In our own lives each of us will wrestle with God, be tempted by women, fight against giants, struggle with our families, and be forced to choose which god to worship. May the example of these Old Testament men remind us to be strong for our families, beneficial to our communities, and faithful to God. Ultimately, the choice to be a man of faith is ours.

Father God, may I remember your men of faith and be remembered as a man of faith, both now and in the days to come. Amen.

JULY

Step Up

STACY L. SPENCER

JULY 1   BE A MAN OF THE NEW ORDER

And by that will, we have been made holy through the sacrifice of the body of Jesus Christ once for all.   (Hebrews 10:10 NIV)

The old agreement between God and man was null and void because of the sinfulness of man. The whole system had been made corrupt because of the actions of the leaders. The kings thought they had accomplished their victories by their own strength. The political leaders had created unjust laws that favored the rich and oppressed those who should have been protected. This time God's people would know him because he would put his laws into their hearts and minds. The new covenant, which is based on our relationship with Jesus, enables us to approach God directly and to have his law in our hearts. It enables us to be free from sin so that we may be reconciled to God. It gives us the power and strength to establish God's Kingdom on earth as it is in heaven.

Even so, we live in a fallen world—a world where the government and church are tainted with man-made agendas. Many of God's warriors are wasting away with disease, infected by their own pride. We must be willing to step up and be men of the new covenant of Jesus Christ—men of the new order. We must be willing to break the cycle of corruption and bring glory, not shame, to God's name.

This month we will explore ways we can "step up" to be men of the new order, men of righteousness.

Dear God, give me again your word so that I might not sin against you. Give me the power and strength to establish your Kingdom on earth. I want to be a man of the new order! Amen.

JULY 2 DON'T BE A DISTANT LOVER

Therefore, get rid of all moral filth and the evil that is so prevalent and humbly accept the word planted in you, which can save you. (James 1:21 NIV)

Marvin Gaye recorded a song called "Distant Lover" in which he lamented about being so many miles from the one he loved. He pleaded with his lover to come back home.

Many times we can be like that distant lover. We can worship God with our lips, but our hearts are far from being yielded to God. We depend on the wrong things to deliver us when we are being besieged. We are drawn away by our own evil desires, and the end result is that, spiritually speaking, we are many miles from God. We can't hear him the way we need to or see him in visions as we used to. But the promise is that if we repent and turn back to God, he *will* restore our sight.

Dear God, I desire to be closer to you than ever before. Too many miles separate us, not because of you, but because of my own drifting. Plant your word in my heart through study, reading, and worship. Draw me nearer to you, blessed Lord. Amen.

JULY 3 DON'T BE FICKLE

He did not need man's testimony about man, for he knew what was in a man. (John 2:25 NIV)

It's amazing that God can move miraculously in our lives, and not long after that, we forget. Jesus didn't get caught up in impressing people with signs and wonders because he knew what was in a man. He knew that even though man can be overwhelmed by God's miraculous power one day, he can be back to business as usual the next day.

Sometimes we're like the Israelites, about whom the prophet Isaiah wrote these words:

> Yet they rebelled and grieved his Holy Spirit. So he turned and became their enemy and he himself fought against them. Then his people recalled the days of old, the days of Moses and his people— where is he who brought them through the sea, with the shepherd of his flock? Where is he who set his Holy Spirit among them? (Isaiah 63:10-11 NIV)

We, too, forget that God rescued us and set us free. So we rebel and grieve his Holy Spirit. And God, as a loving father, disciplines us. Finally, in our desperation and need, we recall God's goodness to us in times past and we cry out to him. The only thing that saves us from total destruction is God's unfailing love.

Thankfully, God knows what is in a man—and loves him still.

Dear God, help me be the kind of disciple who follows you not because of the miracles you have performed but because of who you are. Search me and remove all the human tendencies that cause me to be fickle, replacing them with your Holy Sprit so that I can be faithful. Amen.

JULY 4   DON'T SHRINK BACK

But we are not of those who shrink back and are destroyed, but of those who believe and are saved.   *(Hebrews 10:39 NIV)*

One of the things I always ask the sales clerk when I purchase a new article of clothing is, "When I wash it, will it shrink?" It is important to know that what you made an investment in will not shrink when you use it, so that you are able to use it again. God wants to make sure that after he has invested the blood of Jesus into our lives, we will not shrink back to where we were before he stretched us.

I am always fearfully conscious of where God has brought me. To shrink back would mean to go back to an original shape that is no longer beneficial.

There are things you know that ought to keep you from drawing up and going backward. When you've known and followed God long enough in relationship and he has proved himself, you don't turn back. When you've known what it's like to walk through the fire and through the flood, and your faith has been tried and proved, you don't turn back. After you have done all you know how to do, you must simply stand!

Dear God, make me stretch beyond the ordinary and trifling. Let me reach higher and leave a legacy of righteousness and justice for the next generation to build on. Stretch me for your glory, and don't let me shrink back. Amen.

JULY 5   DON'T GET ENTANGLED

You therefore must endure hardship as a good soldier of Jesus Christ. No one engaged in warfare entangles himself with the affairs of this life, that he may please him who enlisted him as a soldier.   *(2 Timothy 2:3-4 NKJV)*

God calls each of us to a particular mission in life, and we must be faithful to our assignments. When we aren't, we find ourselves embroiled in storms, which are God's way of getting our attention.

When Jonah tried to abandon his mission to the Ninevites, God sent a storm to get his attention. Jonah found himself in the belly of a whale because he was in the belly of a ship trying to get away from the presence of the Lord.

When God calls us into action, we don't have time to be entangled in worldly affairs. In order to please the One who enlisted us, we must be obedient to our assignment even when we don't particularly like where we are being sent. When Jonah accepted his assignment, God used him to save a whole city. What does God have for you that you can't get to because you are entangled? Loose yourself so that God can use you!

ATTENTION! Stand ready, soldier; God is calling your name.

Dear God, I'm ready to disengage from everything that is robbing me of my mission. I'll go wherever you send me as long as you go with me. Amen.

JULY 6   DON'T FALL AWAY

All the nations may walk in the name of their gods; we will walk in the name of the Lord our God for ever and ever.
(Micah 4:5 NIV)

We live in a land of diverse people and cultures. It's easy to get swept away into what everybody else is doing and compromise who we are. Over time, compromise can lead to what I call "falling away." When I think of falling away, I imagine someone abandoning his or her faith in pursuit of what is contrary to the word of God for an extended period of time.

Yet, once we've tasted the goodness of God and had a relationship with Jesus, how can we allow ourselves to fall away? When I think of all Jesus has done for me, I don't want to do anything that would bring him public disgrace. He has done too much for me to fall away! What about you?

Though sometimes we are tempted to fall away, the choice is ours. Let us choose to walk in the name of the Lord our God—today and every day.

Dear God, there's a side of me that wants to get lost for a while, but I know the dangers of getting off your path. Help me remain strong even when the shadow pulls and churns beneath the surface of all that is right. May all I do be pleasing and acceptable in your sight. Amen.

JULY 7   SEEK GOD'S FACE

That is why I was angry with that generation, and I said, "Their hearts are always going astray, and they have not known my ways."
(Hebrews 3:10 NIV)

Growing up in rural Kentucky, I didn't have many choices as to what I was going to watch on television, especially when I was out of school and at the mercies of my grandmother. One of her favorite things to do was to watch soap operas, particularly *As the World Turns*. These shows were intriguing because they were filled with lust, betrayal, adultery, and dysfunction; something dramatic was happening every day. You could miss a month and the same saga would be going on a month later.

Perhaps this is how God feels while watching our drama as the world turns, hoping every day that one generation will finally get out of the cycle of dysfunction. Let us seek his face and return to him.

Dear God, bring my generation out of the cycle of drama and sin. Teach us your ways and heal us. Help me seek your face each and every day. Amen.

JULY 8   PAY ATTENTION

We must pay more careful attention, therefore, to what we have heard, so that we do not drift away. **(Hebrews 2:1 NIV)**

I was out on the lake with my brother-in-law, and the rope to my anchor got twisted around the boat's propeller. It took me about thirty minutes to painstakingly untangle myself. By the time I looked up, the wind and the waves had caused us to drift away from the small island where we had been fishing.

It's so easy to find yourself drifting away when you are preoccupied with something else, especially when your anchor loses its grip. As fishers of men, we have to pay attention so that while we are untangling the affairs of life we don't drift into pop culture or take on the dysfunctional ways of the world.

Sin can become entertaining if you don't pay attention.

Dear God, I pray that I will not be entangled in sin and drift away from you. Keep me connected to the anchor that grips the solid rock. Help me pay careful attention each day to what I have heard and learned of you and your ways. Amen.

JULY 9   SEPARATE YOURSELF

Perhaps the reason he was separated from you for a little while was that you might have him back for good.
(Philemon 1:15 NIV)

Separation is never really easy at first, particularly if you've become dependent upon someone in your life. Philemon was dependent upon Onesimus, his slave; but since Onesimus was now a believer, Paul challenged Philemon to receive Onesimus back as a brother, not a slave.

Separation helps us put things in proper perspective through reflection and internal examination. We see things we might not have seen had we not been away. We don't know what we are slaves to until we separate ourselves from what we are dependent upon.

Recently, on a spiritual retreat at a monastery, I discovered that I was dependent upon luxury, noise, technology, and companionship. But it was good that I separated, so that when I came back, I came back free and not a slave.

What are you dependent upon? Perhaps you need to separate yourself for a time so that you may be set free for good.

Dear God, help me overcome my fears of being alone and facing myself and my dependency on things and people. Help me make wise decisions about my future. Show me the right moves to make and the right relationships to be in. Amen.

JULY 10   CRY OUT IN REVERENT SUBMISSION

During the days of Jesus' life on earth, he offered up prayers and petitions with loud cries and tears to the one who could save him from death, and he was heard because of his reverent submission.   *(Hebrews 5:7 NIV)*

There is so much that can separate us from God if we let it, but the common denominator of it all is sin. Idolatry and waywardness can cause us to be spiritually famished. It is only when we turn back to God and offer prayers in reverent submission that he hears us. When we cry out earnestly, God will hear us and save us.

Hosea 13:6 (NIV) tells us: "When I [God] fed them, they were satisfied; when they were satisfied, they became proud; then they forgot me." When we are well fed, we have the tendency to forget how to cry out to God. It's when we think we don't need anything that we forget to cry out. Sometimes success and prosperity can be an enemy to God. We must be careful not to make those things our God.

Dear God, get me past the point of material comfort and help me mature. Teach me to reverently submit to you. Amen.

JULY 11   ACCEPT GOD'S MERCY AND FORGIVENESS

Who is a God like you, who pardons sin and forgives the transgression of the remnant of his inheritance? You do not stay angry forever but delight to show mercy.   *(Micah 7:18 NIV)*

Even in the midst of judgment and getting what we deserve, God is merciful. Time and time again God took back his people Israel after they had betrayed him.

People are fickle—here today and gone tomorrow. There are relatives who haven't spoken in years because of some falling out. Some business partners left angry because of a disagreement they had. A husband and wife split because of irreconcilable differences. People get mad and hold grudges, but the good news is that God's mercies endure forever.

If we were to attempt to pay for our own transgressions, we couldn't come up with enough sacrifices to cover the cost. Thank God that the lesser is blessed by the greater (see Hebrews 7:7). Jesus lay down his life for us, and that sacrifice covered all our sins forever.

Dear God, thank you that you do not stay angry but delight to show mercy. Thank you for the sacrifice that Jesus made for me, which covers me for life. Amen.

JULY 12   BE RESTORED

"Restore all that was hers, and all the proceeds of the field from the day that she left the land until now."   *(2 Kings 8:6 NKJV)*

There are seasons of famine when nothing seems to be growing in your life. In these times you must remain faithful to all God tells you to do.

Elisha warned the widow to flee to the land of the Philistines for provisions. She had to depend on her enemies for food during the famine. It seemed like a strange command, but she was obedient to the prophet's instruction.

When you're obedient to what God tells you, he has a way of synchronizing his provision with your obedience. While the widow was walking toward the king, the king was inquiring of Elisha's servant about the prophet. He wanted to know more about this great man of God, his miracles, and how God had used him. When the servant saw the woman approaching, he said, "Here comes the widow whose son Elisha raised from the dead." The king said, "Restore!"

When you are obedient through a "famine," going where God tells you, even in the midst of your enemies, God will restore.

Dear God, I might be experiencing some dry places in my life, but I'm believing that you will provide. I trust you, even when I can't trace you. Amen.

JULY 13   LET GOD RAISE YOU UP

You have loved righteousness and hated wickedness; therefore God, your God, has set you above your companions by anointing you with the oil of joy.   *(Hebrews 1:9 NIV)*

All of the kings of Israel and Judah had a choice to love righteousness or to love evil. For those who chose to follow God, he extended their years. It seems that even the good kings started out strong; where they messed up was in not tearing down the high places.

If we would learn how to love what is right and to hate evil, God would raise us up over our companions and anoint us with the oil of joy. Instead, we wind up paying tribute to other kings while exhausting our resources, replicating their worship at the expense of our relationship with God and exposing ourselves to spiritual assignation.

When we follow in the way of David and serve the Lord whole-heartedly, we will experience the raising effect—not the razing consequences of disobedience.

Dear God, teach me to trust you for all that I need. Don't leave me in the hands of the wicked ones. I know I've done wrong, but I ask you to forgive me of my sins and wash me with the blood of Jesus. Amen.

JULY 14   SILENCE YOUR CRITICS

For it is God's will that by doing good you should silence the ignorant talk of foolish men.   *(1 Peter 2:15 NIV)*

How do we silence our critics? By succeeding in the face of opposition. No one knew this better than Nehemiah.

Nehemiah was rebuilding the walls of Jerusalem when his enemies tried to distract him; so he told them he was too busy to come down to talk with them! When you are doing something for God, you don't have time to entertain every negative comment that foolish men bring your way. Let your work speak for you.

My son came to me the other day in tears because people had been teasing him about his short stature. He said, "Daddy, they are saying things that I can't ignore anymore."

I told him that the way to silence those ignorant people was to continue to succeed in life and to pay more attention to those who love him instead of listening to those who don't know what they're talking about.

Don't listen to your critics; concentrate on the work God has given you to do and focus on those who love you. Your success will silence the opposition for you!

Dear God, thank you for being the silencer of those who would come against me. Silence ignorant men and make me resilient in the face of opposition so that I may do the work you have called me to do. Amen.

JULY 15   CONSECRATE YOURSELF

In everything that he undertook in the service of God's temple and in obedience to the law and the commands, he sought his God and worked wholeheartedly. And so he prospered.
(2 Chronicles 31:21 NIV)

There is no success outside of obeying God's word. We must be obedient to what God says do if we expect to receive his blessings.

Hezekiah told the Levites and priests to consecrate them-selves—to clean themselves up—and to remove anything detestable from the temple. After this, the people were able to come back into the Lord's house to make heaps of sacrifices.

What are the detestable things inside your spirit that need to be removed so that you can discover God's will? It's time to reopen God's temple. The apostle Paul writes: "Do you not know that your body is a temple of the Holy Spirit?" (1 Corinthians 6:19 NIV). Every day you must consecrate God's temple with the word of God and fumigate it with prayer.

Dear God, draw me close to you. Help me consecrate myself each day so that I may hear you, receive your direction, and obey. Amen.

JULY 16   BE HOLY

As obedient children, do not conform to the evil desires you had when you lived in ignorance. But just as he who called you is holy, so be holy in all you do; for it is written: "Be holy, because I am holy."   *(1 Peter 1:14-16 NIV)*

It is funny to see my boys imitating me. My four-year-old had on my shoes as he scooted across the floor, mimicking me. It was hilarious. He's not big enough to walk in my shoes, but he was sure trying.

God has some big shoes that we will never fit, but he sent some-one more like us for us to mimic or imitate. His name is Jesus. When we were ignorant, we had certain desires and ways that did not please God; but as we come to have the mind of Christ, we learn how to "walk"—to be Holy, just as our Daddy is Holy.

Though our steps are awkward at first, we become more skilled in our steps as Christ is revealed in us. As Psalm 37:23 (NKJV) says: "The steps of a good man are ordered by the LORD, / And He delights in his way."

In all that you do, let God guide your footsteps so that you can get to where he's trying to take you.

Dear God, teach me to walk in holiness and deny myself of evil desires. My deepest desire is to please you. Walk with me, Jesus, until I get this holiness thing down pat. Amen.

JULY 17   BE ABOUT THE WORK OF
                                                   RIGHTEOUSNESS

The Lord is not slow in keeping his promise, as some under-stand slowness. He is patient with you, not wanting anyone to perish, but everyone to come to repentance.   (2 Peter 3:9 NIV)

It is comforting to know that God is patient with us. How stub-born we are, trying to do what we want even when we know it is wrong. Yet God still loves us. The day is fast approaching when God's judgment will come, and we don't want him to catch us with our work undone.

We cannot give in to the ways of the wicked and serve their gods. We cannot open our beds to them and become intimate with them.

Instead, we must be about the work of righteousness. True righteousness is to do justice and to take care of the poor and needy. God works righteousness through us if we avail ourselves to him.

Dear God, thank you for being patient with us. Thank you for forgiving me of my sins and holding onto me even when I let go. Help me be about the work you have called me to do, so that others may come to repentance and come to know you. Amen.

JULY 18   GROW IN RIGHTEOUSNESS

Therefore, my brothers, be all the more eager to make your calling and election sure. For if you do these things, you will never fall.   *(2 Peter 1:10 NIV)*

Living the way God would have us live is not easy, particularly when we are surrounded by such corruption. But by the power of God, it is possible. God gives us the prescription for growing in righteousness in 2 Peter 1:5-7 (NIV):

> Add to your faith goodness; and to goodness, knowledge; and to knowledge, self-control; and to self-control, perseverance; and to perseverance, godliness; and to godliness, brotherly kindness; and to brotherly kindness, love.

God has given us his divine power to participate in his divine nature so that we can escape the corruption in the world caused by evil desires. God promises that the righteous will stand and flourish. As the psalmist writes: "They will still bear fruit in old age, they will stay fresh and green" (Psalm 92:14 NIV).

Dear God, plant me in righteousness in your house. Help me increase in righteousness and participate in your divine will. Take away evil desires so that I may give you glory, even in my latter years. I need you in order to grow. Amen.

JULY 19   WALK IN A MANNER PLEASING TO GOD

For the eyes of the Lord are on the righteous and his ears are attentive to their prayer.   *(1 Peter 3:12 NIV)*

It is comforting and convicting to know that the Lord is watching over his people. Isaiah says the Lord is a shepherd who carries his lambs in his arms close to his bosom. When we walk in a manner that is pleasing to him, he watches us and listens to our prayers. We must learn how to wait for the Lord so that he can renew our strength. As I am writing this, I am at Saint Meinrad Monastery, waiting for the Lord to renew my strength. I don't want to stumble and fall. Like Paul said, I don't want to be disqualified after having preached to others.

It's important to know that God is watching over us and hears our supplication. In the event that we make mistakes, the good news is that if we confess our sins, God is faithful to forgive us of our sins; and God will turn back to us once again.

Dear God, teach me how to wait for you. Grant me the power to live righteously so that I may help liberate your people from spiritual darkness. Keep me from falling, and let me be a stepping-stone, not a stumbling block. Amen.

JULY 20   WALK ALONG THE RIGHT HIGHWAY

And a highway will be there; it will be called the Way of Holiness. The unclean will not journey on it; it will be for those who walk in that Way; wicked fools will not go about on it.
(Isaiah 35:8 NIV)

There is a road that every believer must travel upon if he is to follow God. Jesus said, "I am the way, and the truth, and the life" (John 14:6). When the early apostles and new believers first went out, meeting in homes, they were the ones who followed the Way.

The righteous are the only ones who can travel this highway. The result of righteousness is peace, quietness, and security. The basis of righteousness is to love God with all your heart, mind, soul, and strength; and to love your neighbor as you love yourself.

I saw a sign the other day that read: "How long must a man travel down a road before he admits that he is lost?" Are you traveling down the wrong road?

162

Dear God, be gracious to me. I long for you. Be my strength every morning and my salvation in time of distress. When I am traveling on the wrong highway, rescue me from myself and send me in the right direction. Amen.

JULY 21   BE STILL AND KNOW

God is our refuge and strength, an ever-present help in trouble.... Be still, and know that I am God.   (Psalm 46:1, 10 NIV)

Oftentimes we scramble around looking for help in all the wrong places. We must be still and know that God is our help. We exhaust ourselves by depending on the wrong people and shutting down God's temple in pursuit of other gods. We must remember that only God can provide for us in supernatural ways and bring life where there was only death.

God is the source and the strength of our lives. When we give God praise, we remind ourselves that he is the author and finisher of our faith; he will finish what he started, and through it all he will be our refuge and strength.

Today, be still and allow God to be your source, your strength, and your ever-present help.

Dear God, teach me how to be still and know that you are in full control. Help me not to turn to ungodly men for help, because in the end I will pay more for not waiting for you. Thank you for being my refuge, my strength, and my help. Amen.

JULY 22   BE PATIENT FOR GOD'S DELIVERANCE

Be patient, then, brothers, until the Lord's coming. See how the farmer waits for the land to yield its valuable crop and how patient he is for the autumn and spring rains. (James 5:7 NIV)

There are seasons of abundance in life. At those times, you are sure of God's providence. Everything seems to be going or falling your way. Then suddenly there is a break—a change. We seem to be stuck between spring and autumn—between the seasons of rain. We wonder if God has removed his favor. But perhaps God is waiting to prove himself, waiting to see if we will be patient for his deliverance.

Hezekiah was one of the greatest kings of Israel. He had been faithful to God in shutting down the high places, but the king of Assyria had laid siege to Judah and destroyed other cities. It looked like Hezekiah was next, but the prophet Isaiah reminded the king that God would come through. Hezekiah was fearful, but he prayed to God. He was stuck between spring and autumn, under siege, but he trusted God even though the world seemed to be against him. And God was faithful.

Dear God, it seems I am stuck between spring and autumn. The rains have stopped, but you have not allowed the storage bin to run dry. I'm shaking, but I'm faithful that you will come through. Amen.

JULY 23   REMEMBER THAT SOMETHING
                           GOOD IS COMING

When a farmer plows for planting, does he plow continually? Does he keep on breaking up and harrowing the soil?
(Isaiah 28:24 NIV)

In order to get the ground ready, a farmer must break up the soil that has been idle and hardened by the winter weather. He must remove the weeds and stones. In days past, rivals who wanted to stop the progress of growth might have tossed those stones into the field.

Spiritually speaking, God must plow our "fields" so that he may plant good seed in us that will produce a sixty- to hundredfold return on our harvest. Our fields can become overrun with weeds, habits, and addictions—or be hardened by grief, tragedy, and financial struggles. Oftentimes, the condition of our fields is a result of what we have allowed to occur in our lives. In order to get our fields ready, God sometimes allows tribulation and testing. The trials of life are God's way of getting a harvest out of what we messed up or what others have tried to sabotage.

When you are in the midst of a trial, remember that it is a time of preparation and will not last forever. Once your field is ready for planting, God will sow seed that will yield a harvest. Something good is coming!

Dear God, turn my "ground" over and sow seed in me that will reap what will give you glory. May something good come out of this inner struggle. Amen.

JULY 24   KNOW THAT YOU CAN'T BE SHAKEN

Therefore, since we are receiving a kingdom that cannot be shaken, let us be thankful, and so worship God acceptably with reverence and awe.   *(Hebrews 12:28 NIV)*

I grew up playing basketball. We prided ourselves in not being shaken. Being shaken meant that the guy you were guarding dribbled so well that he left you standing there confused while he went past you to score. Good defenders would brag, "You can't shake me."

Because we belong to Christ, we can't be shaken. As his heirs, we are receiving his Kingdom, a Kingdom that cannot be shaken. And Jesus himself said: "My Father, who has given them to me, is greater than all; no one can snatch them out of my Father's hand" (John 10:29 NIV).

A time is coming when God will shake the heavens and the earth; only what belongs to God is going to remain. The prophet Isaiah writes: "See, the LORD is going to lay waste the earth and devastate it.... The city is left in ruins, its gate is battered to pieces. So will it be on the earth and among the nations, as when an olive tree is beaten" (24:1, 12-13 NIV).

God is going to shake some things up. But if we belong to Jesus, we can't be shaken.

Dear Heavenly Father, help me hold on to your unchanging hand. When you beat the olive tree, may I be found faithful. Thank you for the promise that you will not allow me to be shaken from your presence. Amen.

JULY 25   WALK FEARLESSLY THROUGH THE FIRE

When you pass through the waters, I will be with you; and when you pass through the rivers, they will not sweep over you. When you walk through the fire, you will not be burned; the flames will not set you ablaze.   *(Isaiah 43:2 NIV)*

In the movie *Little Miss Sunshine*, one of the characters who is depressed, even suicidal, speaks to a young man who has repressed his emotions to the point of silence. This silent young man finally speaks up to say he wishes he could skip though adolescence and just wake up grown. The suicidal man, who has since recovered, quotes an author by the name of Marcel Proust, who said that the times in his life when he suffered were the times when he learned the most. The suicidal man tells the teenage boy that if he sleeps during the high-school years, he will miss all that good suffering.

Our suffering shapes who we are. We must learn to adapt to it, allowing God to use it in our lives. We can trust him, because he has promised to be with us through the fire and to keep us from being burned.

Dear God, thank you for being with me through all of my trials and tribulations. Thank you for blessing me even when I didn't acknowledge you. Thank you for bringing me through the fire. I will come forth as pure gold! Amen.

JULY 26   KNOW WHO IS KEEPING YOU ALIVE

Even to your old age and gray hairs I am he, I am he who will sustain you. I have made you and I will carry you; I will sustain you and I will rescue you.   *(Isaiah 46:4 NIV)*

Carl Jung once said: "The patient must be alone if he is to find out what it is that supports him when he can no longer support himself." Spending time alone with God has brought me to the revelation that God is the keeper of my soul. He is truly the one who is keeping me alive.

It is only when we come to the end of ourselves that we realize

God is the one holding us up. We need to acknowledge that God is the one who has sustained us, carried us, and rescued us. It is not a trick of the ego to believe that if we humble ourselves, God will lift us up. The job of the enemy is to sow doubt into our minds so that we believe we are self-sustaining, but the Spirit reminds us that in God—and in God alone—we "live and move and have our being" (Acts 17:28 NIV).

Dear God, help me stand for righteousness and not succumb to the evil desires of my narcissistic self. Fill me with your Holy Spirit so that I may know your will and be a man of substance, knowing full well that it is you who keeps me. Order my steps and those of my family, church, and business. Amen.

JULY 27   BE A VOICE IN THE WILDERNESS

John replied in the words of Isaiah the prophet, "I am the voice of one calling in the desert, 'Make straight the way for the Lord.' "   *(John 1:23 NIV)*

Ministry is not about self-recognition. It is always tempting to make it about us, but it isn't. We must try to defer attention back to Christ, because a ministry about us dies with us.

God should get all the glory. When people come to any church, it is because Jesus drew them there. The pastor must simply be a voice crying out in the wilderness, trying to make straight paths so Jesus can enter in.

Likewise, each and every believer can be a voice in the desert, helping make a way for Jesus to touch others' lives. Our lives should reflect the glory of Jesus, who was sent "to preach good news to the poor.... To bind up the brokenhearted, to proclaim freedom for the captives and release from darkness for the prisoners, to proclaim the year of the LORD's favor" (Isaiah 61:1-2a NIV).

Dear God, move me out of the way so that people can see Jesus. I am your servant, your slave. Use me to draw others to you and to help connect them to the Body of Christ so that you get all the glory. Amen.

JULY 28   ENTER INTO GOD'S REST

For anyone who enters God's rest also rests from his own work,
just as God did from his.   *(Hebrews 4:10 NIV)*

It is important for us to pull over and rest from all of our work. To
keep grinding without a break can lead us to frustration—and to
the delusion that we are losing when actually we are winning. If
we focus on the wicked, it would seem that they are winning with
their wealth and wicked ways, but God does not forget. God is
mindful of his people even when we are not consistent in what we
should be doing.

   We can wear ourselves out by focusing on the wrong things. Our
focus should not be on those who seem to be doing better than we
are but who are not in the will of God. In due time, God promises
that he will reward us if we do not faint. He reminds us that the
race is not given to the swift or the strong but to those who endure
to the end. Rest is necessary in order to finish what God has for us
to do.

Dear God, help me enter into your rest—as I read your word—
so that I will not enter into the disobedience of the wicked. Help
me not envy arrogant men but trust you in all my ways. Amen.

JULY 29   SEEK THE LORD WHILE
                                           HE MAY BE FOUND

Seek the LORD while he may be found; call on him while he is
near.   *(Isaiah 55:6 NIV)*

God has a "right now" anointing for this generation. So many
young people are poised for spiritual empowerment, yet they are
caught up in worldly pursuits.

   I conducted a funeral for a nineteen-year-old man the other day.
He was such a promising young man, but he got caught up in
youthful pursuits that led to his untimely death. If only he had
sought the Lord while he was near, things could have turned out
differently.

We are in a "right now" season when God is wooing his people back to him, but we must heed his voice. The writer of Ecclesiastes tells us to enjoy our youth and to follow all the desires of our hearts; but he also says that God will bring us to judgment for all that we do. The answer, or the balance, is to "remember your Creator in the days of your youth, before the days of trouble come and the years approach when you will say, 'I find no pleasure in them'" (Ecclesiastes 12:1 NIV).

Will you seek the Lord today? How can you help others seek his face?

Dear God, help all of us wake up and realize that we need you every day. There is a generation of young people that we can help seek your face while there's still time. Give me the courage to speak truth in love and reach your young ones. Amen.

JULY 30   HAVE HOPE FOR A BETTER DAY

They will neither harm nor destroy on all my holy mountain, for the earth will be full of the knowledge of the LORD as the waters cover the sea.   **(Isaiah 11:9 NIV)**

At times it seems that evil has taken over and there is nobody standing for righteousness. Recently, some adults gave a toddler Ecstasy and laughed as they videotaped her reactions. The news replayed the image over and over one morning as authorities looked for the perpetrators.

We shudder at such atrocities. Yet we have hope. God told the prophet Isaiah that a day will come when righteousness and justice will prevail, wild beasts will be tame, and "a little child will lead them" (Isaiah 11:6). We can only hope that this new generation of young people will find a better way, that they will help bring forth a day when crime will come down, racism will desist, and war will be no more. We pray.

Dear God, let your Holy Sprit rest upon us so that we can lead your people in the right direction. Raise up a new generation who will follow you wholeheartedly. Change the nature of the beasts around us so that people can find a better way. Allow the oppressed to beat the yoke of slavery and be free at last. Amen.

JULY 31   KEEP LOOKING AHEAD IN FAITH

He regarded disgrace for the sake of Christ as of greater value than the treasures of Egypt, because he was looking ahead to his reward.   *(Hebrews 11:26 NIV)*

Our faith in God is what pulls us out of difficult times and bad situations. We can act with courage and strength because we know there is Someone who supercedes all natural pursuits who will be working on our behalf. When we begin with the end in mind, it determines much of what we do.

So it was with Moses. His faith in God is what pulled him out of Egypt. He was able to leave the treasures of Egypt behind because of the pull of God on his life. After striking the Egyptian, Moses fled to Midian; and it was there that he had a dramatic encounter with God that led to his life's calling and the freedom of God's people.

It will be the same with you. God will "call you out" and pull you into a life of purpose and freedom—by faith. Keep looking ahead!

Dear God, help me forsake "Egypt" and walk in freedom. I've come this far by faith, and I know you haven't brought me this far to leave me. Help me keep looking and moving ahead in faith. Amen.

AUGUST

Holy and Acceptable Service

JOSEPH L. HARRIS

AUGUST 1   MEN WHO MAKE A DIFFERENCE

Present your bodies as a living sacrifice, holy and acceptable to God. *(Romans 12:1)*

Tom was a busy man. He ran his own company, traveled extensively, and belonged to several civic clubs. When he joined a local church, his schedule prevented him from being as active as he had thought he would be. He became a spectator having little time or motivation to get involved.

Dietrich Bonhoeffer said that being a disciple of Jesus Christ is more than just giving him impressive lip service. We present ourselves for service as our response to the grace that God has showed us. Church membership is more about responsibilities and expectations than privileges and benefits. We are to use our gifts as part of the total ministry of the church.

Tom eventually got involved with his son's Eagle Scout project in the church—a republication of a World War II devotional book. As Tom helped his son complete the book, he found himself becoming more involved with his church. Tom began to realize that God's grace meant that he had to reprioritize what was most important.

This month we will explore what it means to respond to God's grace with lives of devotion and service—service that is holy and acceptable to God. This is what will transform us from spectators in life to men who make a difference.

Lord, help me remember that you call me to serve and not to sit, so that I might make a difference. Amen.

AUGUST 2   A MAN'S THOUGHT LIFE

Whatever is true, whatever is honorable, whatever is just, what-ever is pure, whatever is pleasing, whatever is commend-able...think about these things.   *(Philippians 4:8)*

We men probably get in the most trouble with our thought life. Some of us rationalize that as long as we keep a thought in our mind and do not act on it, it will be OK.

This rationale ignores the fact you are hurting yourself and God. The writer of Proverbs reminds us that "as [a man] thinks in his heart, so is he" (Proverbs 23:7 NKJV). Your thought life can be destructive if it dwells on those things that destroy you rather than build you up.

Bill was in the grips of pornography. He could not stop thinking about the images that it projected in his mind. He finally realized that it was destroying him, and he sought help. His counselor told him to use Philippians 4:8 as a guide every time he started to think about pornographic images. He was to say to himself, "I will put images in my mind of things that are just, pure, pleasing, and commendable." Although he found it difficult at first, repeated use of this exercise eventually freed him from the bondage of a destructive thought life.

Lord, free me from a thought life that is self-destructive, and give me a thought life that reflects whatever is just, pure, pleas-ing, and commendable. Amen.

AUGUST 3   A FEW GOOD MEN

And the doors of the house where the disciples had met were locked for fear.   *(John 20:19)*

The picture we have of the disciples after the Crucifixion is of a group of frightened men behind locked doors. Paralyzed by fear, they thought it was over. Jesus was dead; the cause seemed hopeless and the movement dead.

Danish philosopher Sören Kierkegaard told the story of a fire crew racing toward a burning building. As they got closer, they saw hundreds of townspeople standing in the street with squirt guns!

The fire chief yelled, "What are you doing? Why do you have those water pistols?"

The citizens replied, "We are all gathered here to support your efforts! We all believe in the good work you are doing for our community, and we want to show our appreciation by making a contribution."

The fire chief yelled, "Get out of the way! A fire like this is not for well-meaning people who want to make limited contributions! It demands firemen who are ready to give their lives to put out the flames!"

Jesus' call demands our all, not just occasional contributions. We must be willing to give up our lives to find life. He is calling a few good men to be brave, bold, and fearless.

Lord, help me fulfill the demands of the Kingdom with spirit-led boldness. Amen.

AUGUST 4   AN UNLIKELY PAIR

One day Peter and John were going up to the temple at the hour of prayer.   ***(Acts 3:1)***

One of the most unusual pairings in the Bible is that of Peter and John. These men were partners in fishing, preparing the last Passover meal for Jesus, running to the tomb, and ministering to the Samaritans. They appear to be opposites, yet they were the best of friends. Peter was a doer, often brazen and always bold. John is described as quiet and cerebral—an idealist, poet, and dreamer. How did this unlikely pairing occur?

When I was growing up, my best friend was my opposite. He was short; I am tall. He was white; I am African American. He liked rock; I like soul. What made us good friends was our respect for each other and our mutual love of basketball. This common love helped form a strong bond that overcame any perceived differences.

Peter and John had their love for Jesus in common. They were prayer partners, they were concerned about hurting people, and they desired for everyone to experience the love of Christ. These common interests can help break down any barriers of difference between believers.

Lord, pair me with a brother who has a heart for you so that we might proclaim the saving message of Christ to all. Amen.

AUGUST 5   A MAN OF UNCOMMON LIFE

"And I tell you, you are Peter, and on this rock I will build my church."   *(Matthew 16:18)*

Tiger Woods is a champion golfer. What makes Tiger a champion is his skill, his "fire in the belly," and his unshakeable belief that he can perform his best when it means the most. His willingness to work hard at maintaining an edge through working out, improving his game, and remaining teachable—along with his desire to outwork the average golfer—keeps him at the top. Tiger has the kind of spirit that separates ordinary men from those who achieve extraordinary things.

The disciple Peter had that kind of spirit. He was passionate, bold, and skilled in what he believed. He was not satisfied with the mundane or the ordinary. He seemed to want the best for himself, the movement he was a part of, and those who followed him. He had a "fire in the belly"—a desire to serve Christ and do whatever was necessary for the cause of Christ. He too had the kind of spirit that separates ordinary men from those who achieve extraordinary things. He was a member of the community of the "uncommon life," whose members believe they can accomplish anything for Christ.

Thank you, Lord, for calling me to be, not like other men, but like Jesus, who makes my life "uncommon." Amen.

AUGUST 6   AN IMPORTANT ROLE

Fathers, do not provoke your children to anger, but bring them up in the discipline and instruction of the Lord.
(Ephesians 6:4)

Fathers help shape the lives of children when they are involved with them.

James Hill, a father of three daughters, wrote a book titled *Becoming a Father—The Real Work of a Man's Soul.* In it he describes how his girls lived at home for more than twenty years. Often when he got home they were already asleep. He was there for most emergencies and usually attended special events. He would rationalize that when he had to work long hours, it was for them. Besides, they were girls, and that made their mother the "main parent."

As they grew up, he began to question his involvement in their lives. What were their real interests? What were some of the things that troubled them? What were their hopes, joys, and expectations of life? James concluded that he was not as significant a part of their lives growing up as he could have been.

Fathers play a crucial role in families. The apostle Paul thought the role was so critical that he admonished fathers to take an active rather than a passive role in child rearing and teaching children the faith.

Lord, help all fathers become involved in the lives of their children, particularly in faith development. Amen.

AUGUST 7   MEN WHO CARE

Extend hospitality to strangers.   *(Romans 12:13b)*

Bill ran his own company. His desire was to create a relationship with his workers that was more collegial than boss and worker. He tried to convince employees when he hired them that the atmosphere he wanted in the workplace would be one of equality. He wanted them to know that he cared first and foremost about them as persons.

One day Bill noticed one of his workers was hurting and appeared depressed and distraught. Bill reached out to the employee and asked him what he could do to help. He found out that the employee had just been notified that his wife had been diagnosed with cancer. Bill ordered him to go home and stay home (with pay) until he and his wife had worked through the shock of the news.

Paul told the Romans to share with people in need and to practice radical hospitality to those who suffer. Bill's employees soon found out that he cared as much for them as he did for what they did for his company. Remember, people don't care how much you know until they know how much you care!

Lord, help me care enough for others that I am as sensitive to their needs as to my own. Amen.

AUGUST 8   EGYPTIAN MENTALITY

"Let us choose a captain, and go back to Egypt."
(Numbers 14:4)

A man had completed thirty-four years behind bars. He had become accustomed to prison life, and the thought of being free frightened him. He thought, *Where will I go? What will I do? What will become of me?* After his release, he ended up cold, hungry, and homeless. He decided that he had to get back to the one place where he had a job, food, and a bed. He deliberately broke into a store, let himself get caught, and went back to prison.

The people of Israel, having been freed from slavery, got to a point where they could not handle the responsibility of freedom. They developed a mentality of enslavement that kept them wanting to work in the enemy's camp.

There is a particular kind of African ant that attacks other ants and enslaves them. As they kill off ants in the colony, they carry their larvae to their colony. As the kidnapped larvae hatch, they assume that this is the colony where they were conceived and go to work on behalf of the colony that destroyed their parents.

Christ calls us to live free as people resisting sin.

Thank you, Lord, for the freedom your salvation brings. Help me live free, never wanting to return to the enemy's camp. Amen.

AUGUST 9   END GAME

"But the one who endures to the end will be saved."
(Matthew 10:22)

My dad was a great salt-water fisherman. When he hit a snag in the line while fishing on the bottom, he knew that he had several options. He could release the tension on the line. That might cause the lead or hook to break free on its own accord. He also could cut the line, or simply wait a minute or two. He saved valuable tackle and avoided frustration by waiting. Sometimes a crab might come by and free up the line while pulling at the bait, or the current might loosen it.

The natural reaction to a snag in the line is to jerk it. Sometimes my dad would move around, trying to pull it free from a different angle than where it had snagged. He discovered that if the angle of the line was altered and the pull from above was redirected, the obstruction might give way.

Life is a journey through difficulties and problems. The test of our faith is how we manage to endure the journey with all that comes before us. Waiting, praying, and looking at things from different perspectives allows us to endure life's challenges until the end.

Lord, help me always get new perspectives on life's troubles through waiting, meditation, and prayer. Amen.

AUGUST 10   HIDDEN POTENTIAL

"No one after lighting a lamp puts it under the bushel basket."
(Matthew 5:15)

A story is told about a sheep rancher who could barely afford to keep up with the expenses of his ranch. He depended on government subsidies to keep his family fed. He was considered "land poor," owning plenty of acreage but unable to make it produce financially.

One day a seismographic crew came and asked permission to drill a wildcat oil well. At 1,115 feet they struck a huge oil reservoir. The first well came in at 80,000 barrels a day. Subsequent wells were more than twice as large. In fact, thirty years later the wells were still flowing to the tune of 125,000 barrels a day. The "land poor" rancher became a multimillionaire. He had been unaware of his resources just beneath his feet. He had not tapped into his potential.

Believers are to be the light of this world, showing off our gifts and graces on behalf of God's Kingdom work. We are not to hide our talents or shy away from fully using them. Not sure what gifts you have? Ask God to show you. They may be just below the surface waiting to be tapped!

Lord, help me tap into my God-given potential every day by using the gifts and graces you give me, as everyone, for Kingdom work. Amen.

AUGUST 11　　EXTRAORDINARY RESPONSIBILITY

For the people had a mind to work.　　　*(Nehemiah 4:6b)*

Nehemiah was the cupbearer in the king's army. One day friends visited him from his native Jerusalem and described to him the horrendous conditions in his homeland. The wall that had surrounded the city was no more; the people were hungry and in need. Upon hearing this, Nehemiah was moved to action.

He asked the king if he could take a leave of absence and go back and help his people. Upon his return, conditions were worse than he had been told. The people were demoralized, depressed, and defeated. They felt they could not improve their condition. They lacked a leader who could inspire them.

Nehemiah became that leader. He encouraged them, thought positively, and made plans to rebuild the city. He calmed down those who were afraid of being attacked by reminding them that

God would fight off all attackers. They then developed a mind to work.

Nehemiah could have stayed in the security of his cushy cup-bearer job. However, he felt a responsibility to help his people out of their malaise and defeatist attitude. Our faith walk often requires us to take on extraordinary leadership responsibility for the sake of God's Kingdom work.

Lord, thank you for calling an ordinary person like me to take on extraordinary responsibility in your Kingdom work. Amen.

AUGUST 12   FINDING DIRECTION

There is a way that seems right to a man, but in the end it leads to death.   *(Proverbs 14:12 NIV)*

Men generally do not ask for directions, including life directions. Even if a guy uses a map, it will not show all the roadblocks, detours, and other obstacles in front of him leading to possible destruction. In life, we encounter detours of self-justification, barricades of self-reliance, and wrong turns that lead to dead ends; yet rarely do we get out and ask for help.

Three men felt God calling them to sit with terminally ill patients at the local hospital. One of those patients was my brother, who, despite all my encouragement, had never given his life to Christ. These three men sat with him and led him to Christ. Praise God that these men listened to the calling of God and not to the urgings of men.

The prophet Jeremiah reminds us that "a man's life is not his own; it is not for man to direct his steps" (Jeremiah 10:23 NIV). Renowned British pastor Charles H. Spurgeon once said, "He who is his own guide is guided by a fool. He that trusteth to his own understanding proves that he has no understanding."*

God, help me make decisions about my life and my actions based on directions from you. Amen.

* "An Instructive Truth" (sermon delivered June 22, 1876; published July 21, 1904), www.spurgeon.org.

AUGUST 13   REAL HAPPINESS

*Happy are those who do not follow the advice of the
wicked, . . . but their delight is in the law of the LORD.*
(Psalm 1:1-2a)

The Pharisees of Jesus' day were men who loved recognition; they
played by religious rules and presented an exterior that often did
not match their interiors. They differed little from men today who
live on their own resources and resourcefulness and are self-
centered and self-directed.

The goal of such men often is to live autonomous lives. The
word *autonomy* comes from two Greek words: *auto* (self) and
nomos (law). Men like this often act like a law unto themselves—
independent, accountable to no one, having little time or interest
in others or in God.

Godly men, however, are those who have found true happiness
in always being open and connected to God. They are teachable
because they are lifelong students and are engaged in the
instructions that God gives throughout life. They live out of all
God's revelation for their lives discovered through lifelong reflection, meditation, and study. For these men, God's instructions
are not just rules to be obeyed. They are lifestyles adopted out of
their relationship with the living Christ.

*Lord, help me develop a lifestyle founded on your teachings.
May I grow in the knowledge and grace you offer so that my
happiness is based in that relationship. Amen.*

AUGUST 14   KEEPING UP WITH THE JONESES

I have learned to be content with whatever I have.
(Philippians 4:11)

For some men, a goal in life is to be successful. When success is
not coming as they think it ought to, they do all they know how
to do to acquire it. If someone is achieving things that they think
should be theirs, they can develop feelings of resentment,
jealousy, and envy.

Dan and Phil worked for the same company. Phil had been with the company longer, had been very loyal, and had "paid his dues"; and he felt he deserved the next company promotion. But it was given to Dan. Phil developed resentment and dislike for Dan, feeling that Dan took what was supposed to be his. Dan and Phil never got past this point in their relationship.

Paul told the Philippians he had learned that no matter what he had obtained, he would be content with what God was doing with him at the time. Otherwise he risked focusing on what he did not have rather than on what God had already supplied.

Some men spend too much time pursuing success, which keeps them from focusing on God's call in their lives.

Lord, help my notions of success be rooted in that which I need to do your will. Amen.

AUGUST 15   NO RETIREMENT

Anyone unwilling to work should not eat.
(2 Thessalonians 3:10)

Tom had retired from his business after forty years of service. He decided he just wanted to kick back, travel, play golf, and have fun. After all, he had earned it. His retirement mentality crept over to his attendance and activity in church. He would tell his friends at church, "I had my day; let the younger people take over."

The apostle Paul made the case that there is no retirement when it comes to God's calling. Some Thessalonians had stopped working for God, believing that Christ would soon return. Paul reminded them that nothing can justify idleness in the work of God.

Moses wanted to "retire" after hearing the complaints of the people and facing never-ending conflicts. Although he wanted to hand over his responsibilities to someone else, God asked him to go to the top of a hill and hold up his staff as encouragement. He did not think he could do it, so God got Aaron and Hur to help hold his arms, and the Israelites prevailed (see Exodus 17).

God's work is not something we ever retire from.

Thank you, God, for reminding me that I must never grow weary in doing that which you call me to do for your Kingdom. Amen.

AUGUST 16   PLEASING GOD

Thou hast created all things, and for thy pleasure they are and were created.   *(Revelation 4:11b KJV)*

Some men believe God exists to please them. If we were to sum up a typical man's life, would we say, "He worked hard," "He dressed well," or "He loved life"? Would anyone say, "He pleased God"?

Abraham was a man who understood that the goal of a man's life is to please God. He walked with God so that he could understand God's purposes for his life. He worked on his relationship with God before God asked him to do things so that he would please God.

William Jennings Bryan was having his portrait done by a painter who noticed Bryan's hair hung over his ears. Mr. Bryan proceeded to explain the reason this was so: "When I was dating my wife, she did not like the way my ears stuck out. In order to please her, I grew my hair to cover my ears." The painter replied, "But that was long ago. Why won't you cut it now?" Mr. Bryan smiled, "Because the romance is still going on!"

Our romance with God never ends when we realize we should spend the rest of our lives pleasing him.

Help me spend my life trying to please you, God, by knowing your will. Amen.

AUGUST 17   THE TRANSFORMED MAN

Do not be astonished that I said to you, "You must be born from above."   *(John 3:7)*

When my son was young, he loved playing with Transformer toys. He found he could essentially buy two toys for the price of one. If he bought a Transformer that looked like a car, it could change into a robot with a few twists and turns. It could become completely different from the toy he saw in the store behind the package.

Nicodemus asked Jesus what it takes to inherit eternal life. He thought there must be something he had to do, some deed to accomplish in order to achieve this status. Jesus' answer had nothing to do with what we do or accomplish. It is what the Holy Spirit does through us, from top to bottom, that transforms us into something completely different.

We have an outside package that shows the world one aspect of who we are. Jesus is waiting for us to allow him to change the inside and become new and different persons than we were before he came into our lives.

Lord, thank you for reminding me that change is what you do in my life to transform me from what I am to what I will become. Amen.

AUGUST 18   MAKING PEACE WITH YOUR PAST

"You shall not inherit anything in our father's house."
(Judges 11:2b)

Jephthah was a mighty warrior. He had been conceived from an adulterous relationship that his father had with a prostitute; and his father, who favored his wife's sons, rejected him. He drove Jephthah away from his home saying, "You are not going to get any inheritance in our family because you are the son of another woman." None of this was Jephthah's fault; his father's indiscretion had caused it to happen.

You can imagine the rejection the young man must have felt. He could have quit right there. He could have let bitterness and revenge dominate his life. He was a victim of his father's sins.

When war came to Israel, its leaders, knowing what a skilled warrior Jephthah was, called upon him to be their commander. This could have been his opportunity to get his revenge by refusing to serve. After all, no one helped him in his time of rejection and need.

Jephthah refused to let the circumstances of his life overtake the nature of his mission and calling. He was able to defeat Israel's enemy by not letting his past run his future.

Lord, help me make peace with anything in my past that keeps me from responding to the call you place on my life. Amen.

AUGUST 19   ON BEING A GLOBAL CHRISTIAN

"I truly understand that God shows no partiality, but in every nation anyone who fears him and does what is right is acceptable to him."   *(Acts 10:34-35)*

Rarely do we look to Christians from other nations to help us become more faithful Christians. We tend not to think of Christianity as a worldwide movement.

A man from the Congo became a member of the national board of a large church agency. He would attend meetings, but he did not say much. On September 11, 2001, he came early to the board meeting. That morning the tragic events in New York and Washington, D.C., unfolded. No one knew how to handle what they were seeing. When he arrived, he saw all the devastation and witnessed to us about how God had helped his family through the civil war in the Congo that had killed more than three hundred thousand. That day he became our chaplain, ministering to us about God's sovereignty even in dire circumstances.

Peter understood that all are included in God's invitation and that we must be willing to learn the faith from those we might not consider as having anything to offer us.

Lord, help me remember that yours is a worldwide movement and that I learn from the Body of Christ wherever it is found. Amen.

AUGUST 20   RELIGION OR RELATIONSHIP?

"Woe to you, scribes and Pharisees, hypocrites!"
                                                    (Matthew 23:23)

Jesus' teachings turned upside down virtually every aspect of everyday living. He taught generosity, which contrasted sharply with teachings on acquisition. He changed accepted political practice by declaring that those who wish to lead should serve. He forced people of his day to rethink their notions about family. Rather than being based on blood ties, he described family based on common interest in Kingdom causes.

He interpreted Scripture in a way that drove religious leaders crazy. He ignored religious traditions and rituals when they seemed to interfere with opportunities to minister to hurting people. He placed more importance on relationships with people and on acting justly and mercifully than on observing traditional Sabbath or ritual fasting. The religious leaders of Jesus' day were interested in upholding the legalities of the religious rules. They preached rules they often could not keep themselves!

Christianity has never been about religion; it has always been about relationships—our relationship with God and our relationships with others. Religion can become routine and static; relationships are always dynamic and changing. When we invite people to become Christians, we invite them into developing a lifelong relationship with the risen Savior and all his creation.

Thank you, Lord, for the invitation to be in relationship with you and all your creation every day of my life. Amen.

AUGUST 21   SOMEONE IS COUNTING ON YOU

All who believed were together and had all things in common.
(Acts 2:44)

Bill McCartney, former coach of the University of Colorado football team, tells in his book *What Makes a Man?* how he challenged the team to become more than they thought they could be. He challenged each team member to call someone he admired and loved and tell that person he was dedicating the next game to that person. After the game, Coach McCartney planned to distribute sixty footballs with the final score written on them to be sent to the persons the players had chosen.

Colorado was playing Nebraska, in Lincoln—a place where Colorado had not won a game in twenty-three years. Coach McCartney believed this time would be different because the team would not be playing only for themselves; someone they knew would be counting on them, believing in them, and expecting them to be at their best.

After the game, sixty footballs were delivered to sixty different people with this score written on them: Colorado 27, Nebraska 12.

The believers of the early church counted on one another; they believed they could succeed even in a hostile environment. They held one another accountable so that they could live victoriously through any circumstance or condition that life might bring.

Lord, help me remember those who are counting on me to help them navigate life's challenges and opportunities. Amen.

AUGUST 22   THE SAMSON TRAP

Then Samson called to the LORD and said, "Lord GOD, remember me."   *(Judges 16:28)*

Samson was a gifted man who chose to live in open rebellion to God. Going it alone, he did not allow himself to think he needed God. He became a spiritual outlaw! As long as he had beautiful women, enormous strength, and a keen mind, he believed he could achieve anything.

Samson fell into the sin trap that often snares men: the trap of thinking that as long as you're attractive and successful, and you're not hurting anyone, you can live like you want. But there came a time when Samson needed God. He cried out to God to remember him. God honored that cry and restored him to his special calling and anointing so that he might achieve something great for God.

Samson came to understand that our lives are not measured by what we achieve, accumulate, or do apart from God. Our lives are measured by our ability to remember the purposes we are called by God to accomplish.

God, please help me avoid the traps of life that focus only on my wants and desires. Renew my commitment to achieve the purposes for which I was created. Amen.

AUGUST 23   TRANSFORMATIONAL LIVING

Do not be conformed to this world, but be transformed.
(Romans 12:2)

There's an African American folk saying that goes like this: "We aren't what we want to be; we aren't what we're going to be; but thank God we aren't what we were." This saying recognizes the journey that men of faith are on. We begin at a certain point in our walk with Christ, but we're encouraged to grow in the grace and knowledge of Christ throughout life (see 2 Peter 3:18).

Paul calls this transformation "renewing the mind." It allows us to think as God would have us think, rather than be shaped only by what we see, experience, and know about this world. Transformed minds see the possibilities for life and are not stuck in routine expectations of life.

Transformed men learn to navigate life in the good and bad times. They are not so conformed to the world that they are of no heavenly good.

As I journey through life, Lord, help my transformation be one that overcomes the limitations of this world. Amen.

AUGUST 24   YOUR ATTITUDE DETERMINES YOUR
                                                    ALTITUDE

"But this man has done nothing wrong."   *(Luke 23:41)*

The story of the Crucifixion is a story of three crosses and three men. Although our focus is on Jesus, the two criminals, one on his right and the other on his left, bear some attention; for it is in them that we find how important our attitudes are to where we end up in life.

One of the condemned men suggested to Jesus that if he really were who he said he was, he would save himself. The other criminal understood that the two of them had actually committed the crimes for which they were being punished, but that Jesus was innocent and did not deserve the fate they were facing.

This man's attitude toward Jesus ultimately affected his altitude. His willingness to speak against an unjust sentence, to admit to his own wrongdoing, and to seek forgiveness from the only one who could give forgiveness to him, allowed him to reach new heights in this life and the next.

We men can live lives of negativity, defeatism, blame, jealousy, and ridicule. Or we can approach life with a positive attitude, a willingness to continue to self-examine ourselves, and an attitude of confession and repentance.

Help my attitude reflect the altitude where I want to live for Christ's sake each day. Amen.

AUGUST 25   ACCOUNTABLE MEN

Obey your leaders and submit to them, for they are keeping watch over your souls and will give an account.
(Hebrews 13:17)

William George Ward once said, "Every great person has learned first how to obey, whom to obey, and when to obey."* *Obedience* is another word for accountability. In a society where free will is so cherished, there is a tendency to be accountable to nothing except what the individual desires.

John the Baptist lived and preached in the desert. He had the ultimate expression of free will. Yet when Jesus came to be baptized, John immediately recognized the one to whom he was accountable (see Matthew 3:14). Likewise, when the centurion asked Jesus to heal his servant, he recognized whose authority he was to be accountable to, even though he was not a Jew (see Luke 7:7-8).

The writer of Hebrews understood the importance of men being accountable. Everyone from the top to the bottom of the organization was to "give an account" to someone. Left alone, we tend to do what we want, when we want, to whom we want. Our faith walk is a walk of accountable discipleship in which we hold one another up to accomplish the work of the Kingdom.

Lord, help me be a man who understands the importance of being accountable in my faith walk to those you have put in authority. Amen.

* www.answers.com/topic/william-george-ward.

AUGUST 26   WITNESSING THAT SHOUTS

"And you will be my witnesses . . . to the ends of the earth."
(Acts 1:8b)

I once worked for a company that explicitly prohibited me from proselytizing (making converts). I was a young Christian and thought that everyone needed to hear about what Jesus had done in my life. I was convinced that sharing this good news was what I was required to do, even if people did not want to hear it.

An older, more experienced man in the faith also worked at that company. I shared with him my frustrations of not being able to tell my story. He gave me advice that I remember to this day. This is what he said: "Relax. The work of the Kingdom does not depend solely on you. God has others who are witnessing their faith in a variety of ways. By the way, more people have been converted in this company by what we don't say than what anyone has ever spoken."

He went on to say that unbelievers tend to look more at how we conduct our lives than at what we say. May our lives shout to them of our love of Christ!

Lord, help me live a life that shouts to people my love for you and that moves them to want that kind of relationship with you. Amen.

AUGUST 27   THE DOS AND DON'TS

Do not get drunk with wine, for that is debauchery; but be filled with the Spirit.   *(Ephesians 5:18)*

Scott considered Christianity a bunch of rigid requirements and teachings, and he wanted no part of it. He told his Christian friends, "Your church is about what you can't do more than it is about what you can do. You can't drink, curse, gamble, lie, or cheat. You put people in straightjackets and expect everyone to conform to your sense of values!"

Sam heard this rant and could not hold his peace. He said, "Scott, everything you've just said about the church is true. But you can't seem to get past the don'ts in order to experience the joy and freedom of the dos."

Sam explained that the don'ts are things we do in our own strength, while the dos are what we experience through the movement of the Holy Sprit working in our lives. The dos help us not want to live in the don'ts!

When the apostle Paul wrote about not drinking to excess, his emphasis was on the effect that too much drink would have in limiting what the infilling of the Holy Sprit could do in a person's life. May our actions never limit the Holy Spirit.

Lord, continue to fill me with your Spirit so that all I want to do honors and glorifies your name. Amen.

AUGUST 28   DRAFTED

Select from among yourselves seven men of good standing.
(Acts 6:3)

A critical moment in the early church was when leaders were needed to lead in the distribution of food supplies to the Greek and Aramaic-speaking believers. The apostles were clear that their focus had to be on proclamation and conversion, not on "waiting tables." They encouraged the local congregation to select their own leaders, who would help determine the day-to-day functioning of the faith community.

Stephen was among the first to be drafted into leadership because of how he had already demonstrated leadership qualities in his daily walk with Christ. Others were drafted shortly after that, and the church continued to grow under their leadership.

Men are often asked to serve in leadership capacities throughout the church. Many pastors report that men are the hardest to get to serve, particularly in the areas of prayer, youth, and children's ministries. Many use the excuses of time, availability, interest, and schedule. A good number of these men are draft dodgers when it comes to serving in the church. Some act as if they have a draft deferment when it comes to responding to requests to lead in God's community of faith.

Have you responded to God's draft?

Lord, help me respond to your draft when it relates to leading and serving in the community of faith. Amen.

AUGUST 29   BAND OF BROTHERS

. . . that we may present everyone mature in Christ.
(Colossians 1:28)

The apostle Paul desired to help people mature in Christ. The best way for believers to mature has always been in small groups. In these settings, believers can accept one another (Romans 15:7), love one another (John 13:34-35), encourage and build up one another (1 Thessalonians 5:11), carry one another's burdens (Galatians 6:2), pray for one another (James 5:16), and instruct one another (Romans 15:14)—all signs of Christian maturity.

The miniseries *Band of Brothers*, which first aired in 2001 on HBO and still runs frequently on different television channels around the world, tells the story of a World War II unit that fought and died together. They started as strangers but ended as a family of brothers. They grew to depend on one another, maturing together, sacrificing everything for the cause and for one another.

John and Charles Wesley started the Epworth League. This was a group of men who desired to hold one another accountable for growing and maturing in the faith. These men were the seed for the Wesleyan/Methodist movement that would sweep the world.

The highest goal of Christian small groups is to grow in Christ. Are *you* part of a small group?

Lord, help me find a "band of brothers" who will hold me accountable for spiritual growth and Christian maturity. Amen.

AUGUST 30   GROUNDED

As you therefore have received Christ Jesus the Lord, continue to live your lives in him, rooted and built up in him and established in the faith.   *(Colossians 2:6-7)*

We are called not only to commit our lives to Christ, but also to be "rooted" or grounded in our relationship with him. Some men are not well grounded in Christianity, even after being a member of a church for years.

Bud had been a member of a local church for many years. He rarely went to Sunday school and never attended a Bible study. He developed a terminal illness, and the new pastor of the church came to visit him. The pastor asked Bud if he knew Jesus as his personal Savior. That struck Bud because no one had ever directly asked him that question. Most people assumed that because Bud came to church, he had already been asked that question. Bud's response was that he was not sure. He had little to draw on because he had never studied the Bible or asked any questions concerning it. He thought that going to church meant you were "in," even in the end. He had never been "rooted" or grounded in Christ.

Are you grounded in Christ?

Lord, may I be a man who is grounded in Christ through study, meditation, prayer, and the regular practice of spiritual disciplines. Amen.

AUGUST 31   TROUBLE, TRIBULATION, AND TRIUMPH

"In the world you face persecution. But take courage; I have conquered the world!"   *(John 16:33)*

In the movie *Grand Canyon,* Danny Glover plays a tow truck driver who pulls up as a group of youths surround a man and are about to beat him and strip his car. Danny tells the leader that the world isn't supposed to work this way—that he's supposed to be able to do his job without asking if he can, and that the other man is supposed to be able to wait with his car without being ripped off. Everything, he says, is supposed to be different from this.

Jesus told us that we would have troubles. However, in the midst of trouble, we can take comfort in knowing that we can have peace and experience victory because of what Jesus did on the cross.

One man was heard saying, "I am glad to tell you that I've got peace with God because I have Jesus." Another man said, "I've got something better than that. I have the peace of God." A third man said, "I have something better still. I have the God of peace!"

Lord, thank you for being the God of peace in my life. Amen.

SEPTEMBER

"Body" Building

CHRISTIAN COON

SEPTEMBER 1   A HOUSE FOR THE HOLY SPIRIT

Or do you not know that your body is a temple of the Holy Spirit within you, which you have from God, and that you are not your own? For you were bought with a price; therefore glorify God in your body. **(1 Corinthians 6:19-20)**

Years ago my father took me to see *Pumping Iron,* a behind-the-scenes look at the world of bodybuilding. The star of the documentary was the future governor of California, Arnold Schwarzenegger. I don't remember much about it, but I do recall thinking that these men, in an understatement of huge proportions, took their bodies seriously.

When you hear or read a phrase that puts the words *body* and *temple* together in the same phrase, your first thought might be of someone who takes fitness seriously. That's not a bad thing, but our bodies are much more than opportunities to create six-pack abs or killer triceps. As Paul notes, our bodies are to house the Holy Spirit, which may be the most sacred task of all.

I'd like to take the next month to reflect on the many parts of our body and how each one might create an opportunity to convey the Spirit. My hope is that you'll be engaged in a different kind of "body" building, and it doesn't matter what your body type might be!

God who created me and loves me, thank you for giving me life and for giving me a vessel—my body—to share that life with others. Amen.

SEPTEMBER 2   EVEN THE HAIRS ON YOUR HEAD

"And even the hairs of your head are all counted."
(Matthew 10:30)

Men may think that it's somewhat of a modern phenomenon to be sensitive about hair loss, but it might be much older than we realize: There's a story in 2 Kings 2 where some small boys run up to the prophet Elisha and jeer him by calling him "baldhead"! We don't know for sure whether Elisha needed hair-growth tonic, but it's interesting to think about men from the Bible having similar issues with their hairlines.

It may seem odd to think about our hair being an opportunity to share the Holy Spirit. In order for us to share the Spirit, though, we must feel the Spirit, know the Spirit, and be open to the Spirit. We must accept God's love and welcome God's care for every single part of our being—even our hair. That's one of the points Jesus was trying to make in this passage from Matthew. Do not fear, because God is more powerful than anything. God pays attention to (and loves) the smallest details—even the hairs on your head, no matter how many hairs you may have.

Dear God, you care desperately for everything, even the hairs on my head. Thank you for that love. Amen.

SEPTEMBER 3   HEADSTRONG

You prepare a table before me / in the presence of my enemies; you anoint my head with oil; / my cup overflows. (Psalm 23:5)

One of the most powerful moments for me as a pastor is when I baptize a baby. Whenever I dip my hand into the water and place my hand on the baby's head, her head quickly turns around to see who is getting her all wet. The baby's life has changed.

The Twenty-third Psalm is a passage known by many, but one powerful piece of it that may be overlooked is this notion of God anointing our heads with oil. It's an awesome image to think of God touching our heads, blessing and strengthening us for the day ahead.

When we sense and receive that touch, our lives change too, especially if we turn around to see the One doing the anointing. God's blessing overflows if we bow our heads and allow that anointing to occur.

Dear God, anoint my head today and be an overflowing blessing through me. Amen.

SEPTEMBER 4   WINDOWS TO THE SOUL

"If your right eye causes you to sin, tear it out and throw it away."   *(Matthew 5:29a)*

Someone once said that the eyes are the windows to the soul. Despite the harshness of Jesus' words in this passage from Matthew, I think he was basically saying the same thing.

Jewish teachers often used hyperbole to make their point, and Jesus was doing the same thing here. Jesus knows how powerful the world is with all its images: beauty and ugliness, peace and violence, love and lust. When you think about it, it is astonishing how much we take in each day through our gift of sight.

Because of this, Jesus doesn't want us to take our eyes for granted. We often have a choice of what we see and what we do with the images we ingest. This is not to say that if we look lustfully at a woman other than our wife or greedily at our neighbor's new car, we should flail ourselves. We must, however, be very aware of the power of our eyes. Behold beauty and give thanks. See injustice and act. View the world and know that God is active in it.

Awesome Creator, you have given us so much to see! Help us respond with care when we view your world. Amen.

SEPTEMBER 5   THE NOSE KNOWS

Jesus said, Take ye away the stone. Martha, the sister of him that was dead, saith unto him, Lord, by this time he stinketh: for he hath been dead four days.   (John 11:39 KJV)

A funny thing happens to our faces when we smell something that "stinketh." Our faces scrunch up. We turn away. Maybe we gag or cough. Lazarus's friends and family know this. They are aware of the smell of death. Jesus, though, overcomes death and raises Lazarus.

One chapter later, there's a scene with a different smell. Mary, Martha and Lazarus's sister, anoints Jesus' feet with costly perfume. "The house was filled with the fragrance of the perfume" (John 12:3), the text says. Jesus leads us to believe that Mary is performing this act as a way of preparing him for his own death. But I also wonder if Mary does this as an act of worship.

Smells sometimes make us turn away, but they should also make us turn toward God in worship. Incense has that effect in many churches, but you can probably list many other smells that should trigger a movement toward God. The nose knows. Pay attention to it today.

Dear God, may something as simple as a smell trigger the desire to worship you this day. Amen.

SEPTEMBER 6   YOUR SERVANT IS LISTENING

Therefore Eli said to Samuel, "Go, lie down; and if he calls you, you shall say, 'Speak, LORD, for your servant is listening.'" So Samuel went and lay down in his place.   (1 Samuel 3:9)

I'm going through a bit of withdrawal right now.

Whenever I get into my car, I follow a pretty strict routine. I put on my seat belt, start the car, and turn on the radio. A couple of weeks ago, however, my radio went kaput, so until I get around to having it fixed, I'm driving in silence. I must confess it has been a difficult adjustment, but I think it is good exercise for my ears.

I'm used to listening to so many things. In fact, it's almost as if I've trained my ears to receive music, public radio, and sports talk. When I reflect on how well I've trained my ears to listen to God, however, I know I'm lacking.

Eli taught Samuel how to listen to God, which would be vital for Samuel's ministry as a prophet. The first step is being intentional: putting yourself before God and tuning out everything except God's voice.

God of silence and thunder, you bless us with many sounds. Help us listen to the most sacred sound of all—your voice. Amen.

SEPTEMBER 7   PUT YOUR HAND IN THE HAND

But [Thomas] said to them, "Unless I see the mark of the nails in his hands, and put my finger in the mark of the nails and my hand in his side, I will not believe."   *(John 20:25b)*

My daughter is particularly proud right now of the calluses on her hands, which she has received by being an expert on the monkey bars. Those calluses are little badges of honor that bespeak a girl who's active and willing to use her hands to move forward.

Thomas has been interpreted in many ways, and obviously the "doubter" label is the one that has stuck. An interesting thing about this passage, though, is his willingness to put forth his whole self in the attempt to touch Jesus. He doesn't want simply to glance at the mark of the nails from a distance. He wants to put his *hands* in Jesus' side.

I believe that too many men are timid in their faith—they're unwilling to get their hands dirty, unwilling to put their hands to use to work, touch, heal, or pray. Our hands can do many things, but they're not much use to God if they're not doing the work of Christ.

We are your hands in the world, O God, but you can do nothing if we do nothing with them. Amen.

SEPTEMBER 8   GETTING YOUR ARMS AROUND THIS

"But while he was still far off, his father saw him and was filled with compassion; he ran and put his arms around him and kissed him."   *(Luke 15:20)*

Do you know about the "guy hug"? A youth pastor with whom I worked pointed out that when—or rather, *if*—guys hug each other, they have a certain process for doing so. First, of course, they don't hug too long. Second, they slap each other on the back while they're in the embrace, as if to say, "I'll be intimate with this guy, but not *too* intimate."

That's one reason the story of the prodigal son is so powerful. After the son comes home—the son who blew his inheritance and essentially told his father that he was dead to him—the father breaks all kinds of cultural taboos by running to his son and taking him into his arms.

The father used his arms to hold his son tightly, to squeeze the life back into both of them. How do you use *your* arms? To keep people and the world at a distance or to spread your arms open and embrace all that God has put before you?

You have embraced the world and us, loving God. Help us embrace others in the same way. Amen.

SEPTEMBER 9   THE HEART OF THE MATTER

I will give them one heart, and put a new spirit within them; I will remove the heart of stone from their flesh and give them a heart of flesh.   *(Ezekiel 11:19)*

Whenever I read this passage, it reminds me that sometimes my heart feels like a stone. God, however, wants to give me a heart of flesh, a heart that pumps life through my veins, a heart that loves and breaks.

Something I need to be aware of, however, is whether I'm doing what I can to make sure that this God-given heart stays "fleshy." We read or hear about so many ways we can keep our physical hearts healthy, but what do we do with these hearts of flesh that come from God?

Ezekiel states later that the heart God gives should compel us to follow God's ways. This heart isn't something we can just ignore or toss aside. My daughter made me a heart-shaped valentine last Valentine's Day, and it says, "I love you, Daddy" inside. I treasure this heart and will always keep it. We should do the same with the hearts of flesh that God has given to us.

Give us hearts of flesh, O God, and inspire us to take care of them by staying close to you. Amen.

SEPTEMBER 10   CAN WE TAME OUR TONGUES?

So also the tongue is a small member, yet it boasts of great exploits.   *(James 3:5)*

Whenever an individual running for office comes across as a straight talker, there is an immediate attraction for many. They're tired of politicians who talk in circles, and they want an official who will tell it like it is. Those people probably also like the book of James because James has the same style. A case in point is his treatise from chapter 3 on the tongue and the power that it wields: "No one can tame the tongue—a restless evil, full of deadly poison" (v. 8). James emphasizes later, though, that the tongue can be used for blessing or cursing. It is straightforward talk like this that gets our attention.

We may pay little attention to a sin such as gossip because it seems harmless. But how we use our tongues—what we say about others—has enormous power. There's a reason the word *backstabbing* exists. An insult or disparaging word can damage careers and souls.

The tongue is powerful. Let us use it as an opportunity to bless and not curse those with whom we interact.

Just as you lift us up, Lord, help us build up others with kind and compassionate words. Amen.

SEPTEMBER 11   TALKING WITH FULL MOUTHS

Let the words of my mouth and the meditation of my heart be acceptable to you, O LORD, my rock and my redeemer.
(Psalm 19:14)

Yesterday we reflected on the power of the tongue and how it can bless or tear down other people. What kinds of words fill our mouths in relation to God?

I enjoyed reading the Harry Potter series, and one common theme in those books is the refusal of most of the characters (other than Harry) to mention the name *Voldemort* because of their fear of his mysterious evil.

Tragically, sometimes we, too, allow fear to keep us from mentioning the names *God* or *Jesus*. Now, I'm not suggesting that we are afraid of God! What I mean is that perhaps we're sometimes afraid of embarrassment—of what others might think. We want to be one of the guys, and when the phrase "Jesus is Lord" fills our mouths, we are susceptible to judgment.

But that's the risk we must take. The words of our mouths must include the name of Christ, and we should proclaim it without fear.

Let my mouth be filled with words of praise and love for all you provide, O Lord. Amen.

SEPTEMBER 12   FOOTPRINTS

"By the tender mercy of our God, the dawn from on high will break upon us, to give light to those who sit in darkness and in the shadow of death, to guide our feet into the way of peace."
(Luke 1:78-79)

We have a preschool in our church, and every August the teachers cut out colorful footprints and tape them on the floor to lead everyone to their proper classrooms. This is no doubt very helpful to both children and nervous parents. It shows the way to go.

This passage in the Gospel of Luke is from Zechariah, the father of John the Baptist. After his son is circumcised and after he declares that the child will be named John, Zechariah responds with praise and thanksgiving. He may not fully realize the impact his son will have as one who prepares the way for Jesus, but he has an idea. He knows that this birth will be like a light that guides our feet.

Instead of only looking down for footprints that will guide our feet on our walk with Christ, we also need to look up—and all around. God is ever present, eager to guide our feet on the path of peace.

Guide my feet today, Jesus, and show me the way to walk. Amen.

SEPTEMBER 13   ON YOUR MARK, GET SET . . .

But those who wait for the Lord shall renew their strength, / they shall mount up with wings like eagles, / they shall run and not be weary, / they shall walk and not faint.   (Isaiah 40:31)

I mentioned yesterday that God will guide our feet, yet it is our legs that actually set those feet in motion. Before we move, however, sometimes we must wait.

One of the hardest things for me to do as a runner is to deal with injuries. One of the most obvious things to help an injury heal is, of course, not to run. It's hard, but if I want to be healthy again, I need to wait.

Sometimes men can get inspired and excited by a vision and want to get moving as soon as possible. That's a great feeling to have! Occasionally, as this passage from Isaiah reminds us, we also have to wait for the Lord for strength and direction. If we wait, though, when the time comes we will move our legs with strength and purpose. We shall run and not be weary.

You have exciting things planned for me to do today, God. Help me wait upon you and then move my legs with purpose. Amen.

SEPTEMBER 14   ON YOUR KNEES

At the name of Jesus every knee should bend, in heaven and on earth and under the earth.   (Philippians 2:10)

Though I have been a United Methodist all my life, there's a part of me that has a deep appreciation for the Episcopal Church, including its liturgy and sacredness of space.

Nevertheless, I still find it a bit awkward to kneel on a kneeler whenever I worship in an Episcopal church. I'm not sure why that is, but I do know there's something profound to be said for physically bowing or genuflecting—for getting on our knees as a sign of our obedience and willingness to submit to the love and reign of God.

At times we may go overboard when we think of Jesus simply as our friend. Jesus *is* our friend, and he saw his disciples that way. But Jesus is also Lord, and getting down on our knees reminds us that we serve him and we wait for him to guide, protect, and save us.

Let my knees bend today, dear Christ, as a way of showing that I want to be obedient to your Word. Amen.

SEPTEMBER 15   STANDING ON YOUR TOES

And [Zacchaeus] sought to see who Jesus was, but could not because of the crowd, for he was of short stature.
(Luke 19:3 NKJV)

Many of us know how the song goes. There was a wee little man. His name was Zacchaeus. He climbed the sycamore tree to see Jesus. But this version skips the first part of the story. Before climbing the tree, Zacchaeus tried to see Jesus on his own. How? I believe that, at some point, he stood on his toes.

Despite Zacchaeus's background and the fact that he had cheated many out of a lot of money, something stirred in him that day, giving him a desire to see Jesus. Maybe it was more than desire. Maybe it was desperation. He *had* to see Jesus. So I think he first must have stood on his toes.

Sometimes we may take for granted Jesus' presence in our lives. We assume he'll always be there, so we don't make much of an effort to seek him. On the one hand, that's true. We don't need to stand on our toes. He's within us and within others. On the other hand, it's important to have that same desire, that same need, to see Jesus every day.

Strengthen my desire to seek Christ, O God, so I am constantly aware of his presence. Amen.

SEPTEMBER 16   ARE WE WHAT WE EAT?

"Do you not see that whatever goes into the mouth enters the stomach, and goes out into the sewer?"   *(Matthew 15:17)*

Chips, anyone? Cookies? These two snacks are among my biggest weaknesses when it comes to food. But does it really matter what we eat? After all, Jesus emphasized that it matters more what comes out of our mouth (which proceeds from our heart) than what goes into our mouth and stomach.

Even so, Jesus knew the value of food and used it quite often to make a point (think loaves and fishes). You need to know the value of food, too, especially when you consider how important you are to the mission of Christ. It matters what we put in our stomachs.

Eating well means leading a healthy life. It means having a body with more energy. Not only is that body a gift from God, it also is needed to fulfill what God has called you to do.

Remind me today, O God, that I am needed by you to be Christ's presence in the world. What I eat affects how much of a presence I can be. Amen.

SEPTEMBER 17   YES, THAT BODY PART TOO

"Come, let's make love all night, / spend the night in ecstatic lovemaking!"   *(Proverbs 7:18 The Message)*

When I chose the theme of our bodies as temples of the Spirit, I started writing down all our different "parts." I started at the top—head, then hair, then eyes, and so forth. Halfway through this self-examination, of course, I wondered how I would write about, as the Bible puts it, our "loins."

I thought about many biblical stories related to this topic, but when I came across this passage from Proverbs, I thought, *Here is a biblical statement about the joy of sex!* Then, when I read the passage in context, I realized this was a married woman calling out to a man who wasn't her husband. In a way, however, that may summarize what many of us think about the sex drive: it's something that brings ecstasy but also can bring agony or anxiety.

Your sex life may be filled with joy or frustration—or both! Or perhaps you are single and have no sex life at all because you are being obedient to God's Word. We all need to ask God to guide and bless this part of our lives. It is, frankly, too important to hide from God. I believe God wants our sexuality to be a blessing, and it can be if we allow God to influence our decisions and actions.

Bless all my desires, O God, so that they come from you. Amen.

SEPTEMBER 18   LET LOOSE YOUR LIPS

O Lord, open my lips, / and my mouth will declare your praise.
(Psalm 51:15)

Author Anne Lamott has said that her two favorite prayers are "Thank you, thank you, thank you" and "Help me, help me, help me." These prayers probably wouldn't be included in a modern-day version of the psalms, but their point is pretty clear.

I wonder, though, how many of us spend more of our time using the "help me" prayer. There's nothing wrong with that, of course. God wants us to ask for help, and God is overjoyed when we do. A balanced spiritual life, however, also includes the "thank you" prayer.

God is the one who moves us to great things, including voicing songs of beautiful praise. Open your lips today and, whether you sing like a tenor in an opera or you have a voice that is best heard with a karaoke machine, let your mouth declare God's praise. Your heart will soar when you do, and you'll be much more aware of the help that God provides.

Thank you, O God, thank you—for all that you have done, all that you do, and all that you will do. Amen.

SEPTEMBER 19   LUNG POWER

Then he took a deep breath and breathed into them. "Receive the Holy Spirit," he said.   (John 20:22 The Message)

Whenever I read about prayer, I'm often struck when it stresses the importance of breathing.

At times that's difficult to understand. Breathing? What's so hard about breathing? Shouldn't prayer be more than that?

But then I actually do it. I fill my lungs with air and let it out. I do it again and, more often than not, I find myself much more open to what God might have to say to me. Not only that, but as this verse from John reminds us, God's breath and breathing can be found mentioned throughout the Scriptures, from Genesis (2:7) to Revelation (11:11).

Try it today. Think about your lungs and give them a workout. As you take a breath, think of a name for God that is important to you. As you breathe out, think about an action you'd like God to take.

An abbreviation of what's known as the Jesus Prayer is an example: (Breathe in) Lord Jesus Christ, (breathe out) have mercy on me. That's known as a breath prayer. Use it and see if it makes a difference in your prayer life.

Breathe on me, breath of God, fill me with life anew.* * *Amen.

* "Breathe on Me, Breath of God," Edwin Hatch, 1878.

SEPTEMBER 20   A GOOD RIBBING

And the rib that the LORD ***God had taken from the man he made into a woman and brought her to the man.***   ***(Genesis 2:22)***

There are a lot of Adam and Eve jokes, but here's a good one.

At Sunday school they were teaching how God created everything, including human beings. Little Johnny, a child in the kindergarten class, seemed especially intent when they told him how Eve was created out of one of Adam's ribs.

Later in the week Johnny's mother noticed him lying down as though he were ill, and she asked, "Johnny, what's the matter?"

Johnny responded, "I have a pain in my side. I think I'm going to have a wife."

We may not think about our ribs much, but think about them today and what they might represent. I don't know if Adam had much choice in the matter, but God used a part of him to help another—in this case, to create new life.

We can be selfish when it comes to our bodies. Is there a part of you that God wants to use to help another? Think about your ribs as a reminder of how you can serve.

Use me, O God—any part of me—in your service. Amen.

SEPTEMBER 21   NIPPING AT OUR HEELS

Afterward his brother came out, with his hand gripping Esau's heel; so he was named Jacob.   ***(Genesis 25:26a)***

Esau was first, but Jacob got the notoriety. Isn't that just how it is sometimes?

Many men are driven. They like to create objectives, set goals, and act. But even the best-laid plans can get messed up. Something seemingly nips or even grabs at our heels, which hinders our progress. If only this person or this attitude or this obstacle hadn't gotten in the way, success would have followed.

Esau was supposed to have the birthright and receive everything that Jacob received. But Jacob tricked Esau, leaving him with little. Esau's first reaction was understandable. He wanted to kill his brother, and so Jacob escaped. When they met up later (see Genesis 33:1-17), however, Esau's attitude was one we can admire and copy. Instead of seeking revenge, he embraced his brother, walked alongside him, and gave him gifts. He was not bitter but graceful.

Is there something grabbing at your heels that you wish you could shake off? Perhaps God is calling you to face this person or situation with a change of heart.

Transform my obstacles into opportunities, O God, so that I can show your love. Amen.

SEPTEMBER 22   LOVING WITH YOUR MIND

Jesus replied, "You must love the Lord your God with all your heart, all your soul, and all your mind." (Matthew 22:37 NLT)

Loving God with all our heart makes sense. So does loving God with all our soul. But how do we love God with all our mind?

Some believe there comes a point when it's time to stop thinking and take action. A political leader once accused her fellow citizens of thinking too much. "Enough thinking," she said. "Roll up your sleeves."

Others believe that thinking means you are failing to be faithful. Don't think; just believe!

But there it is in both Matthew and Luke: Love God with your heart, soul, and mind.

Jesus was a teacher and an expert in the Scriptures. The apostle Paul was happy to debate and converse with anyone regardless of his or her philosophy. Using your brain shouldn't be something to fear. Instead, it means being a lifelong student and learning from many different kinds of teachers (not just ones with whom you agree) about how they perceive the world and the divine.

Faith (loving with your heart and soul) and reason (loving with your mind) can be a powerful combination. Just ask Jesus.

Open my mind today, dear Lord, and help me learn more about you and your ways. Amen.

SEPTEMBER 23   AN OBVIOUS REMINDER

Bind [these words] as a sign on your hand, fix them as an emblem on your forehead.   *(Deuteronomy 6:8)*

About fifteen years ago, I worked with a group of guys who swore by their day planners. They spent so much time organizing their lives that I wondered when they actually did their work! They felt, however, that these planners helped them remember what was most important.

When it comes to remembering God's messages—God's Word—we rely on many things. Maybe we use a note card or a sticky note or our memory. Some of our Jewish friends go a step further. They use phylacteries, small leather boxes that they affix to their arms and foreheads. Within these boxes are certain scriptures that they don't want to forget so that they are reminded of the constant presence of God. Not only do these small boxes help them remember to love the Lord their God, but wearing small boxes affixed to their foreheads also makes a definite statement about what's important in their lives.

Christians don't use phylacteries. But if others looked at you, would they know what's most important? Would they know how important it is to you that you love the Lord your God?

Remind me of what's important—most important—O God. Loving you must come first. Amen.

SEPTEMBER 24   THE WEIGHT OF THE WORLD

"Come to me, all you that are weary and are carrying heavy burdens, and I will give you rest."   *(Matthew 11:28)*

Whenever my two-year-old son has a tantrum, one thing I can do to make him stop is carry him on my shoulders. He's usually agreeable to that. I enjoy it, too; and he's still light enough so I can do it fairly easily—at first. After a while, though, my shoulders and neck start to ache, and I have to put him down, much to his disappointment.

Sometimes we feel as if we have the weight of the world on our shoulders, even when that weight seems to be a "good" burden. We take on many responsibilities, and almost all of them are for positive purposes. No matter how productive these burdens are, they weigh on us after a while, and we may think that we can't take them off our shoulders.

Jesus offers another way. He wants to relieve our burdens. He reveals which expectations are in line with his desires. We don't have to shoulder our responsibilities alone.

Ask Jesus to relieve you of your heavy burdens so that you can free your shoulders for something—or someone—better.

It is not all up to me, God in Christ. Take the burdens off my shoulders and give me rest. Amen.

SEPTEMBER 25   LET YOUR FINGERS DO SOME TALKING

When I look at your heavens, the work of your fingers . . . what are human beings that you are mindful of them? . . . Yet you have made them a little lower than God.   (Psalm 8:3a, 4a, 5a)

It's remarkable to think about how we are made. Even small parts of our bodies are vitally important. Take our fingers, for example. Think about all the things we do with our fingers and how challenging it would be to accomplish those tasks without them. (I'm particularly mindful of this as I type these words on my laptop!)

I think there are more than a few men who suffer from low self-worth, which translates into a feeling that they don't have much to offer. They look at their peers or read articles about others in their profession and feel small themselves. And yet every man has something to offer. *Every man.*

The psalmist noted how much God created using only his fingers. Think about your own fingers today—how much you use them, and how life would be tough without them. The work of Christ is similar. He needs every man, no matter how small or large, no matter how seemingly insignificant or famous. Bringing about his Kingdom is tougher when men don't claim their worth.

You have done much with your fingers, O God. Do something with me today. Amen.

SEPTEMBER 26   SHOWING SOME SPINE

"Only be strong and very courageous, being careful to act in accordance with all the law that my servant Moses commanded you."   *(Joshua 1:7a)*

Jim Rome is a sports talk-show host. A number of years ago one of his guests was Jim Everett, who was a quarterback in the National Football League at the time. Rome repeatedly called Jim "Chris" (after Chris Evert, the women's tennis player), arguing that Everett shied away from getting hit. Essentially this was a grown man calling another grown man a woman. Everett didn't like it and attacked him.

I bring up this incident only to illustrate that there are some insults that many men are sensitive about. Most men do not like to have their masculinity questioned. Another insult is being told that they have no courage or, rather, that they're spineless.

Courage can be defined many ways, but Joshua reminds us that before anyone can be courageous, he first must be careful to act within God's parameters. For Christian men, this means following Jesus, who calls us to do seemingly uncourageous things such as turning our cheek or loving our enemies. Society might say that this doesn't show much spine. I believe it shows amazing courage.

True courage starts with listening to you, O God. Help me do that today. Amen.

SEPTEMBER 27   THE NEED FOR WAIST

Stand therefore, and fasten the belt of truth around your waist.
(Ephesians 6:14a)

On a style scale of one to ten, with ten being potential male-model material and one being someone who scrounges around in his clothes hamper for something to wear, I'd say I'm probably a six. I know Jesus said not to worry about what you will wear, but I do pay some attention to what I put on in the morning.

Depending on your "style-scale rating," you may or may not pay attention to the kind of belt you wear around your waist; but we all need to think about the kind of belt that Paul is describing in his Letter to the Ephesians. This is in the middle of a list he makes about other kinds of clothing—or, as he describes it, armor.

He starts with the belt of truth. It's a nice metaphor for us to have. When we slip a belt around our waist, we should think about the need for honesty with ourselves, with others—and most important—with God. We cannot speak the truth of Christ if we are not honest about who we are.

Inspire me to wear the belt of truth around my waist today, O God, so that I can be a man of honesty and integrity. Amen.

SEPTEMBER 28   STICKING YOUR NECK OUT

Greet Prisca and Aquila, who work with me in Christ Jesus, and who risked their necks for my life.   *(Romans 16:3-4a)*

This passage comes from Romans and is one of a series of personal comments that Paul makes to various people in the final chapter. Prisca and Aquila are mentioned elsewhere in the New Testament and appear to have been close to Paul. They were tent-makers, as was he. We don't know, however, what they did on Paul's behalf. Whatever it was, Paul makes it clear that they took a huge risk in sticking their necks out for him.

When was the last time you stuck your neck out for something?

It is certainly easier to be like a turtle, with its head and neck stuck inside its shell, but sometimes Jesus calls us to poke our heads and necks out—to take a risk and work with others in his name.

A risk doesn't have to be dramatic, and it will be an act definitely unique to you. No doubt, you probably know what you can do to push outside your boundaries. Pray about it and know that Christ is with you in the midst of yor risk-taking.

You sometimes invite me to go to risky places of faith, O God.
Go with me as I accept that invitation. Amen.

SEPTEMBER 29   OUR TRUE IDENTITY

For it was you who formed my inward parts; you knit me
together in my mother's womb.   (Psalm 139:13)

It's probably not surprising that DNA isn't mentioned in the Bible, but this verse, I think, gets to the heart of who we really are.

DNA is our unique genetic imprint. We have many things that tell us who we are, including such identifiers as Social Security numbers, driver's license numbers, and credit cards. But our DNA is in us and can't be taken away or stolen. It gives us our biological identity.

Still, our DNA only goes so far. It doesn't tell who we really are or, to borrow a well-known phrase, whose we are. For that, we need the Bible, which reminds us that we are more than cells and molecules. God created us.

In 1971, Jesse Jackson recited a poem on *Sesame Street* titled "I Am—Somebody." The poem emphasizes that we may be different colors or come from different backgrounds, but we are somebody. Before the final line comes this statement, which should remind all of us what our real identity is: "I am / God's child."

My identity isn't defined by anyone but you, O God. I rejoice
that I am your child. Amen.

SEPTEMBER 30   THE BODY OF CHRIST

Then he took a loaf of bread, and when he had given thanks, he broke it and gave it to them, saying, "This is my body, which is given for you. Do this in remembrance of me."   (Luke 22:19)

Our bodies are miraculous works of creation. Each part works in concert with the others to allow us to live and move and have our being (Acts 17:28). Each part is important, and all work together to do the works of Christ.

As we think about how we can use our whole body to further God's Kingdom, however, we also must remember that our whole body is a part of Christ's body—a broken body, a resurrected body. On that night before his death, he tried to tell his disciples that he was giving his life for them. He was giving them his body. It wasn't until after Jesus' death and resurrection that they fully understood this sacrifice.

May you understand what it means to accept the Body of Christ. Receive it so that you may be strengthened when you feel weak, and renewed when you feel weary.

You only have one body to live out the gospel. Use it well.

Open my life, O God, so that I may receive the Body of Christ and then be the Body of Christ in the world. Amen.

OCTOBER

Exercise for Spiritual Fitness

JAMES A. HARNISH

OCTOBER 1   TRYING OR TRAINING?

Spend your time and energy in training yourself for spiritual
fitness. Physical exercise has some value, but spiritual exercise
is much more important, for it promises a reward in both this
life and the next. *(1 Timothy 4:7-8 NLT)*

Every guy who has ever picked up a baseball bat has *tried* to hit
a home run, but the guys who actually hit them are the ones who
train for it. John Ortberg applied that distinction to the Christian
life:

> Trying hard can accomplish only so much. If you are serious about
> seizing this chance of a lifetime, you will have to enter into a life of
> training. You must arrange your life around certain practices that
> will enable you to do what you cannot do now by will power alone.
> (*The Life You've Always Wanted*, Zondervan, 1997, p. 46)

Most of us have learned the hard way that "spiritual transformation is not a matter of trying harder, but of training wisely"
(Ortberg, p. 47). I invite you to think with me this month about the
disciplines that, when practiced over time, will enable us to develop a life of spiritual fitness.

Teach me, O God, to stop trying and start training for a life of
spiritual fitness for this life and the next. Amen.

OCTOBER 2   BEGIN WHERE YOU ARE

As Jesus passed along the Sea of Galilee, he saw Simon and his brother Andrew casting a net into the sea—for they were fishermen. And Jesus said to them, "Follow me and I will make you fish for people."   *(Mark 1:16-17)*

One of my pastoral mentors was chaplain of the University of Florida Gator football team. He said that none of us wants to begin where we are. We all want to begin where we would be if we had started when we should have.

The first time I went to the gym, I saw guys my age who could lift heavier weights and stay on the treadmill longer than I. But my trainer made it clear that I had to begin where I was. He outlined a basic exercise program and led me through rudimentary training that would enable me to start where I was and move ahead.

Jesus met the fishermen where they were and invited them into a lifelong process of training in discipleship. If we want to train for a life of spiritual fitness, we have to begin where we are with the basic disciplines of the Christian life, allowing the Spirit of God to strengthen us along the way.

Thank you, Lord, for meeting me where I am and leading me step by step to become the person you want me to be. Amen.

OCTOBER 3   SOME THINGS TAKE TIME

He went down with them and came to Nazareth, and was obedient to them. . . . And Jesus increased in wisdom and in years, and in divine and human favor.   *(Luke 2:51-52)*

A wise old saint once told me that if God wants mushrooms, they can pop up overnight. But if God wants a Sequoia, it takes a little more time. The same principle applies to both physical and spiritual fitness. Spiritual maturity doesn't happen overnight; it always takes time.

When Jesus was twelve years old, he astonished the teachers in the temple with his adolescent wisdom. In our youth-addicted pop culture, he would have become an overnight celebrity. But Jesus went back with his parents to an out-of-the-way village called Nazareth and was obedient to their parental discipline so that, over time, he would be prepared for the ministry to which God was calling him. Two decades pass in silence in the Gospels until we see him again at his baptism. Even the Son of God could not rush the process of growing up.

Any man who wants to increase in wisdom and in stature needs to be patient. It takes time to become a disciple.

Almighty and infinite God, give me patience that in the finite reality of time I may continue to grow into the likeness of Christ. Amen.

OCTOBER 4   GO FOR THE PRIZE

Do you not know that in a race the runners all compete, but only one receives the prize? Run in such a way that you may win it.   *(1 Corinthians 9:24)*

We don't know if Paul was a runner, but he evidently watched them. He knew enough about running to know that those who enter a race always have a goal in mind. For some, the goal is getting to the finish line first and winning the prize, the way Olympic runners go for the gold medal. But for the vast majority of runners, the goal is not to beat everyone else but to improve their "personal best" time. The prize is constant improvement—being stronger and having more stamina to run this race than they did the last one. They compete against their past performance in order to improve for the next one. The goal is continued improvement.

The point of training for spiritual fitness is not to beat anyone else but to become all that we are capable of being as men who are in training for "the prize of the upward call of God in Christ Jesus" (Philippians 3:14 RSV).

Ever-living God, give me a vision of the prize of your calling in my life, and give me the passion and discipline to run for it with all my might. Amen.

OCTOBER 5   DON'T EXPECT INSTANT GRATIFICATION

I discipline my body like an athlete, training it to do what it should. Otherwise, I fear that after preaching to others I myself might be disqualified.   *(1 Corinthians 9:27 NLT)*

We live in an instant-gratification culture. We are tempted to believe that we can have whatever we want whenever we want it with little or no effort. Just look at some of the clothing advertisements. The pictures of all those perfectly toned and nearly naked bodies would convince us that if we buy the right clothes, we will be just like those guys who have evidently spent their entire lives working out in the gym.

But we all know better. We know that there is no shortcut for building a healthy body; no quick fix for a lack of physical training; no instant gratification that will replace the hard discipline of exercise.

And there's no quick fix spiritually, either. The reshaping of our character around the will and way of Jesus Christ requires an often slow and sometimes painful process of spiritual discipline. But the result is a life that is really our own and is far better than the artificial images in any catalog.

O God, teach me the hard way of discipline that results in life, so that I may become the person you created me to be. Amen.

OCTOBER 6   FITNESS ISN'T GLAMOROUS

Then he said to them all, "If any want to become my followers, let them deny themselves and take up their cross daily and follow me."   *(Luke 9:23)*

Have you noticed the advertisements for glamorous fitness spas where all the "beautiful people" go? It looks as if the only people who go there are the ones who don't need it! But for ordinary guys like me, there's nothing glamorous about the weight room at the gym, and there's nothing glamorous about the way we look when we're working out. We're just a bunch of ordinary guys doing what we can to stay healthy—and we are not particularly concerned about how we look when we do it.

The last time I checked, there was nothing glamorous about self-denial. There is nothing glamorous about the cross. It was the symbol of total rejection, humiliation, ugliness, and shame. Anyone with any sense would be embarrassed to be identified with it. The cross isn't pretty, but it is the only way to the new life of the resurrection.

Lord Jesus, I choose to follow you in the difficult way of the cross in the assurance that it is also the way to resurrection. Amen.

OCTOBER 7   RUN FOR THE CROWN

I have finished the race, I have kept the faith. From now on there is reserved for me the crown of righteousness, which the Lord ... will give me on that day.   *(2 Timothy 4:7b-8)*

The victor's prize in the original Olympic Games was not a gold medal but a laurel-wreath crown. It may not seem like much to us, but the expectation of winning that crown was enough to keep a runner going through the long grueling hours of the marathon.

Paul had evidently seen the winner of a marathon with the crown of victory on his head. He looked toward the end of his life the way a runner looks toward the end of the race, confident that having lived and served faithfully, he would receive "the crown of righteousness" from the One he served. The writer of Revelation painted the same vision of faithful servants of Christ who were crowned with glory at the end of their race.

The life of discipleship is not a sprint but a marathon. One thing that keeps faithful disciples going over the long haul is the assurance that the One who went before them will be waiting for them at the finish line.

Lord, even as you rose victorious over death and reign in Heaven, so give me the strength to run the marathon of life and meet you there. Amen.

OCTOBER 8   THE SHEPHERD'S VOICE

"The sheep hear his voice, and he calls his own sheep by name.... And the sheep follow him, for they know his voice."
(John 10:3-4 RSV)

One of my earliest movie memories is the 1950s classic *A Man Called Peter*. Michael Todd played Peter Marshall, the nationally respected chaplain of the U.S. Senate. In preparation for the role, Todd listened to recordings of Marshall's preaching. He said, "I'm not Peter Marshall. But I can saturate myself with the timbre of the man's voice, with the sparkle of his personality, with the inner essence, until something of the man's spirit shines through" (Catherine Marshall, *To Live Again*, McGraw Hill, 1957, p. 260).

Spiritual discipline does not wipe away the uniqueness of our human personality in some odd attempt to pretend that we are anyone other than who we are. But we can saturate ourselves with Jesus' words, listen for his voice, and soak ourselves in his story in the Gospels so that something of the inner essence of his spirit shines through the uniqueness of our very human lives. Like the sheep, we can know our shepherd's voice and follow where he leads.

Lord Jesus, help me see your life and hear your voice in the Gospels so that something of your life might shine through mine. Amen.

OCTOBER 9   TEACH US TO PRAY

[Jesus] was praying in a certain place, and after he had finished, one of his disciples said to him, "Lord, teach us to pray."
(Luke 11:1)

If you could ask Jesus to teach you anything, what would it be? Something about seeing Jesus pray was so intriguing that it caused one disciple to ask him to teach them to do the same thing. Observing Jesus close at hand, this disciple had evidently figured out that the real power in Jesus' life resulted from his discipline of prayer.

Dorothy Day is remembered primarily as a Roman Catholic social activist. What people often forget is that her activism grew out of a disciplined life of prayer. She said that we are often told that the body needs exercise in order to stay healthy and alive. In the same way, she wrote, "Prayer is that exercise for the soul, just as bending and stretching is the exercise of the body" (*Context*, July 15, 1999, p. 7).

Jesus' example teaches us that if we want to maintain spiritual fitness, we need training in the discipline of prayer.

Lord Jesus, who demonstrated the discipline of prayer in your life with us, even as you taught the first disciples, so teach me to pray. Amen.

OCTOBER 10   OUR FATHER...

He said to them, "When you pray, say: Father, ..." (Luke 11:2)

How do you talk to your father? For some of us, parent-child communication is often a very challenging ordeal. But if the relationship is healthy, the conversation flows freely. There's nothing artificial about it.

What name do you use for your father? Most of us speak to our fathers with personal, intimate, family names like Dad, Daddy, or Pop.

Jesus called God *Abba*, the intimate, family name that literally means "Daddy" or "Papa." It communicates a feeling of warmth, comfort, and welcome. He identifies the God to whom we pray not as some distant, obscure, mean-spirited, capricious being, but as the One who relates to us in the intimacy of healthy family reltionships. The name designates not gender, as if to say that God is male, but relationship, to say that the infinite God relates to us with the intimacy of a loving parent.

If the God to whom I pray is the God whom Jesus called Abba, I can feel at home with him in prayer.

Abba God, I am amazed that you welcome me into your presence as your beloved son. Teach me to trust in you even as a child trusts a loving parent. Amen.

OCTOBER 11   WHAT'S IN A NAME?

He said to them, "When you pray, say: Father, hallowed be your name."   *(Luke 11:2)*

It took me totally by surprise when my daughter and son-in-law announced that they were giving my grandson my name. But then, it's not just *my* name. It belonged to my uncle who was shot down over Holland in World War II. When the family received word of his death, my father vowed to give his firstborn son his brother's name. Now it belongs to my grandson. I bear the name between the past and the future.

On one hand, I would never do anything to dishonor the name of the uncle I never knew. On the other hand, I would never do anything to dishonor the name of the grandson who will follow me. It's all in the meaning that is carried in the name.

We hallow the name of God in prayer because of all that God has done in the past and in the expectation of all that God has promised to do in the future. The name is holy because of the God it represents, the God to whom we pray.

O God, teach me to live in ways that make your name holy in my life and in this world, now and forever. Amen.

OCTOBER 12   FROM HERE TO KINGDOM COME

"Your kingdom come. Your will be done, on earth as it is in heaven."   *(Matthew 6:10)*

Why are freedom-loving Americans whose forebears fought a revolution for independence so fascinated with the British royal family? We are evidently attracted to the pomp and ceremony of a symbolic monarchy. It is the reminder of a time when kings and queens actually ruled in this world, even now, when we live independently of them.

The kingdom of God is not a place or a person so much as it is a relationship that establishes God's authority in our lives. It is the reign of God's grace and the rule of God's will being realized in this world through common men and women whose lives are shaped by the words, way, life, and death of Jesus. God's Kingdom is present in any life lived in obedience to Jesus Christ.

Faithful disciples look to the past to see what the Kingdom looked like in Jesus. They look to the future in the expectation that one day that Kingdom will be fulfilled in the whole creation. They live under the authority of the true King today.

O God who reigns over all creation, reign in me. Allow my life to become a present expression of the future fulfillment of your reign in all the earth. Amen.

OCTOBER 13   LIFE DEPENDS ON IT

"I would feed you with the finest of the wheat, / and with honey from the rock I would satisfy you."   *(Psalm 81:16)*

Jesus teaches us to ask God to provide our daily bread because we can't live without it. As the fast-food commercial declares, "You gotta eat!" Throughout Scripture, bread and water represent the absolute essentials for human survival. It is a reminder that everything we need to sustain life ultimately depends on God.

But Jesus also teaches us to ask God for bread as a reminder of the One upon whom we are ultimately dependent in our spiritual life. To acknowledge our need for bread is to acknowledge our total dependence on the God who provides it.

The writer of Psalm 81 hears God promise that if we will listen for God's voice and follow God's way, then God will satisfy the deepest needs of our lives with the finest wheat and, for good measure, will slather it with honey! The God to whom we pray is the extravagantly generous God who goes beyond the bare necessities and provides us with the fullness and joy of life.

"You satisfy the hungry heart with gift of finest wheat. Come, give to us, O saving Lord, the bread of life to eat."* Amen.

*"You Satisfy the Hungry Heart," Omer Westendorf, 1977, *The United Methodist Hymnal*, p. 629.

OCTOBER 14   FORGIVEN AS WE FORGIVE

Bear with one another and, if anyone has a complaint against another, forgive each other; just as the Lord has forgiven you, so you also must forgive.   *(Colossians 3:13)*

Forgiveness is tough. I think it's the most difficult spiritual discipline. I realized why this is true when I heard someone say that forgiveness means settling for an uneven score.

No matter what game we play, we want the score to be fair. Fans go wild when they think the referee made an unfair call. We hate to lose, but we hate it even more if we think the game was unevenly called. We feel the same way in human relationships. We calculate relationships on the basis of keeping an even score. We want to even up the score of personal hurts and offenses. Tit for tat. Eye for eye.

But forgiveness—God's forgiveness for us and our forgiveness of others—goes beyond trying to even up the score. God's forgiveness always outweighs our sin; it's beyond anything we can earn or deserve. Jesus teaches us to pray that we will experience God's uneven forgiveness as we learn to offer that forgiveness to others.

Forgiveness may be difficult, but that's why it's divine.

O God, even as you go beyond the rules to offer your forgiveness to me, teach me to extend that forgiveness to others. Amen.

OCTOBER 15   LED INTO TEMPTATION

In the spring of the year, the time when kings go out to battle...David remained at Jerusalem. It happened, late one afternoon, when David rose from his couch and was walking about on the roof of the king's house, that he saw from the roof a woman bathing; the woman was very beautiful.
(2 Samuel 11:1-2)

David should have been at work that day. Instead of being where he belonged, David was relaxing on his rooftop patio when he saw

Bathsheba and brought her to the palace for an afternoon of lustful passion. He thought he could get away with it, but as the story unfolds, this moment of temptation sets in motion the downfall of his life.

Temptation—sexual or otherwise—often begins in subtle ways when we are led away from the primary commitments and responsibilities of our lives. The best way to beat temptation is to be where we ought to be, doing what we ought to be doing, so we will not be led in a different direction. Perhaps that's what Jesus intends when he teaches us to pray that we be not led into temptation.

O God, strengthen me in the primary commitments of my life so that I will not be led away from them and into temptation. Amen.

OCTOBER 16   FULLY ALIVE

For this slight momentary affliction is preparing us for an eternal weight of glory beyond all measure, because we look not at what can be seen but at what cannot be seen; for what can be seen is temporary, but what cannot be seen is eternal.
(2 Corinthians 4:17-18)

There's more to *glory* than getting the trophy at the end of the game or making the cover of *Sports Illustrated*. The word comes from a Hebrew root meaning "heavy" or "weighty." Glory isn't a light, ephemeral, esoteric thing. It is God's life made tangible in the weighty realities of this world. It is the infinite life of God made visible in our finite experience.

In the second century, Saint Iraneus said, "The glory of God is man fully alive." The glory of God is revealed in life that models the abundant life Jesus came to bring—life that is nothing less than the life of the risen Christ living in us. God's glory doesn't eliminate my human life; it fulfills it!

Glory belongs to God, which is why Jesus' prayer concludes with the affirmation: "Yours is the kingdom and the power and the glory forever" (Matthew 6:13 NKJV). It is God's glory fully alive in us.

O God of glory, may your life be fully alive in me so that I may bear witness to your glory. Amen.

OCTOBER 17 EXERCISE YOUR PRAYER MUSCLES

When he had entered the house, his disciples asked him privately, "Why could we not cast it out?" He said to them, "This kind can come out only through prayer." **(Mark 9:28-29)**

John Ed Matheson is a championship tennis player. His disciplines of prayer and exercise came together when he wrote:

> Prayer is a spiritual muscle, strengthened when we use it. We don't improve our physical fitness by reading a book about aerobic activity, and we don't build muscles by talking about how strong we'd like to be. In the same way, prayer is something that we get better at only by doing it. (*Treasures of the Transformed Life*, Abingdon Press, 2006, p. 101)

Jesus teaches us to pray the way a tennis coach teaches us to keep our eye on the ball and swing the racket. He not only tells us about prayer; he demonstrates it.

Even for Jesus, there were some things that could be accomplished only through prayer. We learn how to pray by listening to his words and then by doing what he teaches us. He not only shows us how to play in the locker room; he goes with us onto the court!

O Lord, help me not only listen to your words but also follow your example as you teach me to pray. Amen.

OCTOBER 18 DELIBERATE DISCIPLINE

They are to do good, to be rich in good works, generous, and ready to share, thus storing up for themselves the treasure of a good foundation for the future, so that they may take hold of the life that really is life.

(1 Timothy 6:18-19)

Henry David Thoreau once wrote these words:

> I went to the woods because I wished to live deliberately, to front only the essential facts of life, and see if I could not learn what it had to teach, and not, when I came to die, discover that I had not lived. I did not wish to live what was not life, living is so dear; nor did I wish to practice resignation, unless it was quite necessary. I wanted to live deep and suck out all the marrow of life. (*Walden* [1854], in *American Poetry and Prose*, Houghton Mifflin, 1957, p. 566)

Thoreau reminds us of just how easy it is to let real life pass us by in the noisy rush and chaotic confusion of our hyperactive world. It takes deliberate discipline to maintain the healthy spiritual disciplines that enable us to live the abundant life that Jesus promised. But why would we settle for anything less?

Lord, I come into this time of prayer because I want to live deliberately. I want to discover the fullness of life that you intend for each of your children. Amen.

OCTOBER 19   KEEPING YOUR BALANCE

Be careful then how you live, not as unwise people but as wise, making the most of the time, because the days are evil.
(Ephesians 5:15-16)

Karl Wallenda was the patriarch of the world's greatest high-wire circus family. Many thought the winds were too strong for him to go on the wire in San Juan, Puerto Rico, but the overconfident Wallenda started across anyway. Midway through the walk, the wire began to sway in the breeze. Wallenda crouched on the wire, attempting to use his bar to hold his balance. He tumbled to the side, reached out to grab the wire, missed it, and plunged to his death on the pavement below.

Paul used the Greek verb *acribos* to describe what it means to live wisely. To live wisely is to live acrobatically. All of us are capable of losing our balance if we become overconfident in our own strength and power. Paul calls us to live in the power of the Holy Spirit so that we can keep our balance in the winds and currents of the world around us. We find stability as we center our attention on the Spirit of Christ at work within us.

Spirit of God, teach me to live wisely and to keep my life in balance with your purpose and power. Amen.

OCTOBER 20   LOVE AS CHRIST LOVES

Therefore be imitators of God, as beloved children, and live in love, as Christ loved us and gave himself up for us, a fragrant offering and sacrifice to God.   *(Ephesians 5:1-2)*

As a teenager I dated a girl who was a far better Christian than I. We were walking along the midway at the country fair when we came upon a tent that claimed to hold "The Wild Man from the Jungle." We went inside, where we found a dirty, gray-haired, not very sober, older man who was fumbling around with some harmless garden snakes.

I was offended, and ready to protest the way we had been ripped off. But before I could speak, my girlfriend turned to me with a tear in her eye and said, "Just think, Jim. That is a man for whom Christ died." Where I had seen a dirty, drunk old man, she saw a person who was loved so much by God that Jesus would die for him. I haven't always loved like that, but I've never forgotten it, either.

Paul called us to love others as we have been loved by Christ; to see every person we meet as one for whom Christ died.

God of love, teach me to love every person with the love with which you have loved us in Christ. Amen.

OCTOBER 21   LOSE THE WEIGHTS

Lay aside every weight and the sin that clings so closely.
                                                    (Hebrews 12:1)

The writer of the Letter to the Hebrews pictured the Christian life as an Olympic athlete preparing to run the marathon. He evidently had watched as runners, who trained with weights around their ankles, removed the weights from their legs when they entered the stadium so nothing would impede their progress.

In the same way, he calls Christian disciples to get rid of anything that gets in the way or slows us down along the way of faith, particularly the specific sin that affects our lives most directly. The weight could be personal habits, negative attitudes, or unhealthy practices that get in the way of spiritual fitness. If we are attentive to our own spiritual vitality, we can name the "weights" that hold us back. The writer challenges each of us to take decisive action to lay the weights aside so we are free to move into a living, growing, vibrant relationship with God in Jesus Christ.

O Lord, show me those sins that cling closely to me and give me the strength to lay them aside in order to follow you with freedom and power. Amen.

OCTOBER 22   RUN YOUR OWN RACE

Let us run with perseverance the race that is set before us.
(Hebrews 12:1)

One of the things that kept me from getting started as a runner was my internal insecurity about other runners—probably the remnant of uncomfortable memories of seventh-grade physical education classes! How would I keep up with them? What if they could outdistance me? What if I looked downright stupid when I did it? But then a runner friend helped me realize that I did not need to run like anyone else. I could run in my own time, at my own speed, and in my own way; and it would be OK. The important thing was that I kept at it for my own health and well-being.

The writer of Hebrews challenges us to run the race that is "set before us" in the context of our own unique challenges, opportunities, strengths, and weaknesses. We're not responsible for anyone's race—only our own. The athletic-shoe folk got it right in their commercials when they said, "Just do it!"

Lord, give me the strength to run my own race in your strength and Spirit. Amen.

OCTOBER 23   FOLLOW A WINNER

Looking to Jesus the pioneer and perfecter of our faith, who for the sake of the joy that was set before him endured the cross, disregarding its shame, and has taken his seat at the right hand of the throne of God.   *(Hebrews 12:2)*

I was never very good at tennis, but I enjoyed it. Fortunately, I got connected with some players who were far better than I was. Although I could never outscore them, just being on the court with them improved my game. Their patience with my inadequacy helped me become more adequate. If we want to improve, we need to practice with someone who is better than we are but is willing to meet us where we are and encourage us along the way.

Our training for spiritual fitness must be centered in the words, will, and way of Jesus as recorded in the Gospels. He is both the source and goal of our spiritual journey. If we want to be Christlike people, our spiritual trainer is Christ, the one who has already run this race—even when it meant going to the cross—and the one who walked away with the prize on Easter morning!

Lord Jesus, you have run this race before me and won the victory over sin and death. Help me keep my eyes on you. Amen.

OCTOBER 24   WHAT FRIENDS ARE FOR

"I do not call you servants any longer, because the servant does not know what the master is doing; but I have called you friends."   *(John 15:15)*

For my fiftieth birthday my wife invited all the guys who have been my closest friends, and their wives, to a party on the beach. One of those guys has been my friend for more than half my life. Several are members of a clergy retreat group that has been together for more than twenty-five years. They define the meaning of friendship in my life.

I was standing at the side of the room, looking around at this amazing collection of people who have made such a profound difference in my life. The person beside me said, "You know, Jim, you are a very rich man." And he was correct!

When Jesus gathered the men who had been closest to him around the Passover table, he raised human friendship to the level of a sacrament as he identified the disciples not as servants but as his friends. If Jesus needed friends to make it through this life, why would we think we could get along without them?

Lord Jesus, who called the first disciples friends, give me that gift of friendship and teach me to give that gift to others. Amen.

OCTOBER 25   LAMENT FOR A FRIEND

Some friendships do not last, but some friends are more loyal than brothers.   *(Proverbs 18:24 GNT)*

Glenn was seventy-one years old when he died unexpectedly of a massive heart attack. He and his wife were the closest friends my wife and I have. We ate more meals, shared more laughter, and cried more tears together than we can begin to count. Then all too suddenly, totally without warning, he was gone and we were left speechless, numb, broken, and alone.

I'm grateful for the "psalms of lament" in which the writers never hesitate to name their grief, anger, pain, and hurt over what feels like the absolute injustice of what they are experiencing. It was not supposed to be this way! We fully expected to end up as old codgers telling stories in the rocking chairs on the front porch. Now, the stories will have to wait for rocking chairs on the front porch of heaven. But despite the pain, there is nothing I would give in exchange for his friendship. The reason it hurts so badly is that the gift was so good. Every man needs a friend like that.

O God, who gives us the gift of friendship, give us also the assurance of that friendship with you, which can never be taken away. Amen.

OCTOBER 26   A MAN OF HOPE

For in hope we were saved. Now hope that is seen is not hope.
For who hopes for what is seen? But if we hope for what we do
not see, we wait for it with patience.   *(Romans 8:24-25)*

When Glenn died, one of his sons described him as a man who
had no illusions about life but who had hope. He knew about joy
and pain. He knew God did not promise that everything would be
fair, but that God would always love. He believed that God does
not need more angels in heaven as much as God needs people who
will be a part of God's kingdom being fulfilled on earth.

Glenn's gift of hope was passed on to his preschool-age grandson. First thing in the morning he would shout to his father from
the top of the stairs, "New day, Daddy!" or whisper into his grandfather's ear, "New day, Papa!"

The hope in which we live and die is the confidence that, by
God's grace, every day is a new day with new possibilities. Even if
we don't at first see it, we watch and wait for it to be revealed.

God of all hope, help me live without illusions about the world
but with great hope in what you are doing in it. Amen.

OCTOBER 27   LISTEN TO THE COACH

I hear a voice I had not known: ... "O that my people would
listen to me, that Israel would walk in my ways!"
                     (Psalm 81:5b, 13)

Hoosiers, one of my all-time favorite movies, is the inspiring story
of a small-town, underdog high-school basketball team that unexpectedly won the state championship because of a new coach who
demanded that each player give up his stubborn desire for hotshot
basketball stardom and play for the sake of the team. They became
champions when they learned to listen to the coach.

The writer of Psalm 81 hears the Spirit of God offer two alternative ways of living. One way is to live with "stubborn hearts, to
follow their own counsels" (v. 12). It's the way of self-centered

arrogance that is focused on its own interests. The alternative is to learn to listen for God's voice and to walk in God's way. It's the way of self-surrender to God's purpose and obedience to God's will. The divine promise is that the way of listening and obedience is the way that leads to victory.

It worked for the psalmist. It worked in *Hoosiers*. It will work for us!

O God, be the ultimate coach in my life. Teach me to listen for your word and to walk in your way. Amen.

OCTOBER 28   STICKING WITH IT

Let endurance have its full effect, so that you may be mature and complete, lacking in nothing.   *(James 1:4)*

Leroy "Satchel" Paige, baseball's famous philosopher pitcher, said that we shouldn't pray when it rains if we don't pray when the sun shines.

I have no doubt about God's ability to hear the prayers of people who run to him in rain, in the hard times, when emergencies come. But I have great doubt about our ability to experience God's presence in the emergencies if we have not cultivated a growing relationship with God along the way. Powerful prayer grows out of consistency. It is a result of disciplined practice of those who hang in there.

A preacher friend in California pointed out that a weekend golfer sometimes gets off a great shot, but to win the British Open takes more than an occasional experience and natural ability. It calls for disciplined practice over time. Spiritual fitness is the result of consistency, or sticking with it in the good times, so that we will know God's presence in the bad ones.

O God, whose sunshine and rain fall on the just and the unjust, give me strength to walk with you in the sunshine so that I may know your presence in the rain. Amen.

OCTOBER 29   GROWING OLD . . . GROWING
BETTER

Therefore we do not lose heart. Though outwardly we are wasting away, yet inwardly we are being renewed day by day.
(2 Corinthians 4:16 NIV)

I love Ernest Hemingway's description of his aging hunting companion. "His body no longer housed him fittingly. It has gone on and changed, thickening here, losing its lines, bloating a little there, but inside he was young and lean and tall and hard as when he galloped lion on the plain" (*Green Hills of Africa*, C. Scribner, 1963, p. 73).

No matter how well we take care of them, these bodies of ours will show signs of age. They will not always house us fittingly. But if we have maintained healthy spiritual disciplines and if we have continued to grow in our faith, our inner man, the person who lives most deeply inside of us, can continue to be renewed every day.

I've known some men who just keep getting older until they progressively shut down. But I've known other men who, as their bodies age, continue to show the evidence of a lean, tall, energetic spirit—constantly learning, growing, and making new discoveries in their faith. I want to grow up to be like them!

O God, even as my body gets older, may my spirit be continually renewed and reenergized by your spirit. Amen.

OCTOBER 30   OUR CHAMPIONSHIP SEASON

"Do not be afraid; I am the first and the last. . . . I was dead, and see, I am alive forever and ever; and I have the keys of Death and of Hades."   *(Revelation 1:17b-18)*

In the Pulitzer Prize-winning play *That Championship Season*, four members of the starting lineup gather at their old coach's house to celebrate the twentieth anniversary of the night they won the state high-school basketball championship. Unfortunately, what was intended to be a joyful reunion turns into a disaster. None of their lives had turned out as they'd hoped, and the old coach in whom they had put their trust turns out to be a fraud.

My wife and I saw the play with another couple. Our wives didn't like the play. But the other husband, who happened to be a coach, and I could identify with the players' desire to reconnect with a great moment in their past and could feel sympathy for their disappointment at the way their lives had turned out.

The good news is that life doesn't have to turn out that way! Followers of Christ are headed toward a great reunion celebration. The championship season is always out ahead. And whatever happens along the way, we know that we can trust our risen coach to see us through.

O risen Christ, enable me to live in this life in joyful anticipation of the life that is to come through your victory over sin and death. Amen.

OCTOBER 31   SEEING THE END

"The kingdom of the world has become the kingdom of our Lord and of his Messiah, and he will reign forever and ever."
(Revelation 11:15)

Because of a previous commitment, I couldn't watch the Florida Gators play the Ohio State Buckeyes for the 2007 national football championship. I recorded the game to watch the next day. I discovered that knowing who won the game made a big difference in how I watched it. I still knew that the game had to be won or lost in real time. Every play mattered. But knowing how the game came out in the end relieved a lot of anxiety along the way.

The game of human history still has to be played on the field. We're not spectators but participants in God's redemptive work. Every play matters. There will be wins and losses, hits and hurts, and we might be taken off the field before the game is over. But we can throw ourselves with joyful abandon into the vision of God's Kingdom because we know how the really big game comes out in the end!

O risen Christ, may I give myself with total abandon to the work of your Kingdom, confident in the ultimate victory of your reign. Amen.

NOVEMBER

Self-Assessment

JOHN UNDERWOOD

NOVEMBER 1   MY JOURNEY

The LORD shall judge the people: judge me, O LORD, according to my righteousness, and according to mine integrity that is in me.   *(Psalm 7:8 KJV)*

November to me has always been a month of personal assessment. In the United States we celebrate Thanksgiving, and we generally gather as families and groups and think about what we are thankful for. We begin to think about ourselves—where we come from, what we have done, and what we are planning to do. We talk with family and friends; we share new experiences and remember old ones.

Join me in an assessment of self as we take a look at two books in the Bible that tend to lend themselves to the common human experience—through song in the book of Psalms, and through the application of practical wisdom in the book of Proverbs.

Assessment is useful only when we use it truthfully and apply it as a tool to recognize needs in our life. Who are you? Where do you come from? What do you plan to do? How are you going to do it? What kind of experience have you had so far?

I have always been told by my elders that lessons about life are in our songs of praise and stories of experience. Traditionally that is how we learn.

Creator, help me listen for your words of guidance so I can apply them faithfully in my life. Amen.

NOVEMBER 2   GOD'S PRESENCE

Blessed is the man that walketh not in the counsel of the ungodly, nor standeth in the way of sinners, nor sitteth in the seat of the scornful.   *(Psalm 1:1 KJV)*

When I was a child, my father told me that Native American people have always believed that everything in nature is alive—trees, grass, and plants of all kinds—and that God (*O-fun-ga* from the Seminole language, which means "breath giver") is everywhere. So it intrigued me to be in nature as much as I could. I believe those days helped me listen for God's words and respect his works.

People generally act differently when they are at church, God's house, because they sense his presence there. If only we might learn to sense God's presence everywhere.

God is in all of creation; his presence is constant. Until we believe that, the only thing consistent about our behavior will be inconsistency. Let us recognize God daily, for he is all around us.

Father, your daily presence in my life demands respect. Help me live in a manner that is respectful of you—help me to walk not in the way of the ungodly but in the way of the righteous. Amen.

NOVEMBER 3   TRUSTING GOD'S PLAN

Blessed are all they that put their trust in him.
                                        (Psalm 2:12 KJV)

I work in retail, and I have consistently heard one statement that always moves me like the sound of fingernails on a chalkboard: "I pulled myself up by my own bootstraps."

What does that mean? To me, it means that someone has the prideful belief that he or she is the sole reason for all the prosperity in his or her life. To disprove this statement, one needs only to examine the individual's life and take note of all the people who have made a difference.

We all learn from other people. Some people are good examples; some are bad examples. Some people give us breaks; some look to take breaks. Yet each one plays a part in helping us shape our lives in some way.

God's presence in your life is a constant—from the teacher who helped you to love math to the coworker who became your boss and opened the corporate door a little wider. Our choices are the variables. God is constant.

God, help me realize that pride is a barrier between my plan and your plan for my life. Help me trust in you and your plan. Amen.

NOVEMBER 4   STRENGTH FROM RIGHTEOUSNESS

Lead me, O LORD, in thy righteousness because of mine enemies; make thy way straight before my face.

(Psalm 5:8 KJV)

I come from a community that has been choked by poverty for generation after generation. It is currently the poorest county in the state of Oklahoma. Poverty brings hunger, tears, broken hearts, drugs, alcohol, dropouts, and young parents.

I thank God for showing me a way to break out of this cycle of poverty. God helped me realize that to be tough, strong, accepted, and loved, I did not have to say yes to every challenge that was thrown at me. Alcohol wasn't a rite of passage but a barrier to a good future.

It's easy to live a reckless life; anyone can do it. To live a righteous life is much more difficult, but the rewards are great.

Father, thank you for helping me realize that true strength is exhibited by righteousness lived out in the everyday routine I follow to ensure my family's future. Amen.

NOVEMBER 5   CHOICES ARE TRANSPARENT

He made a pit, and digged it, and is fallen into the ditch which he made.   *(Psalm 7:15 KJV)*

God has given us the power of choice, and he does not waiver in his decision. We have the power to change our direction, feelings, place, and beliefs in life at will. This is why bad things often happen to good people. I believe that God does not choose all the whens and wheres; he allows us to choose. He simply starts us out in life and says *choose*. Good people and bad choices are constantly crossing paths. Sometimes it's painful; other times it's deadly.

Look at some of the choices you have made in life and think about the outcomes. The more you look back, the better you can see forward. You have the power to change or implement your life in any way you see fit. What will you choose?

Father, I pray for direction, conviction, strength, and the ability to see the impact of my decisions. Amen.

NOVEMBER 6   FEAR FOCUSES US ON GOD

The LORD also will be a refuge for the oppressed, a refuge in times of trouble.   *(Psalm 9:9 KJV)*

I spent many nights as a child listening to loud thuds, glasses breaking, shouts, screams, and words not meant for the ears of children. I am the product of generational poverty, a broken family, and genocide. I know who I am, where I come from, and where my people came from. As I look back at my life, I would not trade the tears shed or the pain inflicted, for they have brought me closer to God; and I believe that this is the true test of life.

When we are comfortable, we tend to push all thoughts of God to the side; and when we are in times of trouble, we are quick to shout his name. The Lord never leaves us; rather, we often don't notice him until we need refuge. God did not come to me because of the pain; I simply began to notice him because of it. He was always there.

Lord, help me recognize the love you give me, and give me the strength to show my love for you so that others can see and receive your gifts. Amen.

NOVEMBER 7   FORTUNE COMES FROM WITHIN

A good name is to be chosen rather than great riches, and favor is better than silver or gold.   *(Proverbs 22:1)*

The measure of a man is in his deeds. When someone asks us what a man is like, we don't respond with a list of things he owns or his net worth; we generally describe his actions. We might say that he is honest, trustworthy, helpful, considerate, strong, straightforward, and hardworking.These are characteristics that cannot be bought; they must be developed.

Sometimes we get caught up in the perception of fortune and forget about the story of our deeds. What story will you write—the story of the righteous or the story of the wicked?

Dear God, open my eyes to your gifts and help me focus on the wealth of my spirit. Amen.

NOVEMBER 8   MAKE 'EM COUNT

So teach us to number our days, that we may apply our hearts unto wisdom.   *(Psalm 90:12 KJV)*

A coworker sent me an e-mail that told the story of a man who purchased a large number of marbles and placed them in a box in the garage. Each marble represented one day in his life. He separated the correct number of marbles in order to visually represent how many days he had spent. Every day thereafter, he went in and removed one marble, placed it in the spent box, and reflected.

As men, sometimes we don't allow ourselves to fully open up to life's experiences—and I don't mean extreme sports, or extreme anything. I'm talking about making more investments in our everyday lives. It could be hugging your children in the morning or saying a kind word to someone or making an effort to help someone. These are gifts of the spirit; and when we invest in these gifts in a truly meaningful manner, we open ourselves up to receive gifts of the spirit as well.

Don't spend all your marbles before you figure out that life is a series of emotions tied to memories and bound by gifts of the spirit.

Father, help me see that fear of pain closes my heart to the gifts that are available to me. Help me invest myself in every day. Amen.

NOVEMBER 9   THE MEANING OF LIFE

Know ye that the LORD he is GOD: it is he that hath made us, and not we ourselves; we are his people, and the sheep of his pasture.   (Psalm 100:3 KJV)

Love and the experience thereof is the meaning of life. God is the purpose, and God is love. Love is only meaningful if given; it can't be taken. God created people to give his love to; some people return the favor and some do not. We have muddled our minds with so many choices in life that we lose track of our purpose, which is to love God. And the rewards of loving God are infinite.

We struggle with accepting God's love. God lavishes us with love, yet we feel only a small portion of what is offered. When we focus on giving our love to God, we find that there are infinite ways God shows us love—in the eyes of loved ones, the colors of spring, the aroma of hot chocolate on a cold day.

God's love is in the experience; and when we are focused on God, we have the ability to recognize the experience and receive God's love. This is what brings us closer to God.

Help me daily focus my thoughts on you, God, so I can experience your love in greater detail. Amen.

NOVEMBER 10   ONLY THE PRESENT

For a thousand years in thy sight are but as yesterday when it is past, and as a watch in the night.   *(Psalm 90:4 KJV)*

Some cultures believe that there is no past and no future—only the present. The past lives in the mind's eye, and it is saved and shared through various forms, most of which are routinely ignored by many people.

How are you spending the present? Is it a blur of cell-phone calls or e-mails?

What will your life experience be? Will it be a detailed, focused picture of experiences or a muddled blur of time spent "spending time"?

Beauty is in the details of life. Unplug every once in a while and pay attention to the details. It will give you perspective about what is truly important.

Blessed are those who hear your voice and respond. Help me hear your voice. Amen.

NOVEMBER 11   PRAYING TO GOD

Give ear to my words, O LORD, consider my meditation.
                                                   (Psalm 5:1 KJV)

Sitting under an arbor in the summer heat with a stiff Oklahoma wind blowing, I listened as a young person to a sermon that was given by a young man who was something of a prodigy. Not yet ten years old, he traveled and preached at different churches all over Indian country. He always drew in all the young people because when he spoke, he sounded like an old person in a young person's body. He spoke with authority, conviction, confidence, and a loud, clear voice.

One of the things he spoke of on this day was the way in which people pray. He said that reverence, humility, and thankfulness should always be present when speaking with God. I have always remembered that.

When you pray, is it for the ears of those who might hear you, or for God's ears?

Almighty God, thank you for listening to my feeble voice. I love you. Amen.

NOVEMBER 12   CHOOSING YOUR PATH

Even though I walk through the darkest valley, I fear no evil; / for you are with me.   *(Psalm 23:4)*

In the everyday struggle of right and wrong, we are consistently asked to make choices; and those choices determine who we are as people. I have witnessed with my own eyes children who wake up in a house full of drunken people, and I have seen them step over beer bottles and sleeping individuals to make their way to church. God is always present, and God shows us the path back to him. All we have to do is choose to follow his instructions.

Seminoles have a creation story that talks about how we came from underground (darkness) and climbed above ground into the light. This creation story is represented by seven different colors from dark to light in our traditional patchwork, and it serves as a reminder that even in darkness we can find light if we look for it.

Creator, help me see the path you are making for me. Amen.

NOVEMBER 13   AVOIDING VIOLENCE

His trouble shall return upon his own head, / And his violent dealing shall come down on his own crown. (Psalm 7:16 NKJV)

I know a man who has broken his hand, collarbone, arm, jaw, foot, and skull—not all at once but on many different occasions, some of his bones more than once. As he was growing up, he was constantly testing his boundaries and pushing the envelope. When we were young men, it seemed trouble was always close by. He didn't go looking for it; trouble came looking for him. And he was a willing participant once it showed up.

I used to ponder why he was always in fights. I realized later that he stayed close to violence because of the people and places he chose. He placed himself in many of those situations; and when you play the odds with violence, it catches you sooner or later. His thoughts, actions, and memories led him to violence, and he embraced it instead of pushing it away.

Our prisons are filled with young men like the one I speak of, and so are the cemeteries. This man survived his youth and seven stabbings to realize that no one wins with violence. Sometimes we men have to learn this lesson through firsthand experience instead of secondhand stories.

Father, help me recognize my actions and control my thoughts so that I can manipulate my environment, making it conducive to life, not death. Amen.

NOVEMBER 14   PAYING ATTENTION TO GOD'S
                                            DIRECTION

Thou hast enlarged my steps under me, that my feet did not slip.   *(Psalm 18:36 KJV)*

My high school coach once told me, "I think you're good at being a catcher because you have such large feet; it gives you greater balance and a wider range behind the plate." As I look back, I realize that being good at sports gave me larger feet. Sports was the accelerator in my life, keeping me out of trouble, up on my homework, and optimistic about my life. It opened doors for me and gave me hope for a fuller life. The pitfalls of an impoverished community were consistently sidestepped in my life for the opportunity to play ball, and I thank God for shining the flashlight on that path. He gave me an incentive and a focus that helped me be successful in school.

Where is God leading you? The more you pay attention to his direction, the better your decisions will be. If you focus on God, he will show you the way.

Father, help me listen for your direction and hear your voice. We are always given a choice; help me choose the right path. Amen.

NOVEMBER 15   LOOK UP

Mine eyes are ever toward the Lord; for he shall pluck my feet out of the net.   *(Psalm 25:15 KJV)*

I heard a story once about hikers who traveled to a remote location to climb. As they started the hike, they were constantly reminded by the locals to always focus on the peak. They were to look up instead of down, because looking at the goal brought energy and excitement. Looking down and back brought feelings of fatigue and drudgery.

Spiritually speaking, the same holds true for us. We need to focus consistently on God and not on our day-to-day processes.

Take time to look up and give thanks, and God will lighten your footsteps daily.

Thank you, Lord, for your love and guidance, no matter where I may be in life. Amen.

NOVEMBER 16   SETTING AN EXAMPLE

Let integrity and uprightness preserve me; for I wait on thee.   *(Psalm 25:21 KJV)*

There's a saying that it takes a long time to build trust and only a second to tear it down. I was always told that a man is known by his deeds. What story does your life tell at this point? What story would you like it to tell? Are you a man who seeks the gifts of the Spirit or the gifts of the heart? A man is an example to other men, both young and old. We should be strong pillars in our communities and provide positive examples to our youth. Credibility is built on prior examples of what we do. What do you show the people around you?

Lord, help me see the power in my actions and be a good example for you. Amen.

NOVEMBER 17 DON'T FEAR THE UNKNOWN

The Lord is my light and my salvation; whom shall I fear? The Lord is the strength of my life; of whom shall I be afraid?
(Psalm 27:1 KJV)

I remember the teachings of my father. He used to tell me as a child that all things wanted to be round, because that is the natural order of things. He gave me plenty of examples along the way: trees are round, the earth is round, birds build round nests, and the seasons travel in a cycle.

What my father was talking about so long ago was the journey that we all embark on as children—the circle, or journey, of life. We enter the world kicking and screaming into a new and strange environment. We are hesitant to leave the warmth of the womb; however, we find that the new environment has so many things to discover. We travel through the cycle of life and often leave this world as fragile as we were when we came in. We then return to the earth from where we came. In the end, we travel once again into the unknown.

God tells us in the Bible that he is on the other side and that there is a place with no more tears. The circle continues; it just seems to be bigger than we can imagine.

Father, help me see the truth in the things you say and exercise my faith so that it can help me not to be afraid of the unknown. Amen.

NOVEMBER 18 MORE LIKE CHILDREN

Weeping may endure for a night, but joy cometh in the morning.
(Psalm 30:5b KJV)

This passage makes me think about all the children in the world who find themselves in situations that they had no choice in making—from the children in war zones to children in famine-stricken lands to kids in destructive environments right here in the United States. Yet children know better than any other group that there is a light at the end of the tunnel. Tomorrow brings infinite possibilities.

May we be more like children, remembering that although weeping may endure for a night, joy comes in the morning.

Dear God, open my eyes so that I may have the faith that children come by so naturally. Amen.

NOVEMBER 19   WORDS HAVE POWER

Into thine hand I commit my spirit: thou hast redeemed me, O Lord God of truth.   *(Psalm 31:5 KJV)*

"Be careful of the things you say; there is power in the words you speak." This was a common saying of the elders in my community, and I have always tried to heed what they told me. The Bible gives us many examples of the power of the spoken word and of how, when it is combined with true faith, it can move mountains.

I once went to a summer camp for gifted and talented Native American Indian students from all over the country. The concept of the summer camp was to empower native youth through leadership examples, encouragement, challenges, and constant affirmation through the positive words of both speakers and faculty.

The summer camp was a success, and the achievements of the students who attended the camp have far exceeded the expectations of the camp administrators. The camp empowered hundreds of youth through positive words.

If you speak the positive and believe it, you will live it. The spoken word is meant for conviction. If you say something often enough, you come to believe it. And if you believe it, your mind and body will follow.

Gracious heavenly Father, thank you for listening to my feeble voice. Thank you for turning it into a source of strength. Amen.

NOVEMBER 20   BE OF GOOD COURAGE

Be of good courage, and he shall strengthen your heart, all ye that hope in the LORD.   *(Psalm 31:24 KJV)*

Courage is a word that describes one's ability to overcome fear. Fear may be present, but courage does not allow it to rule.

On television our children see constant images of people losing control in every situation imaginable, and very few examples of how to maintain control. When I was a child, my parents constantly reinforced the idea that one should maintain control in all circumstances. They would instruct me to calm down, look at the situation, and figure out what needed to be done. I carry those habits with me still today.

My girls have learned this response as well. When they were young, we did not run to them with dramatic words of pity every time they fell down. I merely told them to get up, asked if they were OK, and gave them advice. Sometimes they repeated their mistakes, and sometimes they learned after the first time. Over time they have become stronger.

God gives us many examples of how he is always there for us—through our loved ones, through the lives of others, and through the Bible. When you know God, courage always follows; and by overcoming fear, strength grows in your heart.

Get up. You're OK. Now, what needs to be done?

Father, thank you for being the cornerstone of courage and for strengthening my heart with every barrier I face. Amen.

NOVEMBER 21   STRENGTH

An horse is a vain thing for safety: neither shall he deliver any by his great strength.   *(Psalm 33:17 KJV)*

Spiritual people think about spiritual things in a spiritual context. The true measure of a man's strength is not the power in his physical form but his belief in himself as a spiritual being.

For years I have thought about painting a picture about strength. I can see the picture in my mind's eye. "Strength" is a figure with a powerful physical form, kneeling with his head bowed and his arms stretched out in front of him. The figure also would have powerful, angelic wings that would be stretched out to cover his arms and head. The background would be mostly dark—lit only by a warm light that descends upon the form. Ideally, it would stir two thoughts about strength, similar to the way some drawings elicit two totally different viewpoints. As you gazed at the painting, you would ponder these questions: Where is your strength—in your physical body or in your spiritual being? Are you stronger standing and fighting or kneeling and praying?

Lord, give me the strength to see my limitations, and the faith to accept the powerful gifts you want to give me. Amen.

NOVEMBER 22   TRUE PROSPERITY

They rewarded me evil for good to the spoiling of my soul.
(Psalm 35:12 KJV)

Prosperity is not found in a new car lot or the latest cell phone. Prosperity lives in the heart. Prosperity is being able to receive the intangible gifts of God. As we live our lives, God fills our hearts with treasures of the spirit—gifts that are spiritual rather than material—and when we leave this world, that is all we carry with us. In the end, that is who we are. Acquisition of material objects interferes with our ability to truly experience the spiritual gifts that God gives us daily.

Today, stop and notice the color purple.

Heavenly Father, keep from spoiling my soul by helping me focus on the spiritual gifts you have laid before me, and help me prioritize my life accordingly. Amen.

NOVEMBER 23   MIND CONTROL

Cease from anger, and forsake wrath: fret not thyself in any wise to do evil.   *(Psalm 37:8 KJV)*

Mind control. What *is* mind control? Is it a sci-fi concept, or is it reality? Hypnotists will tell you that it is reality if you have a willing subject. I believe mind control is a reality, but it is much different from what is depicted in the movies. Mind control is the ability to control your own thoughts—and, of course, you must be willing!

The Bible gives us many examples of how thoughts can manifest themselves into actions, and actions can produce results—both positive and negative. Today's scripture is a warning about the perils of anger and of thoughts of doing evil. We need only to look at the nightly news to see the effects of individuals who allow the seeds of evil thoughts to find fertile ground in their minds.

Mind control is the constant practice of filtering your thoughts each time they enter your mind. Stopping negative thoughts at their conception and focusing on positive thoughts eliminates harmful input so that positive seeds may take root and grow. Positive actions result only when they are powered by positive thoughts. With practice, the filtering gets easier, and negative or evil thoughts find it harder and harder to find fertile ground.

God, help me see the power in the seeds of thoughts, and strengthen my ability to filter the good from the bad. Amen.

NOVEMBER 24 ETERNAL VERSUS TEMPORARY RICHES

A little that a righteous man hath is better than the riches of many wicked. *(Psalm 37:16 KJV)*

In my Bible, the words of Christ appear in red print—and the last time I checked, these words were red: "And again I say unto you, It is easier for a camel to go through the eye of a needle, than for a rich man to enter into the kingdom of God" (Matthew 19:24 KJV). Life as we know it is but one breath when compared to eternity. Live your life accordingly. Do not lose the Kingdom for a life of coveting the riches of the wicked. Knowledge, wisdom, faith, peace, love—these are the riches of a righteous man. Which of these eternal riches would you be willing to trade for any amount of temporary riches?

Thank you, Father, for giving me the insight to see that sometimes what is up is really down, and what is first will be last. Help me focus on eternal riches rather than temporary riches. Amen.

NOVEMBER 25   DISQUIETNESS OF THE HEART

I am feeble and sore broken: I have roared by reason of the disquietness of my heart. **(Psalm 38:8 KJV)**

It was the policy and procedure of the federal government for decades to strip Native Americans of their culture and uniqueness. Children were taken from their families at school age and shipped off to boarding schools around the country. Siblings were separated, and children were psychologically and physically punished for any act that resembled the culture they were born into. The family unit, cultural identity, individual creativity, and the basic needs of love and affection were all attacked with military precision.

Those children grew up with disquietness in their hearts. Their families, in turn, experienced dysfunction because they did not know how to be parents.

I have witnessed firsthand the effects of generational dysfunction and how children continually are the victims of harsh environments. The cycle continues to claim new generations because people do not recognize inhibitors such as alcohol, drugs, lack of education, and poverty. The families have pain because they treat the symptoms of broken hearts rather than the cause of what is breaking them.

Families need to learn how to be families.

Father, help me find the cracks in my heart and fix them for the health of my family. I can't fix everyone's problems, but I can, with your help, keep from passing my own problems on to future generations. Amen.

NOVEMBER 26   DO YOUR BEST

Commit thy works unto the LORD, and thy thoughts shall be established. **(Proverbs 16:3 KJV)**

My father told me one time, "You should always do your best at whatever job you are doing, even when you think no one is watching." I said, "Well, if no one is watching, then who will know?" He said, "You will."

I always thought that my father had an exceptional work ethic. If he was digging a hole, he wanted to dig it faster and bigger than everyone else; and he constantly pushed himself mentally and physically to accomplish the standard he set for himself.

Today my father doesn't do as much physical labor as he once did, but he continues to push the young men of our community when given the opportunity. These days he works for the tribe and the church with the belief that these are the places he is meant to be. He has committed his work to trying to make things better for the community around him, and the Lord blesses him with thoughts of how to do just that. He talks, eats, drinks, and sleeps with thoughts of advancing the lives of the people around him.

God, help me recognize my worth and utilize the tools that you have given me for works that need to be done. Help me be an example for you. Amen.

NOVEMBER 27   SLOW TO ANGER

He that is slow to anger is better than the mighty; and he that ruleth his sprit than he that taketh a city. (Proverbs 16:32 KJV)

A man who is slow to anger is a man who is thoughtful in his actions. A man who rules his spirit is one who controls his destiny.

Anger is like a match surrounded by combustible material: it requires a spark, but once it starts, it can get out of control quickly. Children must be taught how to control their anger because when it is left unchecked, it grows bigger and meaner with a constantly shortening fuse.

An old man told me once that when you allow anger to take over, you lose control of yourself and give control to the thing that has caused the anger. I can think of no positive purpose for anger. Even in combat, anger serves only to cloud the mind and limit judgment. It is a destroyer and should be recognized and dealt with appropriately.

We men should not fuel anger with our thoughts; we must separate it with mind control, self-control, and time. This is what separates us from the beasts of the field.

Gracious heavenly Father, help me recognize the destructive components in my life, and give me the foresight and the vigilance to overcome these obstacles for myself and the people around me. Amen.

NOVEMBER 28   SETTING A GOOD EXAMPLE

Children's children are the crown of old men; and the glory of children are their fathers.   *(Proverbs 17:6 KJV)*

I can remember watching my father work when I was a child. I paid attention to his pace, thought process, strength, and knowledge. I found it intriguing to pick apart what made him tick. I later used what I learned from my father and placed it as a standard of achievement, pushing myself to meet those standards. When I was young it was hard to match the work my father did, but as I grew older it became easier. My father was there to set the bar, and it was my duty to raise that bar for my children.

Some fathers set the bar high, and some set it low. The question is, where will *you* set the bar for your children? How do you work? How do you play? How do you pray?

Lord, help me be a good example for those around me. Amen.

NOVEMBER 29   LOOK TO YOUR ELDERS

The glory of young men is their strength: and the beauty of old men is the grey head.   *(Proverbs 20:29 KJV)*

When I was a child, my father wrestled with me. We were constantly interacting with one another. At the time, I looked at it as playful fun. As I grew older, I looked at it as a challenge. Now, looking back, I see that my father taught me a lot of things about myself with that interaction. By letting me win sometimes, he taught me how to never give up even when it seems impossible to win. I learned that no matter how physically strong you are, sometimes you lose because you didn't use your mind. I learned that I had boundaries and that there were consequences when they were broken. I learned how to laugh at myself. I learned how to compose myself when I lost and how to be gracious when I won. I am thankful for those times.

As teenagers we think we know it all, and as young men we feel that we have to do it all. Sometimes we continually reinvent the wheel instead of turning to our elders. Advice is free. You don't have to use it, but you do have to ask for it.

God, help me open my mind to the knowledge around me and find the information that is useful to the situations I will encounter. Amen.

NOVEMBER 30   KNOW YOUR HEART

Every way of a man is right in his own eyes: but the LORD pondereth the hearts.   **(Proverbs 21:2 KJV)**

You can go into any prison in America and talk with some of the meanest individuals there, and they all will have one thing in common: they have an explanation or a reason for doing the crime that put them where they are. It is a human trait to be able to justify one's actions by one's thoughts. Whether it is a lie or a felony, anyone can justify an action if given enough time to think about it.

A man needs to analyze his actions and his heart. Feed the positive aspects and clean out the negative influences. The heart is the compass of life and requires constant attention in order to navigate the obstacles of life. Sometimes a man needs to analyze his feelings instead of burying them, because they tend to return when you least expect it.

We must know our hearts, because our Father does. Besides, actions are always more powerful then explanations.

Lord, help me see the things I try so hard to hide, and give me the strength to change the aspects of my heart that need repair. Amen.

DECEMBER

Priorities, Promises, and Purpose

SHANE STANFORD

DECEMBER 1   ALL IS WONDER

For it was you who formed my inward parts; you knit me together in my mother's womb. I praise you, for I am fearfully and wonderfully made.   *(Psalm 139:13-14a)*

My wife and I believed we couldn't have children. That was three daughters ago. Sarai Grace, age ten, is quiet and docile. Juli Anna, age seven, is loud and loves to laugh. Emma Leigh, age three, is the discriminating one, easing between being skeptical and jolly with everyone she meets.

We have three wonderful but very different daughters. But as different as they are, I see a common thread in each of them: I can't think of my daughters without being in awe of the wonderfully complex bond we have with the Creator. Even the vastness of the universe cannot surpass this truth. It is deeper than mere emotion—it is wonder!

During this time of preparation, I encourage each of us to think of the wonder in our lives as we prepare for the God who continues to amaze us in complex and simple ways. Happy Advent!

Gracious God, help me slow down and enjoy the wonder of your creation. Don't let me miss your awesome presence this day. Amen.

DECEMBER 2   THE REAL THING

In the beginning was the Word, and the Word was with God, and the Word was God.   *(John 1:1)*

For years, my family put up a live Christmas tree. It was an important event. However, when we discovered that our middle daughter, Juli Anna, is allergic to live trees, we chose to buy an artificial tree. No one was more upset than Juli Anna. Not only did she feel guilty about being the cause of the change; she even wondered if Christmas could take place without the "real thing." We assured her that Christmas trees, real or artificial, reflect the majesty of the home in which they sit. The tree doesn't make the home; the home makes the tree.

The *real thing* at Christmas has nothing to do with trees, decorations, or ornaments and everything to do with our hearts and spirits as we celebrate the birth of a *true original*: our Lord and Savior, Jesus Christ. Don't miss the *real thing* at Christmas by focusing on the temporary things of this world. Christmas comes and goes every year—Christ remains forever.

Gracious God, grant me your presence this Christmas that I might see and experience the real thing, your love for me. Amen.

DECEMBER 3   WATCHING FOR "WOW" MOMENTS

The next day he saw Jesus coming toward him and declared, "Here is the Lamb of God who takes away the sin of the world!"   *(John 1:29)*

Men love "wow" moments. After all, we don't watch sports to see the mundane. We love the excitement and challenge. But what about the birth of your children, fishing with your grandfather, or watching your first baseball game?

Today's Sscripture is a "wow" moment. John the Baptist preached passionately and diligently about the coming of the Messiah. Then Jesus arrived to be baptized. John's reaction says it all: Everyone! *Here he is! Behold!* The promise had come true; faith was not in vain.

Wow moments remind us about God's promise to redeem and restore. However, I am often too busy to recognize the wow moments because I'm so busy trying to get the tasks done and the schedule right. God has wired us to be wowed, to crave wonder and experience awe. During the next days, watch for the wow moments in your life, and you will see how God announces, changes, and transforms the mundane into miracles. Wow!

Gracious God, thank you for creating me to experience and crave wow moments. Help me recognize the amazing ways you are at work in our world. Amen.

DECEMBER 4   WAITING AND ANTICIPATION

When John heard in prison what the Messiah was doing, he sent word by his disciples and said to him, "Are you the one who is to come, or are we to wait for another?"
(Matthew 11:2-3)

We all have to wait at one time or another. I spend a lot of time waiting—waiting for my wife and daughters to get ready, waiting in doctor's offices, waiting at red lights. Waiting is not fun!

But what about anticipation? Isn't that waiting too? What is the difference? Well, anticipation involves a different spirit and meaning. Wait long enough and the situation becomes mundane; but with anticipation, we know that something magical is going to happen.

On our wedding day, I didn't wait for my wife to walk down the aisle; I anticipated her arrival. Too many marriages become more about waiting, losing the anticipation of God's gift and, thus, losing the magic too.

The Jews had waited for hundreds of years for their Messiah. But John taught about anticipation. There is a difference! We do more than wait for Christmas. Our hearts beat with anticipation. Shouldn't it be so every moment with God?

Gracious God, give me the gift of anticipation that I might see the power of your love through this Christmas season. Amen.

DECEMBER 5   THE GOOD SON

*An angel of the Lord appeared to him in a dream and said,
"Joseph, son of David, do not be afraid to take Mary as your
wife, for the child conceived in her is from the Holy Spirit."*
                                                        (Matthew 1:20)

I have often wondered about Joseph's personal expectations for
Jesus. Sure, we know the story of Jesus' birth and of his divine lin-
eage. But, given this, I wonder if Joseph carried the same emotions as other fathers—wanting a son who would make him proud,
live faithfully, maybe even go into the family business.

Before Jesus became the Christ of Calvary, he was a son from
Nazareth. We know a great deal about his ministry, but for the better part of his life we know very little. However, we surmise from
his life that Jesus understood what it meant to be a dutiful son, to
please his parents and obey their wishes.

Christmas testifies to the importance of an earthly relationship,
mirroring God's parental love for us. Yes, Jesus understood the
importance of being a good son, of loving his parents and following their ways.

*Gracious God, help me see the value of my earthly relationships
by watching your love for each of us. Amen.*

DECEMBER 6   ICEBERGS AHEAD

*I appeal to you therefore, brothers and sisters, by the mercies of
God, to present your bodies as a living sacrifice, holy and
acceptable to God, which is your spiritual worship.*
                                                        (Romans 12:1)

Recently, I read a book of personal accounts from survivors of the
Titanic. All lost someone close to them—a father or mother, husband or wife, brother or sister. Several who were children at the
time described the final moments with their fathers. They all
recounted a sense of heroism as their fathers placed them in the
lifeboats. Each of the fathers assured his children that everything

would be OK, but the survivors said they could see the sacrifice being made as they looked into their own fathers' eyes. Those fathers made that choice because of their love for their children.

The apostle Paul calls each of us to present ourselves to God as a holy and living sacrifice. This is the perfect time of year to remember that what began in a stable in Bethlehem led to the cross of Calvary—all done for the love of God's children. God does not ask for much in return, not even a perfect life—just an acceptable one, given faithfully.

God who has given so much to us, help me faithfully and boldly give my life back to you. Amen.

DECEMBER 7   PRIORITIES

"But strive first for the kingdom of God and his righteousness, and all these things will be given to you as well."
(Matthew 6:33)

Priorities. It's a simple word. So why does it seem to cause trouble for so many people?

Throughout my ministry, I've shared many final moments with people. During their last minutes on earth, never did anyone say, "I wish I had worked more," or "Man, I wish I had finished that project." No, the common refrain was about family and friends—priorities.

Perhaps more than any other season of the Christian year, Advent is about priorities. It is a time to prepare, get in order, and be ready. We don't need to wait until the end of our lives to learn the lesson of priorities. Quite simply, it is too late by then. But *now* is a different story. One more dollar can't buy the kind of peace that good priorities offer.

During this season, prepare your heart for God's great gift by getting your focus clear. It will make all the difference—both for today and for tomorrow.

Gracious God, help me seek you first so my priorities for this life will follow. Amen.

DECEMBER 8   CLARITY, PART 1

***The people who walked in darkness / have seen a great light;
those who lived in a land of deep darkness— / on them light has
shined.***   ***(Isaiah 9:2)***

At night, when I look at our Christmas lights without my con-
tact lenses or glasses, the scene is one blurry mass of color. It's
beautiful but without focus. It's nice to view for a while, but I
wouldn't want to spend the entire season this way. I would miss
seeing the ornaments and decorations that make every
Christmas tree special. Clarity means details, and details give us
the nuance of Christmas. The mass of color is wonderful, but
only for a moment.

Clarity of purpose is the same for our lives. We must see past the
mass of color to see wonderful details around us. The first detail
is God's love for us through Christ. John the Baptist saw this when
Jesus appeared to be baptized. "Behold the Lamb of God" (John
1:29 KJV), he said. All that had gone before seemed a blur. This
was the real picture.

What do you see when you look at God's love?

***Dear God, help me look past the confusion of Christmas to see
clearly the love of Christ. Amen.***

DECEMBER 9   CLARITY, PART 2

***"This is my commandment, that you love one another as I have
loved you. No one has greater love than this, to lay down one's
life for one's friends."***   ***(John 15:12-13)***

Yesterday we saw the clarity of God's love for us in Christ. Clarity
at Christmas also reminds us of the love we should have for others. In my family, we love giving gifts, but there's much more to the
season. The best gift is our time together.

God's love teaches us how to treat one another. Nothing could
be clearer in the Gospels. However, at times God's love makes us
uncomfortable because the more we love, the more we reveal our-

selves. And like a picture coming into focus, we watch with joy and anticipation, especially when the right images come to life—images of friendship, commitment, and unconditional love.

To see the real meaning of Christmas, we first must experience and reciprocate Christ's love for us. But it doesn't stop there. That love pushes us to love another. As Jesus instructs, the second points to the first, and they become equally important.

Gracious God, give me clarity of heart and spirit that I might see the power of your love for us through Jesus Christ. Amen.

DECEMBER 10   WHAT IS ENOUGH?

Keep your lives free from the love of money, and be content with what you have; for he has said, "I will never leave you or forsake you."   *(Hebrews 13:5)*

When is enough, enough? Several years ago, I wrote a stewardship article asking that question. I received comments from people around the country sharing their stories of good and not-so-good stewardship habits. Many of them identified spending patterns at Christmas as an example of *missing the mark* for this principle.

Why do we pressure ourselves to overdo our Christmas purchases? One friend calls it Christmas guilt—guilt for not being close enough to people the rest of the year; guilt for not having been generous enough; guilt for not planning ahead. Guilt, guilt, guilt.

The truth is, we often work to *make up* at Christmas for relationships and choices we should have attended to earlier in the year. But *things* cannot replace what our friends really need from us. A genuine connection is the real gift. If we will attend to our relationships throughout the year, perhaps we won't find ourselves trying to *pay off* the previous Christmas in time to *spend again* next year.

Gracious God, help me find my hope in you and know that you are sufficient. Amen.

DECEMBER 11   THE LAZY RIVER

When I am afraid, I put my trust in you. In God, whose word I praise, in God I trust; I am not afraid; what can flesh do to me?
(Psalm 56:3-4)

How much of life do we make happen, and how much of it happens to us? My family loves a local resort's "lazy river." The water's current pushes you with little to no effort. Just sit and enjoy the ride. Nothing is more relaxing than watching my family float leisurely by. *Too bad life is not a lazy river.*

Life reminds me more of a white-water rafting trip. There are moments of peaceful flow combined with some of the most harrowing currents. Half the ride, you sit and relax; the other half, you just hold on. Sound familiar?

Life's been this way from the beginning. Certainly Mary and Joseph would have preferred options other than a stable in Bethlehem, but that's what the journey brought. And so they made arrangements and went with the flow.

We learn from their experience in many ways—notably, that we take life as we find it and trust in God's grace to guide us. God never promised a smooth ride, but God won't let us sink either.

Gracious God, help me go with the flow of your grace and trust in the current of your love. Amen.

DECEMBER 12   HOW MUCH MERCY?

Great is your mercy, O Lord; give me life according to your justice.   *(Psalm 119:156)*

Where do we draw the line when showing mercy? Does one action outweigh another? Do we show mercy only when we understand or rationalize the offense? Or is mercy less about the act and more about the heart—and as much for the one showing mercy as for the one receiving it?

Joseph's feelings about Mary's pregnancy make sense in our culture—as they did in his own. It was an "eye for an eye" world.

Mercy was shown only after certain requirements had been met, not sooner.

So, for God to request Joseph's understanding for Mary's circumstances went against everything Joseph had been taught. But mercy often doesn't make sense, and neither does God's grace.

The world loves to limit mercy. It is much easier to qualify our responses or show no mercy at all than it is to reach deep inside and trust what we do not understand or go where we cannot "see."

Christmas reminds us that God's love looks past our circumstances and loves us anyway. It often doesn't make sense, but it also is such sweet confusion.

Gracious God, thank you for "confusing" us with such amazing grace and mercy. Amen.

DECEMBER 13   HOPE STREET

Now faith is being sure of what we hope for and certain of what we do not see.   (Hebrews 11:1 NIV)

While traveling in a small town several years ago, I found myself at the corner of Main Street and Hope Street. Needless to say, since I am a minister, the wheels began turning. I wondered how many people had stood at this intersection searching for the hope of their lives, asking questions about direction and, more important, a better destination.

The birth of Jesus marked a crossroads for humanity; in fact, Christ's birth is literally the intersection of how we measure time—before and after the "year of the Lord" (A.D.). But isn't it the same with our spiritual lives? God becoming like us, Emmanuel, signals a new place in our relationship with God. God has chosen us as God's own and made our lives the crossroads for God's love. In the end, what seemed like the street corner for one lonely journey after another became a place of new beginnings and better paths.

This Christmas, don't miss the intersection of God's love in your life. Trust me, it is nothing short of life's intersection at "main and hope."

Gracious God, give me direction for my life by following your lead through Jesus Christ. Amen.

DECEMBER 14   PERPETUAL FRUIT

By contrast, the fruit of the Spirit is love, joy, peace, patience, kindness, generosity, faithfulness, gentleness, and self-control. There is no law against such things.   (Galatians 5: 22-23)

When I was younger, my grandfather and I loved to visit a grove of peach trees when they were in season. My grandfather would pick a ripe peach, take out his pocketknife, and cut a piece to taste. We would sit for nearly an hour and eat more than our stomachs needed.

Looking back, those moments with my grandfather meant more than us just sharing a peach together. They taught me the heart of a grandfather, the fragile impressions of childhood, and the joy of spending time with those you love.

Ironically, it didn't cost anything to share those moments together—only a few minutes of time—but they remain the dearest memories of my life. And they continue to teach me about spending time with my own children as some sort of perpetual lesson from my grandfather's heart.

My prayer for each of us is that we not miss the simple ways God teaches us about love and living. Don't miss the sweet taste of God's time with you.

Gracious God, teach me your ways so that I might bear the fruit of your grace in my life. Amen.

DECEMBER 15   CLOTHES MAKE THE PERSON

Put on the whole armor of God, so that you may be able to stand against the wiles of the devil.   (Ephesians 6:11)

We've heard that clothes make the man. In our society, style is big business. Fashion dominates newsstands and plays a huge part in defining our culture. One friend described the issue for men this way: "Of course, the measure of a man is more than what he wears, but what he wears describes how what we measure matters." I hope we are not this shallow, but I also understand the comment.

Paul says that what we wear in our spiritual lives matters too—not for the same reasons as our physical clothes, but with similar impact. What we "put on" spiritually provides a glimpse into our relationship with God. Just look at Paul's suggested wardrobe for us: truth as the belt, salvation as the helmet, faith as the shield, peace as our shoes, and righteousness as our breastplate.

What we wear in our journey becomes the measure of life in Christ. So, dress well. It matters!

Gracious God, you clothe us in your grace. Help me not miss the splendor of what you have in store for me. Amen.

DECEMBER 16　　MY FAVORITE CHRISTMAS MOVIE

May the LORD give strength to his people! / May the LORD bless his people with peace!　　(Psalm 29:11)

I love National Lampoon's *Christmas Vacation*. I still laugh at such scenes as a flying snow-disk ride, a gift-wrapped cat, and a "killer" squirrel. Clark Griswald, the main character, constantly loses his cool in search of the perfect Christmas experience. However, not only does his ideal Christmas not turn out well, but his guests don't appreciate his hard work or frustration.

By the end of the movie, which involves a S.W.A.T. team and an exploding gas line, Christmas plays a secondary role to the mayhem. Sure, many of us will never have a Christmas tree explode, but losing our focus for the season is not uncommon.

The Griswalds' absurdity may seem out of place, but the hectic pace of our modern Christmas celebrations is not. This Christmas don't let the craziness of the season keep you from seeing the real meaning: welcoming the Prince of Peace.

Gracious God, help me trade the hectic nature of the season for the Prince of Peace. Amen.

DECEMBER 17   DISAPPOINTMENT

I can do all things through him who strengthens me.
(Philippians 4:13)

Have you ever been disappointed by a friend, family member, or colleague? A wounded relationship is a difficult feeling. Our natural instinct is to be angry and to refuse to forgive. We want the other person to feel the same emotions we are experiencing. Yes, an "eye for an eye" is easier and more rewarding if we measure disappointment by human emotions.

However, God measures disappointment by grace. Imagine how the God of the universe must feel when we disappoint, fail, or disobey. What if God's first instinct were to remain in anger? Where would we be?

Thankfully, God's response to disappointment was to send Jesus as our example, friend, and Savior. Christ's life, death, and resurrection mark an end to disappointment and begin a new chapter in our relationship with God. Instead of an "eye for an eye," God teaches us to turn the other cheek and to offer a new relationship of restoration and hope.

This Christmas, don't miss the opportunity to begin again in your relationships. God seized such a moment, and that has made the difference for you and me.

God of forgiveness and new beginnings, help me begin again in my relationships with others as you began again with me. Amen.

DECEMBER 18   THE BEST GIFT

When he [Zechariah] did come out, he could not speak to them, and they realized that he had seen a vision in the sanctuary. He kept motioning to them and remained unable to speak.
(Luke 1:22)

Recently, a friend asked me what the best gift I have ever received was. After some thought, I told him it was a piece of advice from my grandfather: "Silence is often the wisest voice in the room." At the time, I didn't fully appreciate the words. But in the years since, I have come to understand the meaning and spirit of this advice.

Sometimes our words speak volumes, but at other times our silence speaks even more. In a world where words are taken for granted, learning to listen is even more valuable. Often our advice is not what is needed. Instead, what is needed is our willingness to be available in the situation.

Zechariah learned that God needed his heart, not his words or understanding. Our doubts, advice, and opinion matter less than our presence. Not only will this be an incredible gift to those in need; it is a blessing for us as well.

Gracious God, help me listen for your word in my life and not miss how that word can transform my world. Amen.

DECEMBER 19   THE DADDY DILEMMA

"Look, the virgin shall conceive and bear a son, and they shall name him Emmanuel," which means, "God is with us."
(Matthew 1:23)

I love golf. No player is more exciting to watch than Tiger Woods. Like him or not, one must admire his talent and tenacity for the game. Over the first decade of his career, Tiger dominated the tour with dozens of victories and countless majors. Since the age of two, golf had been Tiger's life, and he played like it.

But in 2007, Tiger Woods became a father. Suddenly, within moments, golf was no longer most important. His world changed, and incidentally, Tiger appeared to like it. In the weeks following the birth of his daughter, Tiger changed his schedule, not to mention his focus. He entered what I call the "Daddy Dilemma"—that moment when the once "most important thing" ceases to be so.

Sure, Tiger will always love golf and probably will continue to dominate the game. But, as Joseph no doubt experienced, a small child should change us and create in us the sweetest dilemma we will ever know. It's our job not to miss it.

Gracious God, give me the presence of mind to watch for impor-tant things in my life and not miss you working in our midst. Amen.

DECEMBER 20   RELUCTANT CHARITY

Each of you must give as you have made up your mind, not reluctantly or under compulsion, for God loves a cheerful giver.
(2 Corinthians 9:7)

At Christmas, our congregation takes a special offering. Individuals and families bring gifts of money, canned goods, clothes, and other items for those who are underresourced in our community.

We ask our children to give from their allowances in order to share funds or goods for the offering, and we encourage them to give as God leads. Last Christmas, my middle daughter dreaded the offering because she had planned to spend her money on her-self. However, she knew that we expected her to give.

As the special offering drew near, she planned how she could give *anything* other than her money. Finally, we suggested that she not give, at least until she could give for the right reasons.

At first, she was relieved, but when we arrived at the service and we heard the Christmas story, her heart changed. She gave her entire allowance.

The Christmas story reminds us of God's unwavering, unselfish love for us. There is no reluctance in God's heart; neither should there be in ours.

Gracious God, help me give out of my love for you so that I might see your eager gifts through Christ to us. Amen.

DECEMBER 21   99 PERCENT CHRISTIAN

Therefore, my beloved, be steadfast, immovable, always excelling in the work of the Lord, because you know that in the Lord your labor is not in vain.   *(1 Corinthians 15:58)*

Too often I am 99 percent Christian. That's when a person gives 99 percent of his or her life to God but, for one reason or another, holds back the final 1 percent. Recently I received a very large hospital bill. I remember the anxiety of wondering how such costs would affect the security and future of my family. My first instinct was how I would fix the problem.

However, I realized that I could not address the problem alone. Even 1 percent is too much without God; so I prayed for guidance. Over the next days, friends and family offered guidance and assistance. It was humbling and overwhelming. God's plan for our lives means working in community and trusting the guidance of others.

Christmas is a time for families and friends to come together. Yet the birth of Jesus unifies us every day, not just once a year. Don't miss the potential of giving 100 percent to God, and better yet, of doing so with others.

Gracious God, help me give 100 percent to you because you gave everything to me through Christ. Amen.

DECEMBER 22   YOU KNOW, RED-STRIPED
CHRISTMAS CANDIES

It is no longer I who live, but it is Christ who lives in me. And the life I now live in the flesh I live by faith in the Son of God, who loved me and gave himself for me.   *(Galatians 2:20)*

Yes, I mean *peppermints*. The day my wife sent me to the store, my mind went blank. I couldn't think of peppermints, candy canes, or anything even similar. So I described what I needed. Finally, after using all of my "big words" for the day, I managed, "You know, the red-striped Christmas candies."

"You mean peppermints?" the clerk asked sadly. By this point, I could tell she felt sorry for me. "Yes!" I exclaimed.

It is frustrating to know what you are looking for, yet be without the right words to describe it. Ever felt like that? God understands our questions better than we know how to ask them. All we have to do is be willing and open to what we find.

Christmas is a season for discovering the best of what God offers—namely, God's Son. Don't miss the gift, even if you can't describe it. God knows what you are looking for, and that is all that matters.

Gracious God, thank you for sending me what I need even before I know I need it. Amen.

DECEMBER 23   LIGHTS, TINSEL, GARLAND . . .
CHIPMUNKS?

Beloved, let us love one another, because love is from God; everyone who loves is born of God and knows God. (1 John 4:7)

Oh, the things we did for our grandparents! Sure, they spoiled us rotten. So, when my grandmother asked me to dress up like Alvin from the Chipmunks and perform Christmas carols on the neighbor's doorstep, I cleared my throat and sang. To say this was the highlight of my grandmother's season would be an understatement. To say this was the thorn in mine—well, you get the picture.

My grandmother is feeble now and lives in a nursing home. But even today, if she asked, I would gladly suit up and sing away. In fact, I would do anything for my grandmother, because her entire life she did anything for me. That is the nature of unconditional love—loving even in the ways, places, and spaces that make us most uncomfortable.

Christmas shouts this kind of love because it reminds us of when God dressed up like us to stand at the doorway of our lives, singing a new song. Why? Because God is unconditionally in love with us. Shh . . . hear the music? Open the door!

Wonderful God, help me always hear the music of your unconditional love. Amen.

DECEMBER 24   NEW EVERY MORNING

Let me hear of your steadfast love in the morning, / for in you I put my trust. Teach me the way I should go, / for to you I lift up my soul. (Psalm 143:8)

Scarlett O'Hara was right: *tomorrow is another day*. Several weeks ago, I underwent open-heart surgery. One morning, I felt a tightening in my chest. The next morning, I had a stress test. Several mornings later, I was in the intensive care unit. For more than a week, each morning seemed like a new struggle.

In difficult periods, many of us feel that each morning is another opportunity for things to get worse. As our despair grows, the joy leaves and each morning becomes a dreaded event.

But God sent Jesus to restore the morning. Christ's presence in our history and our hearts provides each day with hope the world can't take away.

Several mornings ago, I sat on my porch to watch the day begin. I heard the birds, watched the sun rise, and felt the presence of God. It was the first morning I didn't feel overwhelmed or fearful about my situation. I realized those mornings were gone; this was a new day. Praise God! This is your new day!

Gracious God, thank you for difficult mornings that remind me of each new day to be with you. Amen.

DECEMBER 25   EXTRAORDINARY PEOPLE

"To you is born this day in the city of David a Savior, who is the Messiah, the Lord. This will be a sign for you: you will find a child wrapped in bands of cloth and lying in a manger."
(Luke 2:11-12)

It amazes me how often in Scripture God uses ordinary people to do extraordinary things. We know the stories: Joseph was a slave, Moses an outcast, Rahab a prostitute, David a shepherd, Jeremiah a complainer, Daniel an exile. All of these heroes in the faith were once, shall I say, like you and me.

So it should come as no surprise that when God decided to enter our world, the result was rather simple and common. The cast on that Christmas morning was ordinary. Joseph was a carpenter; Mary was a young girl. The setting? Nothing more humble than a stable. No glitz or glamour.

God's way uses the ordinary to proclaim the amazing!

Today is just another day, yet there is nothing ordinary about it. As Christmas unfolds for us, don't miss the power of God's extraordinary love. It is nothing short of amazing!

Merry Christmas.

Gracious God, thank you for using the ordinary to do extraordinary things—and for making me a part of the plan through your Son, Jesus. Amen.

DECEMBER 26   YESTERDAY WAS CHRISTMAS DAY!

The shepherds returned, glorifying and praising God for all they had heard and seen, as it had been told them.   (Luke 2:20)

No, a bomb did not go off in your home—yesterday was Christmas Day! It amazes me that what takes so much time and energy to decorate and wrap can be dismantled within a matter of hours—perhaps minutes. On December 24, everything sits perfectly in place. Today, December 26, seems like a whole new world.

It takes even less time for our lives to unravel from the pristine aura of the holiday, returning to the mundane. But that is not God's intention. Each day, whether Christmas Day or the day after or any other day, provides an opportunity for us to serve in God's name and make a positive difference in our world.

Sure, the clutter often returns, but the mayhem doesn't have to. What matters most is celebrating the 26th like the 25th, only without the presents. It is no less a time to remember God's amazing love for us; in fact, it may be even more so.

My prayer for you on your "day after Christmas Day" is that the God of Christmas morning will become even more your friend and strength the morning after. Merry Christmas Day— plus one!

...ing God, thank you for the gift of Jesus—on this day and day after. Amen.

DECEMBER 27   THE PARTY

For just as the body is one and has many members, and all the members of the body, though many, are one body, so it is with Christ. *(1 Corinthians 12:12)*

My family loves a party. We celebrate everything—birthdays, anniversaries, the Fourth of July! Each person has a special responsibility. My wife prepares the food. I make sure the yard looks nice. My daughters help arrange the food and set the table. They also put away the various toys. Everyone does something. Working together makes each occasion even more special.

The Body of Christ lives like this, too. Christmas reminds us that God includes us in God's "special events." Scripture says we have been given a place in the work of God and a gift to live out our responsibility. We experience the fullness of God's love by serving in those special ways that God has planned. Sure, we may choose not to be a part, and someone might even take up our task for us, but it will never be the same as if we had done it.

Dear God, thank you for the special event of Christmas and for sending your Son. Help me be prepared and be a part by serving in the way you have planned. Amen.

DECEMBER 28   JUST A JANITOR

Whatever your task, put yourselves into it, as done for the Lord. *(Colossians 3:23)*

"How many degrees you got?" the man asked.

"Two," I said as I straightened papers and books on my desk in my new office.

"I didn't graduate from high school. Ain't got no papers to hang on my wall," the gentleman quickly replied.

"What do you do here?" I asked.

"Oh, I'm nobody—just the janitor," the man responded.

Just the janitor. Over the next years of my ministry in that congregation, I learned the real importance of my new friend,

Jack. Sure, on paper he appeared uneducated or unimportant. But every day we called on Jack for his help and common wisdom. In fact, there was little in my day that did not involve his help. Jack didn't have "papers on the wall," but his worth was more than evident!

Sometimes we believe that we need the right pedigree, degree, or past for God to truly love us. However, what we really need is a willing heart. We need to be available to be and do as the child God created in us.

Dear God, give me a sense of your presence in me to know my worth and value to you. Amen.

DECEMBER 29   THE MOST WONDERFUL TIME
OF YEAR?

"A voice was heard in Ramah, wailing and loud lamentation, Rachel weeping for her children; she refused to be consoled, because they are no more."   *(Matthew 2:18)*

"Christmas is the most wonderful time of the year—right?" The young lady asked me the question during a counseling session. She was beautiful, smart, and outgoing, but Christmas reminded her of a broken family and difficult upbringing. Her view of Christmas was connected to how others, especially her parents, shaped her young memories of the holiday.

Often we forget that Christmas, along with all the celebration, is also a time of sadness and brokenness for many. This Christmas season pray for those whose lives do not experience the season as a time of joy and peace. And if Christmas is a struggle for *you,* know that the Body of Christ belongs to the broken lives of our world. Let's not miss the opportunity this Christmas to watch the power of healing and hope born anew in our hearts. It will make all the difference, both this season and for generations to come.

acious God, give me a sense of joy and peace this season—
to experience the power of Christmas for myself and to
it with others. Amen.

DECEMBER 30   AS A HEN GATHERS HER CHICKS

"Jerusalem, Jerusalem....How often have I desired to gather your children together as a hen gathers her brood under her wings."   *(Luke 13:34)*

When I was seven, my mother and I moved to my grandmother's farm. My mother set up chores for me, including feeding the chickens and gathering the eggs. I had never been around chickens before, and I was amazed at how protective hens are of their chicks—not that I should have been, for nothing seems more natural on this earth than to gather our little ones under our care.

The saddest story of the Christmas season involves Herod's response to the birth of a "king." It calls forth some of the bloodiest parts of Scripture as we imagine mothers and fathers gathering their children close to protect them.

God's grace happens in spite of our imperfections. Jesus enters the best and worst of our journey and knows the struggle of God's people to find peace. But redemption comes regardless of the situation. It is the promise of God. God gathers God's children at the most difficult times. It is more than an act of God; it is God's nature.

Gracious God, thank you for gathering all of us under your care even in the midst of the world's imperfections. Amen.

DECEMBER 31   WHAT IS A RESOLUTION AND
                                     DO I NEED ONE?

"For surely I know the plans I have for you, says the LORD, plans for your welfare and not for harm, to give you a future with hope."   *(Jeremiah 29:11)*

Tomorrow the new year begins, and most people will *say* they have a new year's resolution. I've heard resolutions for years and wondered whether or not I really need one.

Dictionary.com defines resolution in many ways. My favorite is "determining upon an action or course of action." Sounds good, but given that definition, haven't all of us been moving somewhere whether we know it or not?

New year's resolutions are great as long as we are *resolved* to follow them (all puns intended). A course of action is only as successful as the commitment to see it through. A resolution without follow-through is just another good idea.

God resolved that we should begin a new relationship. And so God saw the resolution through with the gift of God's Son. It wasn't just a good idea; it changed the course of human history.

Make resolutions if need be, but also make one to keep the rest. Such determines everything.

Gracious God, thank you for new beginnings. Give me the strength and wisdom to make the most of them. Amen.